TRADE AND THE ENVIRONMENT

T0382770

Trade and the Environment

A New Zealand perspective

Edited by
RAVI RATNAYAKE
Department of Economics
The University of Auckland

Routledge
Taylor & Francis Group

LONDON AND NEW YORK

First published 1999 by Ashgate Publishing

Reissued 2018 by Routledge
2 Park Square, Milton Park, Abingdon, Oxon, OX14 4RN
52 Vanderbilt Avenue, New York, NY 10017

Routledge is an imprint of the Taylor & Francis Group, an informa business

Publisher's Note
The publisher has gone to great lengths to ensure the quality of this reprint but points out that some imperfections in the original copies may be apparent.

Disclaimer
The publisher has made every effort to trace copyright holders and welcomes correspondence from those they have been unable to contact.

A Library of Congress record exists under LC control number: 9973392

ISBN 13: 978-1-138-36787-6 (hbk)
ISBN 13: 978-1-138-36788-3 (pbk)
ISBN 13: 978-0-429-42961-3 (ebk)

Contents

List of Figures   *vii*
List of Tables   *viii*
List of Appendices   *xi*
List of Contributors   *xii*
Acknowledgements   *xiii*

PART I: ISSUES AND POLICIES

Introduction   3

1   Trade and the Environment: An Overview of Current Issues and
    Evidence
    Ravi Ratnayake   9

2   The Effects of Trade Liberalisation on New Zealand's CO_2
    Emissions: A Computable General Equilibrium Assessment
    Blair Townsend and Ravi Ratnayake   29

3   Stringent Environmental Regulations and International
    Competitiveness: Evidence from New Zealand
    Ravi Ratnayake   49

4   Agri-Environmental Policy and Market Developments in the
    EU and Their Potential Impact on New Zealand Trade
    Caroline Saunders   83

5   Foreign Direct Investment and the Environmental Regulatory
    Regimes of the Countries of the APEC Region: Where Does
    New Zealand Stand?
    Michael Wydeveld   97

PART II: SECTORAL STUDIES

6   Trade and Environmental Linkages in New Zealand Fisheries
     Basil Sharp   129

7   Agricultural Trade and Environment: Exploring the Linkages
     Mia Mikic   149

8   Trade and Environmental Linkages in Manufacturing Industries
     Ravi Ratnayake   173

9   Forestry Export Restrictions and Carbon Emissions in New
     Zealand
     John Gilbert   195

10   Reconciling Trade and Environment Concerns: Summary of
     Policy Conclusions
     Ravi Ratnayake   231

List of Figures

Figure 1.1   The R&D decision with a regulated standard   15
Figure 6.1   Simple model of optimal fisheries management   131
Figure 6.2   Impact of subsidies on economic surplus   132
Figure 6.3   Optimal allocation of the total allowable catch   137
Figure 6.4   Subsidies and trade flows   139
Figure 6.5   Export growth in an output constrained fishery   142
Figure 6.6   Harvesting New Zealand's exclusive economic zone   143
Figure 6.7   Growth in the total value of seafood exports, 1981-97   144
Figure 6.8   Destination of fishing industry exports, 1986-95   145
Figure 6.9   Changes in the composition of the value of fin fish
             exports   146
Figure 7.1   Trade liberalisation and environmental quality   154
Figure 7.2   Mechanisms of linkages between agricultural trade
             liberalisation and the environment   156
Figure 7.3   Trade and welfare effects of a Pigovian tax in a small
             exporting country   161
Figure 7.4   Trade and welfare effects of an optimal Pigovian tax in
             a large exporting country   162

List of Tables

Table 2.1   Simulation Results   43
Table 3.1   ES and NES Shares in New Zealand's Total Exports by
            Country Groups (Percentage)   55
Table 3.2   Direction of New Zealand's Exports (Percentage)   56
Table 3.3   Composition of New Zealand's Imports (Percentage)   56
Table 3.4   ES and NES Shares in New Zealand's Imports
            (Percentage)   57
Table 3.5   Frequency Distribution of RCA for New Zealand's
            Total Exports of Manufactures 1980-1993   58
Table 3.6   Highest and Lowest Values of RCA for New Zealand's
            Trade in Manufactured Exports   60
Table 3.7   New Zealand's Exports: Percentage of Environmentally
            Sensitive and Non-Environmentally Sensitive Goods by
            2 Digit SITC   62
Table 3.8   Determinants of International Competitiveness in
            Manufactured Exports   69
Table 3.9   Variable Addition Test   71
Table 4.1   Financial, Public Exchequer and Social Value of
            Livestock Output £ per Livestock Unit   85
Table 4.2   Extent of Measures Related to Environmentally
            Friendly Farming   86
Table 4.3   MAFF (UK) Expenditure on Agri-Environmental
            Schemes   87
Table 4.4   Current and Proposed Prices and Subsidies in the
            Cereal, Dairy, and Beef Regimes   91
Table 5.1   Trade Correlations and the Share of Inward and
            Outward FDI in GDP for the APEC Countries, 1992   102
Table 5.2   Restrictions/Prohibitions on Inward FDI with Possible
            Environmental Impact, 1994   107
Table 5.3   Environmental Laws and Corporate Competitiveness,
            1992   109

Table 5.4	Categories of Industries Surveyed	110
Table 5.5	Results of the Survey	112
Table 5.6	Results of the Survey	114
Table 5.7	Results of the Survey	116
Table 5.8	Growth of Inward FDI in Pollutive Industries / Growth of Total Inward FDI	124
Table 7.1	Potential Negative Environmental Consequences of Agricultural Production (selected examples)	152
Table 7.2	Agricultural Reforms / Agricultural Trade Liberalisations and Potential Effects on Environment in New Zealand since 1984	165
Table 7.3	Producer Subsidy Equivalents 1996 (estimate)	167
Table 8.1	Competitiveness Perceptions - Plastics and Synthetics	177
Table 8.2	RMA Impact Against Environmental Degradation - Plastics and Synthetics	177
Table 8.3	Significance of Regulations in Investment Decisions - Plastics and Synthetics	178
Table 8.4	Destination of Exports - Plastics and Synthetics	179
Table 8.5	Possible Responses to Regulations - Plastics and Synthetics	180
Table 8.6	Competitiveness Perceptions - Iron and Steel	182
Table 8.7	RMA Impact Against Environmental Degradation - Iron and Steel	183
Table 8.8	Significance of Regulations - Iron and Steel	184
Table 8.9	Destination of Exports - Iron and Steel	184
Table 8.10	Possible Responses to Environmental Regulations - Steel	185
Table 8.11	Competitiveness Perceptions - Paper	186
Table 8.12	RMA Impact Against Environmental Degradation – Paper	187
Table 8.13	Significance of Regulations - Paper	188
Table 8.14	Destination of Exports - Paper	188
Table 8.15	Possible Responses to Regulations - Paper	189
Table 9.1	Areas of New Zealand Forested and Non-Forested Land	197
Table 9.2	New Zealand Regional Base Cut Wood Supply Forecasts (000m^3 per year)	200
Table 9.3	Estimated New Zealand Consumption of Roundwood (000m^3 RWE) 1971-1995	201

Table 9.4	Value of Exports of Forestry Products From New Zealand by Destination 1985-1995 ($000)	203
Table 9.5	Production and Trade Effects	213
Table 9.6	Final Demand and Energy Usage	214
Table 9.7	Carbon Emissions and Summary Statistics	215
Table 10.1	The Environmental Effects of Trade Liberalisation and Policy Responses	234

List of Appendices

Appendix Table 3.1	Frequency Distribution of RCA for New Zealand's Trade in Manufactures with the OECD 1980, 1985 and 1993	76
Appendix Table 3.2	Frequency Distribution of RCA for New Zealand's Trade in Manufactures with ASEAN 1980, 1985 and 1993	76
Appendix Table 3.3	Frequency Distribution of RCA for New Zealand's Trade in Manufactures with DCs 1980, 1985 and 1993	77
Appendix Table 3.4	Highest and Lowest Values of RCA for New Zealand's Trade in Manufactured Exports with the OECD	78
Appendix Table 3.5	Highest and Lowest Values of RCA for New Zealand's Trade in Manufactured Exports with ASEAN	79
Appendix Table 3.6	Highest and Lowest Values of RCA for New Zealand's Trade in Manufactured Exports with DCs	80
Appendix 3.1	Variable Definitions and Data Sources	81
Appendix 5.1	Some Aggregate Data on FDI Flows in Pollutive Industries	124
Appendix 9.1	Equations of the Model	223
Appendix 9.2	Definitions of Variables and Parameters	226
Appendix 9.3	Input Output Database for New Zealand 1993	228
Appendix 9.4	Parameter Values	230

List of Contributors

John Gilbert, Lecturer, Department of Economics, The University of Auckland, New Zealand

Mia Mikic, Senior Lecturer, Department of Economics, The University of Auckland, New Zealand

Ravi Ratnayake, Senior Lecturer, Department of Economics, The University of Auckland, New Zealand

Caroline Saunders, Senior Lecturer, Commerce Division, Lincoln University, Canterbury, New Zealand

Basil Sharp, Associate Professor, Department of Economics, The University of Auckland, New Zealand

Blair Townsend, Economic Consultant, London, United Kingdom

Michael Wydeveld, Economist, Ministry of Housing, Wellington, New Zealand

Acknowledgements

Financial support from the project on "APEC Integration: Implications on New Zealand" funded by the Foundation for Research, Science and Technology (FoRST), Wellington is gratefully acknowledged for preparation of some of the chapters in this volume (chapters 1, 3, and 8). Several other papers (chapters 4, 6, 7 and 9) have been presented at the workshop on trade and environment held in March 1998, at The University of Auckland, organised by the above mentioned project. I am very grateful to all my colleagues who contributed to the book with very interesting papers. I would like to thank Dr Mia Mikic for intellectual support and encouragement and Trish Marsters for assistance in the preparation of this book. Finally, to my family (Kumudu, Nithya and Dinithi) for their love, understanding and support while I was preparing the manuscript.

PART I:

ISSUES AND POLICIES

Introduction

Background and Objectives

This book is about the link between trade and the environment which has been subject to enormous discussions and debates over the years and has become a very important national issue for all countries. In particular, this issue is important to the countries which have been undergoing lengthy periods of trade and investment liberalisation programmes recently. This also has become an international issue of tremendous current interest given its implications on the global environment and trading system. International organisations such as WTO, OECD and the United Nations and regional trading agreements such as NAFTA, EEC and APEC have been actively involved in this policy debate.

Despite the critical importance of trade-environment issue, less is known about the linkages between the two. The purpose of this book is to present a New Zealand perspective on this topic. New Zealand is a case study of global interest due to two major reasons. Firstly, many countries, both developed and developing are taking the New Zealand economic reforms as a model for restructuring their economies. Those countries will be very interested to see how New Zealand achieved the so called economic miracle while maintaining a "clean and green" image. Secondly, New Zealand is going to become a member of APEC (Asia Pacific Economic Co-operation) by 2010 (developed countries) and 2020 (developing countries) together with 17 other countries in the area. The book is expected to contribute significantly to the current debate on this issue and to assist in the process of reconciliation of trade and environmental policies for sustainable economic development in the context of APEC integration.

Structure of the Book

The book is basically divided into two parts: general studies and industry-specific studies. The first part consists of the empirical studies dealing with some selected issues involved in the debate of trade and environment. These studies which are inter-industry in nature, attempt to test empirically various hypotheses on the linkages between trade and environment. The second part is a collection of industry studies investigating the issues discussed in the first part at a sector or industry level.

The first part starts with chapter 1 where I present an overview of issues involved in the debate with a particular emphasis on New Zealand. I start from more broad issues such as economic growth and environment and trade liberalisation and environment and move onto more specific issues such as international competitiveness and pollution haven hypothesis. Then I move onto more general issues such as the use of trade restrictions for environmental purposes, the impact of environment policies on trade and the perspective of WTO on this debate.

In chapter 2, Townsend and Ratnayake attempt to assess the effects of trade liberalisation on welfare and emissions levels in the New Zealand economy, and the degree to which these effects are influenced by environmental policy. This analysis is performed by constructing a trade and environment focused multisectoral computable general equilibrium model for New Zealand and simulating two policy scenarios. The effects of trade liberalisation in the absence of a carbon tax, and the effects of trade liberalisation in the presence of a carbon tax. Trade liberalisation on its own is found to have negative effects on the level of emissions, with total emissions increasing by 2.9 per cent, however, the effect on welfare remains ambiguous. The simulation of trade liberalisation in the presence of an endogenous carbon tax maintaining the current emissions level, is on the other hand, found to have an unambiguous positive effect on welfare.

In chapter 3, I attempt to answer the question "do stringent environmental regulations lead to loss of international competitiveness in terms of declining exports and increasing imports compared with those from the countries which have lower environmental standards and regulations?" The paper examines this issue by conducting an inter-industry analysis of New Zealand manufacturing industries. By analysing the patterns and determinants of comparative advantage of 109 industries over the last 13 years, we found no strong evidence to suggest that environmental standards lead to loss of competitiveness.

Saunders in chapter 4 discusses the implications of developments in the European Union and its environmental policy for New Zealand. While the importance of the European Union as a market for New Zealand produce has diminished, it is still significant accounting for 17 per cent of exports (6 per cent of which are to the United Kingdom) especially as a high value market and in commodities such as sheepmeat, fruit and dairy. It is because of the importance of primary products in New Zealand trade with the European Union and the fact that much European Union environmental policy intervention and market changes are in the primary products sector that this chapter will concentrate upon European Union environmental policy and its impact on agriculture.

Wydeveld in chapter 5 address the issue of pollution hypothesis using New Zealand data in the context of the Asia-Pacific Economic Co-operation (APEC). The APEC region is one of the most dynamic regions of the world, with rapidly accumulating material wealth. The maintenance of such growth requires that countries adopt sustainable management of resources as one of their key policy objectives. An appropriate conception of sustainable management includes both aspects of efficiency and sustainability. It is the argument of this paper that the current concerns raised in some quarters as to the anti-competitive nature of many environmental regulations does not stem from legitimate differences between countries over what levels of pollution are sustainable, but rather from the failure of domestic governments to introduce sufficiently adaptive environmental regulatory regimes. It is the hypothesis of this paper that such adaptiveness would reduce many of the apparent conflicts between sustainability and efficiency, thus, helping to retain the competitiveness of certain pollutive, or resource intensive, sectors as international economic integration proceeds. There is evidence that some APEC countries have been particularly more adept at mitigating efficiency and sustainability conflicts than others. New Zealand stands out as a country which has been particularly successful in this regard.

Sharp in chapter 6 illustrates the linkages between property rights, trade and sustainable resource use. Most of harvest from New Zealand's exclusive economic zone (EEZ) is exported and so the links between trade and sustainability are transparent. A simple model of fisheries policy is developed to discuss the outcomes observed under regulated access. Then trade is analysed within the context of the rights-based QMS. Again, a simple model is used to illustrate the economic implications of an unsubsidised producer competing with a subsidised producer. Performance of the New Zealand fishing industry is described and offered as evidence of the successful adjustment of government policy away from subsidies to rights-based sustainable fisheries management. It has been shown that the management regime of regulated access coupled with subsidies contributed to serious depletion of high value fish stocks and minimal economic surplus in the fishing industry. Subsidies and non-transferable property rights had combined to produce unsustainable outcomes. However, an unprofitable fishing industry has been transformed to a dynamic profitable industry within the framework of rights-based fishing introduced since 1986. The study shows that in terms of biological sustainability and economic wealth in the fishery, the QMS easily out-performs regulated access.

In chapter 7, Mikic explores the two-way relationship between agricultural trade and environment. Firstly, mechanisms and evidence for the impact of agricultural trade liberalisation on environmental quality are reviewed. Secondly, the impact of environmental policies on agricultural trade is examined. The paper provides a brief review on how the concerns on agriculture and environment have been handled in New Zealand, a leading country among the OECD members when it comes to elimination of assistance to agriculture. It has been concluded that in the case of agriculture, trade liberalisation in general results in improved economic efficiency and economic growth. On the other hand, it has been found that it is possible for environmental policies to weaken competitiveness and thus invoke renewed demand for protection.

In chapter 8, I analyse examine some selected linkages of trade and environment in three environmentally sensitive manufacturing industries: plastics and synthetics, steel, and paper industry. My investigation is based on a sample survey conducted in these three industries. According to the survey, the majority of firms are of the view that New Zealand's environmental regulatory system is very well adapted or acceptable. It was also found that the Resource Management Act has little direct effect on output levels of companies participating in the survey. The cost of compliance in all industries was found to be insignificant in investment decisions of New Zealand. The majority of firms in the survey exported their goods to advanced developed countries where relatively high environmental standards are in place. I also examined the impact of environmental regulations on innovations. The question asked was how would firms respond to more stringent environmental regulations. Again the majority of firms stated that they would introduce new technologies to combat this constraint.

Gilbert, in chapter 9, considers the issue of export restrictions from the perspective of their impact on net carbon emissions, and the policies required to meet the FCCC obligations. He develops a CGE model of the New Zealand economy, which explicitly incorporates emissions data from manufacturing and the absorptive capabilities of the forestry sector. The model is used to simulate the effect of log export restrictions on net carbon emissions, and development estimates of the carbon taxes required to fulfil FCCC obligations with and without log export restrictions. It has been demonstrated that inclusion of environmental costs in this manner strengthens the usual neo-classical case against export restrictions for the small economy.

Finally, in chapter 10, major policy conclusions are summarised.

1 Trade and the Environment: An Overview of Current Issues and Evidence

RAVI RATNAYAKE

Introduction

Increasing concern for the quality of the environment and rapid globalisation of the world economy have resulted in a large body of academic and policy-oriented discussions at both national and international arenas on the interaction between trade and the environment. On the one hand, concerns for environmental protection have intensified recently as our awareness for environmental problems such as air and water pollution, deforestation and soil degradation at national level and acid rain, climate change and ozone layer depletion on a global scale increased. On the other hand, the world economy is getting more and more integrated through liberalisation of foreign trade and investment supported by the WTO multilateral trading system.

Supporters of the environment protection argue that international trade leads to more pollution and environmental degradation through increased economic activities (i.e. more production and consumption). Supporters of free trade show that the additional income gained from more international trade can be used for more environmental protection. It has been shown that if all environmental costs are internalised worldwide and if there are no barriers to trade, international price mechanism would make sure that such goods and services are produced always in the countries where the required environmental factor is most abundant (Kulessa, 1992). This, however, assumes that there is no cross-border pollution and no global common goods.

These concerns are widespread in New Zealand which has been undergoing a lengthy period of trade liberalisation multilaterally, bilaterally and unilaterally over the last two decades. Trade barriers including tariffs and quantitative restrictions have been eliminated or lowered on exports as well as imports, making significant changes in the patterns of trade. On the environmental side, New Zealand is an active participant in almost all international agreements and discussions on environment organised by international organisations such as the United Nations, OECD and GATT/WTO. Internally, all environmental matters are being well looked after by the Resource Management Act which recognise the concept of sustainability explicitly. The concerns for environment are clearly witnessed in the recent Report on Environment released by the Ministry of Environment.

The purpose of the chapter is to provide an outline of the issues involved in this debate. We first discuss the major issues giving particular emphasis on New Zealand's situation and then offer some thoughts on reconciling trade and environmental concerns.

Economic Growth and the Environment

It has been argued that when the economy expands, both production and consumption increase, leading to a depletion of the resource base and environmental degradation. On the contrary, others argue that rising incomes associated with economic growth induce greater public demand for a cleaner environment and generate additional resources for greater environmental protection (e.g. Copeland and Taylor, 1994; Radetzki, 1992; Lopez, 1992). According to this literature, income growth has three distinct effects on the levels of pollution (e.g. Lopez, 1992; Holtz-Eakin and Selden, 1992, Shafik and Bandyopadhyay, 1992; Anderson, 1990). First, the "scale effect" which associates increased economic activities (higher economic growth) with increased production and consumption thereby increasing pollution. Second, the "technical effect" which associates higher levels of cleaner technology with higher income. There is an incentive for firms to look for environmentally friendly technology because there is a demand for such goods resulting from higher incomes. Third, the "composition effect" that arises if income growth causes changes in the preferences of society from pollution-intensive goods to cleaner goods. It is argued that there is some level of income at which the composition and technical effects outweigh the scale effect, resulting in a reduction in pollution.

The relationship between economic growth and the environment can take many forms (Grossman and Krueger, 1995; Selden and Song, 1994). First, when the level of income increases the environmental conditions improve, so the curve declines over time. It has been shown that technical change, income effects and public pressure for cleaner environment, all associated with higher economic growth, lead to lower environmental degradation and less pollution intensity of production (O'Conner, 1994). Second, the environmental conditions monotonically deteriorate when the level of income increases, so the curve is upward sloping. Third, as income increases, the levels of pollution can increase, decrease and then increase again forming a N-shape relationship. Fourth, the relationship can take the form of a U-shape where pollution decreases first and after reaching a minimum, can increase again. Finally, the curve can show an inverted U-shape relationship between income and pollution, a form which has been subject to careful analysis of a number of researchers[1]. According to this view, at lower levels of income the environmental condition deteriorates, reaches a peak, and then gradually declines when the level of income increases.

Recently, an influential paper by Grossman and Krueger (1995) has examined this U-shape relationship between per capita income and various environmental indicators and found no evidence to suggest that environmental quality deteriorates with economic growth indefinitely. They found that "economic growth brings an initial phase of deterioration followed by a subsequent phase of improvement". Barrett (1997) identifies three major forces behind the inverted U-shape relationship. First, at lower levels of income, economic growth can expand the industrial sector at the cost of the agricultural sector and then at the higher levels of income the service sector takes the lead at the expense of the industrial sector. Second, higher income levels can accompany greater democratic freedom giving citizens an opportunity to voice "their preferences for an improved environment". Finally, as income rises the income elasticity of demand for environmental improvements can increase.

Trade Liberalisation and Environment

Trade liberalisation may have both positive and negative environmental impacts. The impacts of trade liberalisation result from its obvious purpose, which is to change existing trade policies in the direction of freer trade. Because of this trade liberalisation can have significant positive impacts on the environment by correcting existing trade policy intervention failures. It may also have some negative impacts related to an expansion of trade in the absence of correcting other existing market and policy intervention failures. In addition to the product, scale, and structural effects, OECD (1994a) identifies a further category of effects trade liberalisation may have, namely regulatory effects, in its implications for environmental standards and policies[2].

Townsend and Ratnayake (1998) have examined the effects of trade liberalisation on welfare and emissions levels in the New Zealand economy, and the degree to which these effects are influenced by environmental policy. In order to estimate the consequences of trade and environmental policies a computable general equilibrium model of the New Zealand economy incorporating a trade and environment focus was constructed. While acknowledging that the estimation of these effects using the CGE model employed in this study should be used to complement other approaches to their estimation, the application of the model does show this method to be valuable for developing policy responses. In this sense the relevance of this study is not solely confined to the case of New Zealand, but has implications for many other small open market based economies contemplating freer trade policies.

According to Townsend and Ratnayake (1998), trade liberalisation on its own is found to have negative effects on the level of emissions. When the impact of this increase in emissions on welfare is ignored, welfare is seen to rise following trade liberalisation, however when the impact of increased emissions is considered, the effect on welfare is ambiguous. The simulation of trade liberalisation in the presence of an endogenous carbon tax maintaining the emissions level, is on the other hand, found to have an unambiguous positive effect on welfare, with emissions remaining constant. Furthermore, the policy of trade liberalisation accompanied by environmental policy is also seen to generate superior welfare outcomes than the present protectionist trade policy, while leaving the environment unaffected.

Environmental Regulations and Competitiveness

Researchers are divided on the nature of the relationship between environmental regulations and international competitiveness. First, it is claimed that stringent environmental regulations impose significant costs on the domestic firms and industries reducing their international competitiveness in terms of declining exports, increasing imports compared with those from the countries which have lower environmental standards and regulations. The loss of competitiveness is said to be greater in the so-called "pollution-intensive" industries[3]. Second, an entirely opposite view, mainly due to Porter (1991), was that environmental regulations lead to productivity improvements because of a more cleaner environment and to innovations because of the stimulating effects of such regulations. Furthermore, countries adjusting early and investing in environmentally friendly technology would be able to create comparative advantage in these environmentally sensitive industries[4]. Compliance with higher environmental regulations could also be an additional source of structural adjustment in particular for developing countries as these regulations will promote less pollution-intensive industries (Sorsa, 1994).

Although comparisons of empirical studies on this issue are difficult due to different methodologies used, Dean (1992) has summarised three major results of these studies. First, on average environmental control cost[5] (ECC) is a smaller share of total costs of production. For example, average annual overall ECC for US exports was 1.75 per cent of the value of exports for 1968-70 while that for US imports is 1.52 percent. However, it has been shown that some individual industries such as construction, mining and plastics could suffer from loss of competitiveness due to high ECC (Walter, 1973). Second, generally, reductions in output caused by abatement costs are insignificant although some individual sectors have been affected. For example, one study based on 14 United States industrial sectors (Yezer and Philipson, 1974) found that the percentage decrease in output resulting from high ECC is less than 1 per cent. Third, the patterns of trade have not been affected significantly by the costs associated with environmental regulations.

The previous studies have been carried out either for the United States or for other large industrial countries. Trade/environment relationship issues in respect of small open economies such as New Zealand have not been studied, mainly due to the unavailability of data, in particular on environmental aspects. Although a number of government agencies including Ministry of Foreign Affairs and Trade (MFAT), Ministry of Agriculture and Fisheries (MAF) and Ministry for the Environment and researchers including Hewison (1995) have identified issues relevant for New Zealand, economic analysis on the subject of trade and environment in New Zealand is surprisingly limited. One noteworthy study was by MAF (1994) which examines the environmental effects of agricultural subsidies in New Zealand for the period of 1975 to 1990. The study finds that agricultural trade liberalisation, in particular the removal of subsidies has had some positive effect on environment. Second, with the exception of Tobey (1990) and Grossman and Krueger (1993), the previous studies have not attempted to analyse the relative role of environment stringency in explaining inter-industry differences in trade performance in the framework of trade models. Tobey specifies net exports as a function of country characteristics and estimates on a sample of 23 countries using 1975 data while Grossman and Krueger regress United States imports from Mexico on factor shares on a sample of 135 industries using data for 1987. Both studies have not examined the role of industrial characteristics and trade policy induced variables in explaining trade flows between countries. Since international trade patterns are determined by many factors rather than factor endowments, it is important to specify environment stringency as a possible determinant of trade flows along with other industrial characteristics, factor intensities and trade policy measures.

Ratnayake (1998) attempts to fill the gap in the empirical literature by analysing the environment and competitiveness link in the context of New Zealand. In particular, it addresses the question "do environmental standards lead to loss of international competitiveness?" The study found no evidence to suggest that New Zealand has lost its comparative advantage of environmentally sensitive (ES) goods during the period under consideration. It was also shown that it was not an important determinant of New Zealand's international competitiveness. In terms of econometric results, there is no substantial evidence to suggest that environmental stringency leads to a loss of international competitiveness. The results give some support to the proposition that New Zealand has gained or increased comparative advantage in exporting some environmentally sensitive goods to some country groups, in particular, OECD.

Innovations and Environmental Regulations

It is reasonable to assume that increased environmental regulation in an industry will increase the associated pollution abatement expenditures, because tighter standards will compel firms to invest in additional equipment and/or extra workers in order to reduce pollution levels. As the burden of abatement rises, as measured by the ratio of abatement expenditures to sales, we expect the incentives for firms to invent either cleaner technology or more efficient abatement technology to increase. Figure 1.1 illustrates this point.

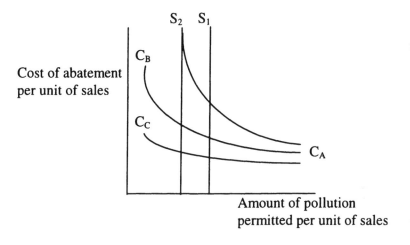

Figure 1.1: The R&D decision with a regulated standard

S_i (i = 1,2...n) represents the standard in period i. It can be seen that as the standard becomes stricter (e.g. moving from S_1 to S_2), in which case less pollution is permitted, the cost of abatement per unit of sales increases. This is likely to occur because of technological constraints. When technology is constrained, the marginal cost of reducing pollution increases as abatement laws become stricter. The line C_A represents the abatement costs of an arbitrary firm given present technology. The firm can reduce abatement costs in two major ways. Firstly, it can embark upon a R&D project to increase the efficiency of the abatement process thereby shifting the firms cost curve down to C_B. Secondly, the firm can invest in another project to reduce the output of emissions from the production process, shifting the firm's cost curve further down to C_C. The former reduces the firm's costs by reducing the cost of abating the emitted pollution, while the latter reduces the firm's costs by reducing the amount of pollution that must be abated. From the diagram it can be seen that as the amount of pollution permitted falls, the cost savings to the firm from either R&D project increases.

The above discussion shows a positive relationship between environmental compliance costs and environmental abatement technology. However, this contradicts with an influential argument which postulates a negative link between the two. According to this view, environmental regulations undermine innovations and restricts firms in pursuing cutting-edge technology (e.g. Breyer, 1982; Caincross, 1992)[6]. It has been shown that high compliance costs associated with environmental regulations use the resources that would otherwise would be invested in innovations. It should be noted, however, that this relationship can be affected by the nature of regulations. So called "poor" regulations of "command and control" type can act as a barrier to technological change while "good" regulations acting as market incentives can encourage such investments. The poor regulations constrain the choices of technology and depend on end-of-pipe and clean-up measures (Porter, 1991).

Pollution Haven Hypothesis: Environment and Investment

In terms of neo-classical trade theoretical setting capital movements or FDI across countries may be seen as a partial substitute to exports[7]. It follows that if environmental regulations are tightened in countries well endowed with assimilative and regenerative capacities that the production conditions of the pollution-intensive sector will be adversely affected, as the production costs in these sectors rise[8]. At the same time, the relative cost advantage of the country poorly endowed with assimilative capacity increases. This implies that if capital is internationally mobile, in a two country model, capital of the environmentally rich country will be transferred to the environmentally poor country because now the locational disadvantage of the latter is lower than previously. Under such a scenario multinational firms will be involved in producing pollution intensive goods in the foreign country[9], despite the fact that this locational shift may be ecologically antagonistic to the country's natural resource endowments[10].

Walter (1982) in a study of shifting plant locations examines the percentage of capital spending for pollution control by United States' MNCs in their domestic operations and in their overseas operations. He identifies eight pollutive industries for examination[11]. He examines the years 1970-76 and discovers, with the sole exception of mining, that in all these pollutive sectors the percentage of capital investment required for pollution controls abroad were significantly lower than in the United States indicating that if everything is equal, there is a clear advantage for overseas production over domestic production. However, Walters' information does not contradict the evidence presented above that ECCs are insignificant when evaluated against total costs.

If one country has higher ECCs vis a vis another country then that country is said to have more stringent environmental regulations (Jaffe et al., 1995). To substantiate the pollution haven hypothesis would then require that these ECCs are significant in providing a motivation for relocation. The empirical evidence, however, suggests that although in aggregate ECCs appear large, when compared against total costs or value added they are generally found to be insignificant[12]. A major limitation of these studies is that frequently only the direct costs, such as spending on *"end of pipe"* abatement equipment have been considered in the estimates of ECCs. The indirect costs such as costs associated with improving worker health, transitional costs, government administration costs and other social impacts have been ignored[13].

However, even when we include these indirect costs most studies still find ECCs to be relatively insignificant. Dean (1992) summarising available evidence on ECCs suggests that these costs, on average, constitute a small proportion of total industry costs and reduce output insignificantly, though in some particular industries ECCs may be significant. It is those industries in which ECCs have proved to be significant that have then been termed pollution intensive (e.g., Low and Yeats, 1992).

For New Zealand, Wydeveld (1998) conducted a survey consisting of 21 firms across a variety of manufacturing categories[14]. Those firms with the greatest potential environmental impact were identified[15]. According to this survey, there was a general perception that good environmental practices brought a positive business image which then benefited the firm. A precise quantification of ECCs was difficult in New Zealand. This can be traced largely to the failure of many firms to operate an environmental management system (EMS). When ECCs are recorded they tend to be segmented to various areas of the financial accounts making aggregate ECCs difficult to determine. Despite this quantification problem the majority of firms still perceived ECCs an insignificant cost. However, some managers made mention that significance depended to a great degree on the ferocity of competition. One also alluded to the possibility of cross-subsidisation of environmental costs from sales in markets were competition is a little less fierce. As industry groups it appears that only the Auto Parts and Accessories, and the Pulp and Paper and Furniture found ECCs to be a significant cost. The majority of firms in other groups finding them insignificant.

Given this information, it could be speculated that ECCs are unlikely to be a significant determinant for New Zealand firms, in their investment decisions or overseas competitiveness. However, this must be qualified, as there were several firms who suggested that the capitalisation costs of environmental regulations were a significant cost and influenced decisions as to whether new plants would be constructed or older plants upgraded. Further, the uncertainty surrounding the ability to gain ongoing resource consents also have affected the level of investment.

Of the firms surveyed who undertook outward FDI, the greater number when questioned on their motivation highlighted greater market access, including access to retail and wholesale outlets, as an overriding factor. All saw environmental regulations as an insignificant determinant in their decision. However, some firms raised the possibility that it may become more important in the future.

Environmental Policies Affecting Trade

Environmental measures affecting trade can be discussed under three major headings: trade provisions in multilateral environmental agreements (MEAs), environmental taxes and charges, eco-labelling, packaging and recycling requirements. The major issue here is how to use these measures for legitimate environmental objectives without undermining free trade principles based on the multilateral trading system.

Trade measures in MEAs

An increasing interest can be seen in using trade measures as enforcement mechanisms in international environmental agreements. These treaties were signed by countries who have a common interest in reducing transboundary pollution or conserving natural resources such as animals or birds and plants or preserving global commons such as ozone layer. According to the Register of International Treaties and other Agreements in the Field of the Environment, 24 out of 200 MEAs as of October 1994 had trade measures. Some important MEAs include Basel Convention on the Control of Transboundary Movements of Hazardous Wastes and their Disposal (1989), Montreal Protocol on Substances that deplete the Ozone Layer (1987), African Convention on the Conservation of Nature and Natural Resources (1968) and International Convention for the Protection of Birds (1950). The commonly used trade provision in these MEAs are the bans on exports and imports of the items which need to be preserved or the items which need to be restricted. For example, under the Montreal protocol, parties are required to ban importation of CFC-containing products and export of controlled substances.

The issue here is whether these trade provisions are the best in achieving environmental objectives. Given the well-known problems associated with the use of trade measures, it is important to make sure that these trade measures are necessary and effective in achieving environmental goals. If there is no other alternative, it is important to use the least restrictive trade measures which do not violate GATT/WTO principles.

Environmental taxes, charges and subsidies

Some taxes and charges designed to internalise environmental costs such as a carbon tax can affect trade. It has been claimed by business communities that the goods and services subject to these levies become less competitive in the world markets compared with those sourced from countries which do not impose such taxes on business. However, as discussed before there is no evidence to prove that this claim is true. As regards imports, generally these taxes do not become barriers to trade as long as they are applied to both imports and domestically produced goods at the same rate.

There are also other interventions such as subsidies for environmental purposes and laws relating to animal welfare which can affect trade. For example, some European countries such as Britain and Denmark give subsidies to encourage farmers to adopt organic farming methods. These subsidies can create additional costs in terms of loss of competitiveness to the producers from the countries like New Zealand and Australia where such subsidies are not granted.

Eco-labelling, packaging and recycling

Another type of environmental regulations which have been designed recently are eco-labelling, packaging, eco-standards and recycling requirements. The purpose of these is again to internalise externalities and protect the environment. Eco-labelling can take the form of either "single issue labels" or "life-cycle" types The first type is used for managing one environmental quality such as energy efficiency in refrigerators while the second type of labels are designed for "cradle to grave" management of products. Similarly, eco-packaging schemes are being used to encourage recycling, reuse and proper disposal of the waste. In addition, some countries use eco-standards for environmental management. For example, products such as pesticides, metals and foods are subject to a variety of standards in many countries.

Although most standards based on products can be justified in terms of the WTO Agreement on Technical Barriers to Trade (TBT) and they are much better than the use of trade measures for environmental purposes, these measures have a great potential for mis-use, acting as new barriers to trade. In particular, these measures can be used to favour domestic producers over imports and are likely to violate GATT/WTO principles. For example, it has been claimed that the German Packaging Law introduced recently imposed enormous costs on exports to the German market in relation to local German firms (Drake-Brockman and Anderson, 1994). Therefore, it is important for countries involved in trade to work towards mutual recognition and harmonisation of such measures.

These measures are being used by New Zealand as well as other countries including North-American and certain Asian countries which are important destinations for New Zealand exports. For example, New Zealand's eco-labelling scheme is managed by International Accreditation New Zealand (IANZ). It has granted labels for some products including paints and carpets while it has already developed criteria for a number of other products including detergents, plastic products and batteries.

Trade Policies for Environmental Protection

An increasing interest can be seen within the environmental community in the use of trade policy measures for environmental protection. It is believed that trade policy measures can be used for the purpose of improving environmental standards locally and internationally and encouraging countries to become parties to MEAs. One such use of trade policy measures is to impose restrictions on the imports from the environmentally lower standards countries. The argument is that these standards impose additional cost on the firms in environmentally higher standards countries and make them internationally less competitive.

A number of arguments have been presented against the use of trade policy measures for environmental purposes. Firstly, it has been shown that trade policy measures do not attack "the root causes of environmental problems and provide no positive incentives for sustained improvement" (Drake-Brockman and Anderson, 1994). Secondly, these measures can violate the important principles of GATT/WTO as they are discriminatory in most cases where there are differences in environmental standards between the WTO member countries. Thirdly, there are instances where trade restrictions have been applied on imports on the basis of production process and methods. A well-cited example is the United States ban on Mexican tuna fish because they do not use dolphin-safe nets. Sometimes these restrictions can be extended to goods which are entirely unrelated to the goods being restricted. For example, advanced developed countries can restrict imports of textile and clothing from certain developing countries where logging of tropical timber is carried out in an unsustainable manner. Therefore, trade policies are not only likely to be misused but also sometimes they tend to be environmentally counter productive. Some examples are the ban on ivory trade (International Convention on Trade in Endangered Species) and the export ban on Australian native birds. Environmental protection policies such as taxes and charges seem to be the best solutions to most environmental problems.

Trade and Environmental Concerns and WTO

The member countries of WTO are concerned with two conflicting policy objectives of protecting the environment and promoting multilateral trading system. It is interesting to see how WTO can accommodate both of these objectives in its overall programme of liberalising international trade in goods and services. In January, 1995, the Committee on Trade and Environment (CTE) was established by General Council to examine the issues involved in the trade and the environment debate[16]. It is now accepted by WTO that these two objectives should not be in conflict anymore. What is needed is coordination rather than choosing between trade and environmental policies themselves. It is clear now that environmental policies can be accommodated within WTO rules and regulations. We outline below some of the recommendations made by the CTE on the main items of the agenda[17].

One of the main items in the CTE work programme is to examine the relationship between the provisions of the multilateral trading system and trade measures for environmental purposes. First, it was concluded after lengthy discussions that there is already scope under WTO provisions to use trade measures for environmental objectives provided that they do not undermine WTO members' rights against unjustifiable discrimination. The most important GATT/WTO obligations are non-discrimination against members i.e. different sources of imports (most favoured nation - MFN) and non-discrimination between domestic products and imports. Second, it was agreed during the course of the discussions that the most preferred way of coordinating global and transboundary environment problems is to embark upon multilateral environmental agreements (MEAs). This may not be that difficult given that only 20 out of existing 200 MEAs use trade measures of which most notable are the Montreal Protocol, the Basel Convention and CITES. In particular, this may be much easier in the case where all WTO members ratify an MEA. A major problem arises, however, when a party to a MEA applies discriminatory trade measures against a non-MEA party who is a WTO member. In this case, this non-MEA member can complain against the MEA member for violation of WTO rights.

A number of options have been suggested to resolve the conflicts which can arise from coordinating MEAs and WTO provisions. These include the WTO dispute settlement mechanism, granting waivers to members to a WTO obligation which needs to be approved by a minimum of three-quarters of the membership, and amending or interpreting the WTO provisions in order to use some trade measures for environmental purposes. The last option, in particular, attracted considerable attention of the members and facilitated a number of proposals for implementing it. The purpose of this option is to create an "environmental window" for incorporating MEAs into the WTO system.

While a number of member countries of WTO presented proposals to reconcile the conflict in using trade measures for environmental purposes, the proposal made by New Zealand is worth mentioning. New Zealand proposed a scheme in which trade measures specifically mandated in a MEA are to be subject to differentiated treatment depending on whether the countries concerned are parties to a particular MEA. Under this proposal, trade measures which are used between parties to the MEA could not be challenged through WTO dispute settlement as they override the WTO obligations. If the measures are taken between non-parties, those should be accommodated under WTO rules and be subject to dispute settlement mechanism. Those measures should be implemented only if they receive adequate support from the member countries and were shown to be "necessary", "effective", and the "least trade restrictive" option available[18].

The other important items that were discussed at length at the CTE were: the relationship between the provisions of the multilateral trading system and requirements for environmental purposes relating to products, including standards and technical regulations, packaging, labelling and recycling (Item 3B); the provisions of the multilateral trading system with respect to the transparency of trade measures used for environmental purposes and environmental measures and requirements which have significant trade effects (Item 4); the effects on environmental measures on market access, especially in relation to developing countries, in particular to least developed among them, and environmental benefits of removing trade restrictions and distortions (Item 6); the issue of the export of domestically prohibited goods (Item 7). The CTE has made some important recommendations on these items. Some issues such as trade in services and the environment, the relationship between environmental policies relevant to trade and environmental measures with significant trade effects and the provisions of the multilateral trading system (Item 3), and the relationship between the provisions of the multilateral trading system and charges and taxes for environmental purposes (Item 3A) are still being discussed.

Notes

1   See Barrett (1997) for a recent survey of this literature.
2   The product, scale and structural effects of trade liberalisation on the environment are well known, see Grossman and Krueger (1992), and Copeland and Taylor (1994). OECD (1994a) provides an excellent summary of these effects.
3   Pollution-intensive industries are defined in the literature as the ones with products whose direct and indirect abatement costs are equal or greater than 1.85 per cent of total cost of production in the United States These include iron and steel, ferrous and nonferrous metals, paper and paper products and wood and wood products [see Low and Yeats (1992) for details].
4   This view, however, has been criticised by a number of economists including Oates et al. (1993) and Palmer et al. (1995). Some others have analysed the link between pollution control and technological advance [see for instance, Magat (1978), Millman and Prince (1989) and Barrett (1994)].
5   Environmental control costs include capital costs of environmental control equipment, depreciation on existing such equipment, operational costs associated with environmental management and research and development expenditure for compliance for environmental standards.
6   See Sanchez (1997) and Jaffe et al. (1995) for reviews of this literature.
7   Conversely relocation may stimulate trade. Colgate and Featherstone (1992) suggest that there are two lines through which capital relocation may stimulate trade. First, the imports of the home country may rise as the country imports products produced by foreign subsidiaries. Second, exports of the home country may rise as foreign subsidiaries require capital goods and intermediate inputs and parts for production.
8   Yet, this rise would be less than had they been poorly endowed with such capacities.
9   The theory of product life cycle provides another trade based argument for international capital flows (Vernon, 1966). Similarly, there are other explanations to capital movements which are based on the modern theory of FDI. These include locational advantage approach, ownership advantage theory and the internationalisation theory based on transaction costs, which were combined by Dunning in his "eclectic theory" of FDI and international production. [See Dunning (1988) for details.]
10   It is frequently assumed that LDCs are well endowed with assimilative and regenerative capacities, because of their large stock of untapped resources.

However, it should be recognised that some eco-systems are particularly fragile and that a quantification of the environmental capacities, not just the stock of resources, is required.

11   They include: Iron and steel and nonferrous metals; Fabricated metals; Stone, clay and glass; Chemicals; Pulp and paper; Rubber; Petroleum; and Mining.

12   For the United States, studies have estimated total ECCs of between $81 billion and $125 billion in 1990, Rutledge and Leonard (1993), Environmental Protection Agency (1990). In 1991, 65.5 per cent of total ECCs, estimated above, were incurred by business, 26.3 per cent by Government and 8.3 per cent by personal consumption, Rutledge and Leonard (1993).

13   Leonard (1988) makes a similar observation but stops short of terming them indirect ECCs. He argues that other factors, such as social blockage of new plants and constraints on hazardous production, which result in MNCs incurring negotiation and legal costs, must also be considered.

14   The Survey was conducted by phone and worked from a standard questionnaire. However, the phone survey had advantages in that I was able to explore tangent issues which were of particular significance for the firm. It also allowed me to qualify answers or pose further questions.

15   Pollutive industries were identified by Walter (1982), Tobey (1992), and Low and Yeats (1992). 25 firms were targeted in all, with 21 providing responses. Of the firms surveyed only two had less than 60 per cent of the operation engaged in manufacturing, with the lowest having only 30 per cent of its operation devoted to manufacturing and the remainder engaged in distributing other related products.

16   The CTE was able to build on previous discussions in 1992-93 within the GATT Group on Environmental Measures and International Trade (EMIT) and the discussions in 1994 within a Sub-Committee on Trade and the Environment of the WTO Preparatory Committee.

1⁊   See the Report (1996) of the Committee on Trade and Environment, WTO for details.

18   See the discussion paper on "Item 1: The relationship between the provisions of the multilateral trading system and trade measures for environmental purposes, including those pursuant to multilateral environmental agreements (MEAs)", Ministry of Foreign Affairs and Trade, Wellington, February 1996.

References

Barrett, S. (1997), *Environment and Growth*, mimeo, London Business School.
Breyer, S. (1982), *Regulation and its Reform*, Cambridge, MA: Harvard University Press.
Caincross, F. (1992), *Costing the Earth*, Boston: Harvard Business School Press.
Colgate, P. and Featherstone, K. (1992), "Changing Pattern of FDI in the Pacific Region: New Zealand." New Zealand Institute of Economic Research, Pacific Economic Cooperation Council, *Changing Pattern of Foreign Direct Investment in the Pacific Region,* 2, 216 - 30.
Copeland, B.R. (1994), "International Trade and the Environment: Policy Reform in a Polluted Small Open Economy", *Journal of Environmental Economics and Management*, 26, 44-65.
Copeland, B.R. and Taylor, M. (1994), "North-South Trade and the Environment", in *Quarterly Journal of Economics*, 109, 755-787.
Dean, J. (1992), "Trade and the Environment: A Survey of Literature", in P. Low (ed), *International Trade and the Environment*, World Bank Discussion Papers, 159, 15-28.
Drake-Brockman, J. and Anderson, K. (1994), "The trade/environment debate and its implications for Asia-Pacific", Policy Discussion Paper, Centre for International Economic Studies, University of Adelaide.
Dunning, J. (1988) *Explaining International Production*, London; Boston: Unwin Hyman.
Grossman, G.M. and Krueger, A.L. (1993), "Environmental Impacts of a North American Free Trade Agreement", in P. Garber (ed), *The US-Mexico Free Trade Agreement*, Cambridge, MA: MIT Press.
Grossman, G.M. and Krueger, A.L. (1995), "Economic Growth and the Environment", *Quarterly Journal of Economics*, 110, 353-375.
Hewison, G. (1995), *Reconciling Trade and the Environment*, Wellington: Institute of Policy Studies.
Jaffe, A.B., Peterson, S.R., Portney, P.R. and Stavins, R.B. (1995), "Environmental Regulation and the Competitiveness of U.S. Manufacturing: What does the Evidence Tell Us?", *Journal of Economic Literature*, XXXIII, 132-163.
Kulessa, M.E. (1992), "Free trade and protection of the environment: Is the GATT in need of Reform", *Intereconomics*, July/August, 27, 3, 105-117.
Leonard, H.J. (1988), *Pollution and the Struggle for the World Product: Multinational Corporations, Environment, and International Comparative Advantage*, New York: Cambridge University Press.
Lopez, R. (1992), "The Environment as a Factor of Production: The Economic Growth and Policy Linkages", in P. Low (ed), *International Trade and the Environment*, World Bank Discussion Papers, 159, 137-156.

Low, P. and Yeats, A. (1992), "Do 'Dirty' Industries Migrate?", in P. Low (ed), *International Trade and the Environment*, World Bank Discussion Papers, 159, 89-103.

MAF (1994), *Impacts on the environment of reduced agricultural subsidies: A case study of New Zealand*, Wellington: Ministry of Agriculture and Fisheries.

O'Connor, D. (1994), *Managing the environment with rapid industrialisation: Lessons from the East Asian Experience*, Paris: OECD Development Centre.

Radetzki, M. (1992), "Economic Growth and Environment", in P. Low (ed), *International Trade and the Environment*, World Bank Discussion Papers, 159, 121-134.

Ratnayake, R. (1998), "Do stringent environmental regulations reduce international competitiveness: Evidence from an inter-industry analysis", *International Journal of the Economics of Business*, 5, 1, 77-96.

Ratnayake, R. (1998), "Does Environmental Regulation Stimulate Innovative Responses? Evidence from US Manufacturing", *Working Papers in Economics*, 188, The University of Auckland: Department of Economics.

Rutledge, G. and Leonard, M. (1993), "Pollution Abatement and Control Expenditures, 1987-91", *Survey of Current Business*, 55-62. (May)

Selden, T.M. and Song, D. (1994), "Environmental Quality and Development: Is There a Kuznets Curve for Air Pollution Emissions", *Journal of Environmental Economics and Management*, XXVII, 147-62.

Siebert, H. (1987), *Economics of the Environment*, Berlin; New York: Springer-Verlag.

Tobey, J. (1990), "The Effects of Domestic Environmental Policies on the Pattern of World Trade: An Empirical Test", *Kyklos*, 43, Fasc.2, 191-209.

Townsend, B. and Ratnayake, R. (1998), "The effects of trade liberalisation on New Zealand's CO_2 emissions: A CGE assessment", unpublished internal paper, Department of Economics, The University of Auckland.

Walter, I. (1973), "The Pollution Content of American Trade", *Western Economic Journal*, 11, 61-70.

Walter, I. (1982), "Environmentally Induced Industrial Relocation to Developing Countries", Rubin, S. and Graham, T. (eds), *Environment and Trade*, Allanheld, Osmun & Co. Publishers.

Wydeveld, M. (1998), "FDI and the environmental regulatory regimes of the countries of the APEC region: Where does New Zealand stand?", unpublished internal paper, Department of Economics, The University of Auckland.

Yezer, A. and Philipson, A. (1974), "Influence of Environmental Considerations on Agriculture and Industrial Decisions to Locate outside the Continental US", Public Interest Economics Centre.

2 The Effects of Trade Liberalisation on New Zealand's CO_2 Emissions: A Computable General Equilibrium Assessment

BLAIR TOWNSEND and RAVI RATNAYAKE[1]

Introduction

The link between trade and environment has been a prominent issue for most of the nineties. The number and scope of environmental concerns is growing rapidly and intensifying public interest in environmental issues. Increasing economic openness has led to concerns about possible detrimental effects on the environment. Expanded trading opportunities in natural resources and hazardous products and the possibility that trade liberalisation could significantly undercut domestic environmental policies through trade diversion have augmented fears about the environment. At the same time, pressures have mounted to use trade instruments to achieve environmental ends. There is an emerging consensus in the environmentalist community opposing free trade (Drake-Brockman and Anderson, 1994). While some economists see this as merely another excuse for protectionism, recent work has begun to investigate the theoretical and empirical relationships between international trade and environmental quality.

Supporters of trade liberalisation and of environmental protection share a common goal, to improve social welfare, and a common problem, the need to promote multilateral cooperation to fully achieve that objective. However, the benefits of freer trade are well known by supporters of liberalised trade, but environmentalists tend to see trade policy as merely a potential instrument to achieve their objectives (either to "compensate" domestic producers for high domestic environmental standards or to entice other countries to raise their environmental standards) (Drake-Brockman and Anderson, 1994).

Free traders tend to take exception to the environmentalists impinging into the free trade debate, especially when they believe that freer trade is environmentally friendly, not only in the sense that it allows more efficient allocation of the world's resources, but also in the sense that, by raising living standards, it enables a greater allocation of resources to protecting the environment.

Liberalisation and expansion of international trade, growth, and protection of the natural environment are all compatible with the concept of sustainable development. There is however, the possibility that certain restrictive trade policies, adopted in response to environmental concerns, could be sufficiently inefficient so as to worsen welfare in many countries. Furthermore these restrictive trade policies in some cases may even heighten rather than reduce environmental degradation. As such, there is a demand for an improved understanding of the various interactions between trade and the environment, and between environmental and trade policies, as well as their respective effects on welfare.

New Zealand provides an interesting case study for analysing environmental effects of trade liberalisation. There has also been a recent intensification of interest in environmental matters in New Zealand which has, in conjunction with New Zealand's reliance on environmental quality to maintain it's international "clean-green" image, raised the profile of the trade and environment debate in New Zealand. These issues are of particular relevance for New Zealand because of its dependence on international trade, and the removal of trade-related protectionist measures. Growth in the New Zealand economy has been predicated on economy-wide reforms, in particular trade and investment liberalisation, and this trend towards a more open and deregulated economy is forecast to continue (Hewison, 1995). Environmentalism is now a significant influence on public policy development in New Zealand as in other countries and is likely to continue to increase in importance. In response to these increasing environmental concerns New Zealand has recently introduced innovative environmental policies which promote sustainability. Furthermore, New Zealand is expected to implement additional environmental policies in the near future such as a carbon tax to limit carbon dioxide emissions[2]. Following the formation of the

Comprehensive Strategy on Climate Change New Zealand established a domestic carbon dioxide target consistent with the Framework Convention on Climate Change (FCCC). New Zealand's primary carbon dioxide objective is to take precautionary actions to help stabilise atmospheric concentrations of carbon dioxide, in order to reduce risk from global climate change and to meet New Zealand's commitments under the FCCC. Specifically, to return net emissions of carbon dioxide to no more than their 1990 levels by the year 2000 (but to aim for reduction in net carbon dioxide emissions to 20 per cent below their 1990 levels by the year 2000 if this is cost effective, will not harm our international trade, and has a net benefit to New Zealand society) and to maintain them at this level thereafter (Ministry of Environment, 1995). These factors, in conjunction with the present lack of trade and environment related studies on New Zealand, mean that an investigation of the likely effects of trade liberalisation on welfare and carbon dioxide emissions, both in the absence of, and presence of, a carbon tax is particularly pertinent.

International Trade and the Environment

It is postulated that international trade may have both positive and negative effects on the environment (OECD, 1994a). In most sectors the direct effects of trade are small, largely due to the fact that only a small share of environmentally-sensitive goods are traded, and because trade is only one of many factors that affect the environment. Less well understood are the indirect effects trade may have on the environment by its influence on world prices and market conditions. In general, trade is not the fundamental cause of environmental problems, which are predominantly the result of market and intervention failures (OECD, 1994a). Market failures result from the inability of the market to correctly value and allocate environmental resources and the failure to internalise environmental costs in commodity prices. Intervention failures occur when government policies (environmental, trade and others) do not correct for, create or exacerbate market failures. Trade expands the scale of economic activity and market growth, which can provide additional resources for environmental protection, but which may also be environmentally detrimental in the presence of market and intervention failures. Trade also facilitates the international diffusion of environmentally beneficial products and services, but similarly it is also the means by which environmentally harmful goods are exchanged internationally.

The impacts of trade liberalisation result from its obvious purpose, which is to change existing trade policies in the direction of freer trade. Because of this trade liberalisation can have significant positive impacts on the environment by correcting existing trade policy intervention failures. It may also have some negative impacts related to an expansion of trade in the absence of correcting other existing market and policy intervention failures. In addition to the product, scale, and structural effects, OECD (1994a) identifies a further category of effects trade liberalisation may have, namely regulatory effects, in its implications for environmental standards and policies[3].

CGE Analyses of the Effects of Trade Liberalisation on Environmental Quality

There are only a few studies to examine the environmental effects of trade liberalisation using CGE modelling framework. One such study is by Espinosa and Smith (1995) who uses a CGE model to investigate these effects for the EC, the United States, and Japan. The model incorporates morbidity and mortality effects of particulates, sulphur dioxides, and nitrogen dioxides and uses nonmarket valuation estimates, with a specification for consumer preferences that allows changes in atmospheric emissions to diffuse in different amounts to each region and have feedback effects on market demands. Because the ambient environment is treated as another mechanism (beyond markets) for interactions between economic agents, all policy interventions can, in principle, have market and nonmarket impacts on Hicksian welfare measures. The analysis presents both impacts by comparing the results of model specifications with and without environmental feedback effects to evaluate trade liberalisation and environmental degradation scenarios.

The results indicate that the impact of environmental effects is minor when the policy scenario focuses on parameters linked to market transactions. When the mortality effects of pollution are included with those of morbidity, a more pronounced difference in the impact of removing trade barriers is seen. However, even without the mortality effects, the increased domestic production of durables induced by the substitution and income effects of reduced trade barriers, generates more pollution which in turn increases health costs and therefore the subsistence needs in the services sector. A reversal of the welfare effect was engineered by increasing the emission rate, this had a negative welfare effect even when excluding mortality effects. Overall, trade liberalisation is found to have a negative effect on the environment, but when accompanied by an environmental policy, it is found to be environmentally beneficial and welfare enhancing.

Beghin, Roland-Holst and van der Mensbrugghe (1995) analyse the environmental implications of growth and opening up of trade in Mexico based on an empirical economy-wide model. In particular, they analyse how tradeoffs between growth and environmental objectives can be minimised by using targeted policies on pollution emissions in coordination with outward oriented trade strategies. Pollution emissions in the model are linked by using polluting inputs rather than polluting output.

The results show economic integration will not exacerbate environmental degradation in Mexico, and that the pollution elasticity with respect to growth is very stable in Mexico, and is not affected by trade. The new patterns of resource allocation, trade, and production are found to be less pollution intensive after trade liberalisation, however a strong scale effect dominates this and economic growth increases pollution in most sectors. It is concluded that environmental policy reforms that target the use of polluting good are the best way to achieve pollution mitigation and that it would be appropriate to target a subset of sectors and pollutants, to lower administrative costs while achieving high abatement levels.

Perroni and Wigle (1994) present a general equilibrium model of the world economy with local and global environmental externalities, and use it to investigate the relationship between trade liberalisation and the environment. Their results show international trade has little effect on environmental quality and that the magnitude of the welfare effects of environmental policies is not significantly affected by changes in trade policy. They also find the size and distribution of the gains from trade liberalisation appear to be little affected by changes in environmental policies. It is argued that using trade policy for environmental objectives may be very costly as trade accounts for a small share of world production, a large share of trade is in environmentally clean goods, and pollution-intensive traded goods have abatement costs which are only a small percentage of total costs. Furthermore, even without environmental policy, trade liberalisation may promote a more efficient use of world resources.

The majority of the literature on trade and the environment is theoretical in nature with most analyses agreeing that trade policies are a poor substitute for domestic environmental policies, and that trade liberalisation and environmental protection can be treated as separate objectives[4]. However there has been very little attention paid to the empirical or computable quantification of these results[5]. This is particularly so in the case of the effects of trade liberalisation on the environment with little empirical evidence in existence and computational evidence in the form of CGE analyses in it's infancy.

Economic analysis of the relationship between trade and the environment in New Zealand is scarce[6]. One significant study on this issue examines the impact on the New Zealand environment of reduced agricultural subsidies in New Zealand for the period from 1975 to 1990 (MAF, 1993). This study points out that from 1975 to 1984, New Zealand maintained restrictive and managed economic policies as well as relatively high agricultural assistance levels, especially for pastoral farming, compared with other countries. In 1984 as part of the reforms to open the New Zealand economy product price and farm input subsidies were removed. Most of the agricultural assistance that remained has since been dissociated from production and mostly consists of research, disaster relief and exit grants. The elimination of agricultural subsidies after 1984 had instantaneous effects on both farm inputs and outputs. In particular, the study notes that the use of phosphate fertiliser, pesticides and the rate of development of marginal lands (which was often indigenous forest) into pasture, declined substantially. The effects of these changes were to reduce the likelihood of off-site contamination, in particular water bodies and degradation of newly developed land. In addition the environment benefited from a fall in sheep numbers and the diversification of pastoral farming away from sheep to deer, goats, horticulture, and forestry, particularly from the reduced intensity of sheep grazing in certain hill country areas of New Zealand. The study found that agriculture liberalisation, in particular the removal of subsidies, resulted in some very positive environmental outcomes.

However, the study also noted that the legacy of poor land management practices in the past was still apparent. The study concluded that the liberalisation led to a cut in input use and stocking, but also meant farmers faced increasing income restraints. As a consequence in certain areas the farmlands vulnerability to the effects of droughts and storms has increased. In many cases, farmers have lacked the income to adequately maintain land resources, invest in soil conservation, manage pests such as rabbits and possums, or convert marginal land into forestry. The vulnerability of certain farming areas to the effects of adverse climate conditions and degradation of land resources are problems which remain from the "development" (as opposed to "conservation") oriented policies of the past.

A Trade and Environment Focused Multisectoral CGE Model of New Zealand

This study attempts to assess the effects of trade liberalisation on welfare and emissions levels, and the degree to which these effects are influenced by environmental policy. It is expected, based on theoretical analyses, that the results will show trade liberalisation to be welfare enhancing, and for it to have a minimal impact on environmental quality, in the presence of environmental policies which internalise environmental externalities.

Although this study concentrates on the effects within the New Zealand economy, the results subsequently obtained will be widely applicable to other small open market based economies. Based on theoretical analyses, it is anticipated that the results will show trade liberalisation to be welfare enhancing in the presence of environmental policies which internalise environmental externalities. Because the questions raised in this study have economy-wide implications, this study assesses the consequences of trade and environmental policies by incorporating a trade and environment focus into a computable general equilibrium (CGE) model for the New Zealand economy. This question is easily examined in a general equilibrium context and the results of the two policies not only on the environment, but on the rest of the economy, can be compared. The advantage of CGE models over other empirical models is that they can capture the numerous complex relationships between variables in the model economy, many of which may not be apparent or expected before the analysis. Furthermore only a general equilibrium evaluation of these policies can assess the impacts of their respective effects on welfare.

The model is relatively simple and closely follows neoclassical theory, however interindustry linkages, sectoral protection, and sectoral emissions are explicitly modelled. The model that will be employed is in part based on the work of De Melo and Tarr (1992), who have developed a CGE model for the United States economy to analyse the effects of trade liberalisation under various scenarios. By using a similar type of model but specifically including the environment (in the form of emissions), it will be possible to achieve an analysis of environmental effects of trade liberalisation in New Zealand, and whether it remains a welfare enhancing policy change. This analysis is performed both with and without an emissions tax to evaluate trade liberalisation and environmental degradation scenarios[7].

Overview of the Model

The model is a simple neoclassical model for a small open economy, focusing on international trade and the environment. The model is designed to analyse the medium and long run effects of trade liberalisation on welfare and the level of carbon dioxide emissions both with, and without the presence of an emissions tax. It is also assumed that all consumers have identical preferences so that their behaviour is modelled by a "representative consumer". The government collects tariffs and environmental taxes, where the government's budget surplus is distributed to the consumer as a lump sum payment. The single representative consumer purchases domestic and foreign goods and maximises utility, given income and prices. The consumer's income is determined endogenously.

The exchange rate is flexible and is assumed to adjust to maintain the current account position, expressed in foreign units, which remains unchanged as a result of policy simulation. Thus any exogenously given current account deficit that exists in the year for which the model is benchmarked will continue to prevail after the policy simulation. This treatment of the current account guarantees that there will be no permanent capital transfers taken from or given to the rest of the world in the policy simulations. This assumption makes welfare analysis of changes in policy more meaningful and transparent.

Producers maximise profits subject to a constant returns to scale technology. Given technology, and output and input prices, the representative firm in each industry purchases primary factors and domestic and foreign intermediate inputs so as to minimise the costs of producing a level of output. Production substitution possibilities utilise two level nesting. At the first level is a Leontief input-output production function. At this level firms use a composite of primary factors of production, emissions, and n composite intermediate intermediates inputs, one from each sector. At the second level each of the composite functions is defined. The primary factor of production is a composite of two primary factors, capital and labour, which substitute smoothly for each other through CES value added functions. Intermediates from different sectors, as well as emissions (in the form of a nontraded intermediate input), enter production with a fixed coefficient (Leontief) technology[8].

For consumption demand a Stone-Geary linear expenditure system (LES) allows for cross price effects in demand. Products produced by New Zealand and the rest of the world are treated as differentiated, with substitution possibilities between domestic and foreign produced goods of the same category being represented by a nested CES function.

A final issue is whether New Zealand would face fixed terms of trade for the trade policy changes to be modelled. This study's view is that in most cases the small country assumption for New Zealand in world markets is a good first order approximation. However it is also assumed that New Zealand would face a noninfinite foreign elasticity of demand for its agricultural exports[9].

It is reasonable to assume that the amount of capital in each sector is fixed at the beginning of the period being modelled, but since we are interested in finding an equilibrium configuration for some future year without actually modelling the path to it, then it is sensible to allow the model to determine sectoral capital stocks endogenously. The specification of the production set of the economy is incomplete without factor availability restraints, here we assume capital and labour stocks are fixed. Each sector of the economy is treated as made up of many similar firms maximising profits and bidding for the scarce factors. We assume producers maximise profits and that demanders minimise the cost of purchasing a given quantity of composite good.

Finally, it should be emphasised that an applied CGE model cannot be seen as a short run projections model and is not intended for that purpose. It is better suited to explain medium to long run trends and structural responses to changes in policy. This is not to say the CGE model should not produce good predictive performance. In fact, they should be able to predict, conditional upon policy variables, trends in sectoral structure, intersectoral terms of trade, and trade performance, and do so more consistently than linear models or more informal methods.

For analysing the effects of trade liberalisation, and carbon dioxide emissions the economy is aggregated into five sectors: Agriculture and Food; Textiles, Apparel and Leather; Chemicals; Manufactures; and Services. This aggregation was chosen because it enables the isolation of separate industries in the model which are of significance in terms of trade restrictions and emissions levels, furthermore, accurate data is readily available for these industry classifications. Since both the average level of protection and the dispersion of protection across sectors contribute to the cost of protection, in principle it is always preferable to disaggregate further[10]. However, dissaggregation is difficult in an economywide context, as it is often difficult to obtain reliable elasticity estimates. For assessing the costs of protection in the textiles and apparel, and manufacturing sectors, and emissions in the agriculture, manufacturing, and chemical sectors, this aggregation is adequate as these sectors remain explicitly treated, isolated sectors of the economy[11].

In order to model the effects of trade liberalisation on the environment, sectoral emissions are incorporated into the model. Each sector uses emissions as an intermediate good, in the form specified by the Leontief technology in the production. This amounts to a linear relationship between emissions and production. This relationship is detailed in equation 1 where Z_i^x is the total production emissions of carbon dioxide by sector i, and ϕ_i^x is the rate at which output in sector i, X_i, produces carbon dioxide.

$$Z_i^x = \phi_i^x X_i \tag{1}$$

This assumption of Leontief technology does however limit the ways in which firms can respond to a ceiling on emissions, or a carbon tax. Firms are restricted to lowering output in order to lower their emissions, they cannot substitute between inputs with different emissions rates, nor can they utilise less polluting technology.

In addition to emissions being incorporated as an intermediate good in production, the consumption of goods is also treated as generating emissions. This relationship is analogous to that above for production and is detailed in equation 2, where Z_i^c is the consumption emissions of carbon dioxide by sector i, and ϕ_i^c is the rate at which consumption of sector i, C_i, produces carbon dioxide.

$$Z_i^c = \phi_i^c C_i \tag{2}$$

Thus, the total emissions attributable to each sector from both production and consumption can be seen in equation 3.

$$Z_i = Z_i^x + Z_i^c \tag{3}$$

In some of the policy scenarios to be modelled the aggregate level of economy-wide emissions, shown in equation 4, is required to meet the condition represented in equation 5. This is, in effect, what is required by the FCCC whereby carbon dioxide emissions must not exceed the level that existed in 1990. In order to enforce this condition in the model it is desirable to include an endogenous emissions tax. This requires the price of both domestic production and consumption goods to include the cost of that good's contribution to economy-wide emissions, so that the most polluting goods have to pay the highest tax. This has the effect that consumers will react by substituting away from these higher priced goods, and so their production and/or consumption will fall along with their contribution to emissions.

$$Z = \sum_{i=1}^{n} Z_i \tag{4}$$

$$Z \leq \overline{Z_{1990}} \tag{5}$$

Simulation Results

Two trade and environment policy scenarios are examined in this study:

1) The effects of trade liberalisation are examined in the absence of a carbon tax,
2) The effects of trade liberalisation are examined in the presence of a carbon tax.

In each case the simulations are performed for both the medium and long run. The medium run is calculated by limiting capital expansion in any one sector to twenty per cent above its initial equilibrium. In the long run there is no limit on sectoral capital stocks.

Case one: the effects of trade liberalisation in the absence of a carbon tax

Trade liberalisation in the absence of a carbon tax can be simulated by implementing the model with all tariffs set to zero, and the endogenous emissions tax also set to zero. The effects of this policy simulation on utility and emissions can be seen in Table 2.1.

The generation of emissions follows a linear form and as such the production and consumption emissions within any sector are in direct proportion to the output and consumption in that same sector. However these emissions are generated at different rates and so the expansion of a more polluting sector at the expense of a decline in the cleaner sectors will lead to an increase in economy-wide emissions even if total production within the economy has remained constant. Production emissions in the medium run following trade liberalisation rise by 2.8 per cent, this is mainly due to the increase in manufacturing which has a high emissions rate. As the gains from trade are realised then production shifts into textiles with a consequent increase in textiles production emissions. In the long run analysis production emissions are seen to increase by 3.3 per cent. The fall in price of consumption goods following trade liberalisation leads to an increase in consumption both in the medium and long run, and this in turn leads to an overall increase in consumption emissions of 1.8 per cent in the long run. Following the removal of the tariffs economy-wide emissions are seen to increase by 2.3 per cent in the medium run, and by 2.9 per cent in the long run.

The effects of trade liberalisation on welfare are well known, and the expected welfare improvement is also found in this case. Because a Stone-Geary utility function is used as the measure of welfare in this model the percentage change in its value is not relevant as the utility function is merely ordinal not cardinal[12]. However its value can be used to see if the representative consumer is better or worse off under the new policy scenario. Following trade liberalisation it can be seen in Table 2.1 that the representative consumer is in fact made better off (in the long run), insofar as the utility function includes all factors influencing the representative consumer's welfare. In this case however, that cannot be said since the utility function does not include the level of ambient emissions either as a non-separable or separable effect on preferences. As such, this estimate of welfare is upwardly biased when accompanied by an increase in the level of emissions. Therefore despite the representative consumer appearing to be better off following trade liberalisation, this cannot be said with certainty, and so the effect of trade liberalisation on welfare is ambiguous. Whether the representative consumer is in fact better or worse off following trade liberalisation depends on whether the associated disutility due to the increase in emissions is smaller or greater than the change in utility as measured by the utility function.

In summary, it can be seen from the results that trade liberalisation does lead to a decline in environmental quality in terms of emissions, and as such has an ambiguous effect on welfare. Therefore it cannot be determined at this stage whether trade liberalisation in the absence of a carbon tax is a welfare enhancing policy strategy.

Case two: the effects of trade liberalisation in the presence of a carbon tax

Trade liberalisation in the presence of a carbon tax can be simulated by implementing the model with all tariffs set to zero and by enforcing the relationship given in equation 5 where emissions are capped at their 1990 level (as required by the FCCC). This latter constraint is equilibrated by the endogenous carbon tax when generating the new equilibrium.

In this policy simulation, total emissions are subject to a constraint which caps them at the same level as the benchmarked equilibrium. As such trade liberalisation in the presence of an endogenous carbon tax will not increase total economy-wide emissions. However as mentioned in case one above emissions are generated at different rates in each sector and as such the carbon tax will affect each sector to varying degrees. This is most evident in the case of manufacturing production and chemicals consumption, which exhibit the highest emissions rates. Manufacturing production emissions decline by 18.1 per cent in the long run (3.3 per cent in case one), and chemicals consumption emissions fall by 5.7 per cent in the long run (rises by 3.4 per cent in case one). Overall production emissions decline by 7.2 per cent as production falls in the medium run and consumption emissions fall by 3.6 per cent. This results in a reduction in economy-wide emissions in the medium run of 6.4 per cent. In the long run analysis production emissions rise by 0.6 per cent, whereas consumption emissions fall by 2.1 per cent, resulting in total economy-wide emissions remaining unchanged.

In the discussion on welfare effects in case one above it was acknowledged that the use of the utility function in this model lead to a biased estimate of welfare when the level of emissions changed. However, in the policy scenario examined here, the total emissions level remains unchanged through the use of an endogenous emissions tax. Because of this the utility function can be employed as an unbiased estimate of the level of welfare attained by the representative consumer. The fact that the total level of emissions is unchanged (in the long run) means that there can be no disutility from an increase in emissions and so their effects on welfare can be ignored when we are simply comparing the case two policy simulation with the initial equilibrium. From Table 2.1 it can be seen that trade liberalisation in the presence of a carbon tax is in fact welfare enhancing, with the level of utility attained being slightly less than that attained in the case one scenario. From this it can be said that the representative consumer is unambiguously made better off through a policy of trade liberalisation in the presence of a carbon tax.

In summary, it can be seen from the results that trade liberalisation in the presence of a carbon tax has no affect on environmental quality in terms of emissions, and as such unambiguously enhances welfare[13]. Therefore it can be determined that trade liberalisation in the presence of a carbon tax is a superior policy strategy to the protectionist trade policy present in the initial benchmarked case.

Table 2.1: Simulation Results

Variable		Value					Per cent Change			
		Initial	Case 1 Medium Run	Case 1 Long Run	Case 2 Medium Run	Case 2 Long Run	Case 1 Medium Run	Case 1 Long Run	Case 2 Medium Run	Case 2 Long Run
Utility		1.318	1.318	1.332	1.320	1.330	0.0%	1.1%	0.2%	0.9%
Production Emissions	AGF	3.785	3.668	4.053	3.281	4.305	-3.1%	7.1%	-13.3%	13.7%
	TEX	0.283	0.132	1.374	0.129	1.688	-53.4%	385.5%	-54.4%	496.5%
	CHE	0.383	0.335	0.346	0.321	0.343	-12.5%	-9.7%	-16.2%	-10.4%
	MAN	7.199	8.109	6.963	6.030	5.897	12.6%	-3.3%	-16.2%	-18.1%
	SER	6.906	6.833	6.429	7.459	6.438	-1.1%	-6.9%	8.0%	-6.8%
Total		*18.556*	*19.077*	*19.165*	*17.220*	*18.671*	*2.8%*	*3.3%*	*-7.2%*	*0.6%*
Consumption Emissions	AGF	0.226	0.225	0.226	0.225	0.226	-0.4%	0.0%	-0.4%	0.0%
	TEX	0.077	0.081	0.082	0.081	0.081	5.2%	6.5%	5.2%	5.2%
	CHE	2.450	2.498	2.534	2.233	2.310	2.0%	3.4%	-8.9%	-5.7%
	MAN	0.622	0.624	0.634	0.621	0.629	0.3%	1.9%	-0.2%	1.1%
	SER	2.305	2.297	2.305	2.316	2.317	-0.3%	0.0%	0.5%	0.5%
Total		*5.680*	*5.725*	*5.781*	*5.476*	*5.563*	*0.8%*	*1.8%*	*-3.6%*	*-2.1%*
Total Emissions	AGF	4.010	3.894	4.278	3.506	4.531	-2.9%	6.7%	-12.6%	13.0%
	TEX	0.359	0.213	1.456	0.211	1.770	-40.7%	305.6%	-41.2%	393.0%
	CHE	2.833	2.834	2.880	2.553	2.654	0.0%	1.7%	-9.9%	-6.3%
	MAN	7.821	8.733	7.597	6.651	6.526	11.7%	-2.9%	-15.0%	-16.6%
	SER	9.211	9.130	8.734	9.775	8.755	-0.9%	-5.2%	6.1%	-5.0%
Total		*24.235*	*24.803*	*24.946*	*22.696*	*24.235*	*2.3%*	*2.9%*	*-6.4%*	*0.0%*

Conclusion

The objective of this study was to assess the effects of trade liberalisation on welfare and emissions levels in the New Zealand economy, and the degree to which these effects are influenced by environmental policy. In order to estimate the consequences of trade and environmental policies a computable general equilibrium model of the New Zealand economy incorporating a trade and environment focus was constructed. While acknowledging that the estimation of these effects using the CGE model employed in this study should be used to complement other approaches to their estimation, the application of the model does show this method to be valuable for developing policy responses. In this sense the relevance of this study is not solely confined to the case of New Zealand, but has implications for many other small open market based economies contemplating freer trade policies.

The main focus of this study was to assess the effects of trade liberalisation both in the presence, and in the absence of a carbon tax, on the environment (emissions) and welfare. The results of these two policy scenarios, namely, the effects of trade liberalisation in the absence of a carbon tax, and the effects of trade liberalisation in the presence of a carbon tax have resulted in the following effects being identified with respect to emissions and welfare. Trade liberalisation on its own is found to have a negative effect on the level of emissions, with total emissions increasing by 2.9 per cent. When the impact of this increase in emissions on welfare is ignored, welfare is seen to rise following trade liberalisation, however when the impact of increased emissions is considered, the effect on welfare is ambiguous. The simulation of trade liberalisation in the presence of an endogenous carbon tax maintaining the emissions level, is on the other hand, found to have an unambiguous positive effect on welfare, with emissions remaining constant. Furthermore, the policy of trade liberalisation accompanied by environmental policy is also seen to generate superior welfare outcomes than the present protectionist trade policy, while leaving the environment unaffected.

The results obtained in this study compare favourably with those found by Smith and Espinosa (1995), as well as those reported by Beghin, Roland-Holst and Van Der Mensbrugghe (1995). Both of these studies find trade liberalisation, when considered alone, to have a negative effect on the environment, and trade liberalisation when accompanied by environmental policy to be environmentally beneficial and welfare enhancing. The results presented in this study are also consistent with those based on theoretical analyses, such as Anderson (1992a), who shows that, "...there is an unambiguous welfare gain from trade for a small country provided something approaching the optimal environmental policy is also introduced..." Furthermore, the hypotheses that trade policies are a poor substitute for environmental policies, and that trade liberalisation is welfare enhancing in the presence of environmental policy, have been confirmed in this analysis.

The results of the two policy simulations as presented above have clear-cut policy implications, both for New Zealand, and more generally for other small market based economies contemplating liberalised trade regimes.

It is apparent from the results that the use of trade policy (namely, tariffs) to protect the environment is second-best. Furthermore, the results clearly demonstrate that the optimal policy is one of trade liberalisation accompanied by an environmental policy. It has been shown that this policy can realise gains from trade liberalisation without compromising environmental quality. Trade liberalisation on it's own does lead to environmental degradation. However, these negative environmental effects are shown to exist only when there is a lack of appropriate environmental policies in place. As such it can reasonably be concluded that there is nothing to fear from trade liberalisation with respect to the environment, provided an appropriate environmental policy is present. Therefore New Zealand's policy of continued trade liberalisation is unlikely to have serious environmental impacts (in terms of carbon dioxide emissions), given that the implementation of a carbon tax is expected in the near term.

Notes

1   The financial assistance from the Foundation for Research, Science and Technology (FoRST) project on APEC Integration: Implications on New Zealand, is gratefully acknowledged.

2   See Ministry for the Environment (1994).

3   The product, scale and structural effects of trade liberalisation on the environment are well known, see Grossman and Krueger (1992), and

Copeland and Taylor (1994). OECD (1994a) provides an excellent summary of these effects.

4   See for example Bhagwati (1981).

5   For a survey of empirical studies see Dean (1992) and Beghin, Roland-Holst, and Van Der Mensbrugghe (1994). Computable general equilibrium studies have been undertaken by Perroni and Wiggle (1994), Smith and Espinosa (1994, 1995), and Beghin, Roland-Holst, and van der Mensbrugghe (1995).

6   Because of the difficulty of obtaining environmental data small open economies such as New Zealand have not been studied. However, a number of government agencies including Ministry of Foreign Affairs and Trade (MFAT), Ministry of Agriculture and Fisheries (MAF), and Ministry for the Environment (MfE) have identified relevant issues for New Zealand.

7   The emissions tax is levied against carbon dioxide emissions and is essentially the same as the carbon tax to be implemented in New Zealand in the near future. Here the terms emissions tax and carbon tax will be used interchangeably.

8   In virtually all applications an inter-industry table is used, and intermediates from different sectors usually enter with a fixed coefficient (Leontief) technology, De Melo and Tarr (1992). Existing CGE models have often retained the assumption of fixed coefficients for intermediate technology. This choice of functional forms has the practical advantage of reducing considerably the number of parameters necessary for implementing the model.

9   While New Zealand is not significant in overall world trade, in terms of world agricultural trade New Zealand is considered an important player (MFAT, 1993). For example New Zealand is far and away the largest sheepmeat exporter in the world, the second largest dairy exporter and a significant exporter of beef, and horticulture, particularly kiwifruit and apples.

10   It is well known that the costs of protection are a function not only of average tariff levels but also of their dispersion, see Johnson (1960).

11   The costs of protection as well as emissions are assessed for all sectors, however these industries exhibit the highest levels of protection and emissions respectively.

12   It is easy enough to construct a measure of the change in welfare, such as equivalent variation or compensating variation, from the Stone-Geary utility function in order to measure how much better or worse off the representative consumer is in the simulated equilibrium (see De Melo and Tarr, 1992 for an example of such a measure). However, the purpose of this study is not to investigate how much better or worse off the representative

consumer is, but rather whether or not they are better or worse off, as such this specification is sufficient.

13   This result is supported in theoretical analysis, see Anderson (1992a).

References

Anderson, K. (1992a), "The Standard Welfare Economics of Policies Affecting Trade and the Environment", in Anderson, K. and Blackhurst, R. (eds), *The Greening of World Trade Issues*, New York: Harvester.

Anderson, K. (1992b), "Agricultural Trade Liberalisation and the Environment: A Global Perspective", *The World Economy*, 15(1), 153-171.

Beghin, J., Roland-Holst, D. and van der Mensbrugghe, D. (1994), "Trade and Pollution Linkages: Piecemeal Reform and Optimal Intervention", *OECD Development Centre Technical Papers*, 99.

Beghin J., Roland-Holst, D. and van der Mensbrugghe, D. (1995), "Trade Liberalisation and the Environment in the Pacific Basin: Coordinated Approaches to Mexican Trade and Environment Policy", *American Journal of Agricultural Economics*, 77, 778-785.

Bhagwati, J. (1981), "The Generalised Theory of Distortions and Welfare", in Bhagwati, J. *International Trade: Selected Readings*, Cambridge, MA: MIT Press.

Copeland, B.R. (1994), "International Trade and the Environment: Policy Reform in a Polluted Small Economy", *Journal of Environmental Economics and Management*, 26, 44-65.

Copeland, B.R. and Taylor S.M. (1993), "Trade and Transboundary Pollution", *University of British Colombia Discussion Paper*, 93-46.

De Melo, J. and Tarr, D. (1992), *A General Equilibrium Analysis of US Foreign Trade Policy*, Cambridge, MA: MIT Press.

Dean, J. (1992), "Trade and Environment: A Survey of the Literature", in Low, P. (ed), *International Trade and the Environment*, Washington DC: World Bank.

Drake-Brockman, J. and Anderson, K. (1994), "The Trade/Environment Debate and its Implications for Asia-Pacific", Paper prepared for the Australian Committee of the Pacific Economic Cooperation Council (AUSPECC), Centre for International Economic Studies, University of Adelaide.

Grossman, G.M. and Krueger, A.B. (1992), "Environmental Impacts of a North American Free Trade Agreement", *CEPR Discussion Paper*, 644.

Hewison G. (1995), *Reconciling Trade and the Environment: Issues for New Zealand*, Victoria University of Wellington: Institute of Policy Studies.

Johnson, H. (1960), "The Costs of Protection and the Scientific Tariff", *Journal of Political Economy,* 68, 327-345.

Ministry of Agriculture and Fisheries (1993), *The Environmental Impact of the Reduced Agricultural Subsidies, Case Study of New Zealand,* Wellington.

Ministry for the Environment (1994), *Climate Change: The New Zealand Approach,* Wellington.

Ministry for the Environment (1995), *Environment 2010 Strategy: A Statement of the Government's Strategy on the Environment,* Wellington.

Ministry of Foreign Affairs and Trade (1993), *New Zealand Trade Policy: Implementation and Directions; A Multi-Track Approach,* Wellington.

OECD (1994a), *The Environmental Effects of Trade,* Paris: Joint Committee on Environment and Trade.

Perroni, C. and Wiggle, R. (1994), "International Trade and Environmental Quality: How Important are the Linkages?", *Canadian Journal of Economics,* 27, 551-567.

Smith, V. and Espinosa, J. (1994), "Environmental and Trade Policies: Some Methodological Lessons", Working Paper, University of British Columbia.

Smith, V. and Espinosa, J. (1995), "Measuring the Environmental Consequences of Trade Policy: A Nonmarket CGE Analysis", *Journal of American Agricultural Economics,* 77, 772-777.

Walter, I. and Ugelow, J. (1979), "Environmental Policies in Developing Countries", *Ambio,* 8, 102-109.

3 Stringent Environmental Regulations and International Competitiveness: Evidence from New Zealand[1]

RAVI RATNAYAKE

Introduction

Over the last two decades a widespread environmental concern has developed nationally as well as internationally around the issues related to water and air quality, protection of the soil, waste treatment and disposal, noise control and the management of natural resources. The interest in environmental problems such as greenhouse gas emissions, ozone layer depletion, tropical deforestation, pollution of the ocean and the loss of biodiversity has intensified recently. These concerns for environmental quality have generated many issues regarding the interaction between trade and environment. One such important issue is the link between environmental standards and loss of competitiveness[2].

There are two major views on the relationship between environmental regulations and international competitiveness. First, it is claimed that stringent environmental regulations impose significant costs on the domestic firms and industries reducing their international competitiveness in terms of declining exports, increasing imports compared with those from the countries which have lower environmental standards and regulations. The loss of competitiveness is said to be greater in the so called "pollution-intensive" industries[3]. Second, an entirely opposite view, mainly due to Porter (1991) and Porter and Linde (1995), was that environmental regulations lead to productivity improvements because of a more cleaner environment and to innovations because of the stimulating effects of such regulations. Furthermore, countries adjusting early and investing in environmentally friendly technology would be able to create comparative advantage in these environmentally sensitive industries[4]. Compliance with higher environmental regulations could also be an additional source of structural adjustment in particular for developing countries as these regulations will promote less pollution-intensive industries (Sorsa, 1994).

There is a large body of literature which uses neo-classical trade models to examine the impact of environmental regulations on competitiveness [eg. Siebert (1985); McGuire (1982); Blackhurst (1977); Copeland (1991); Tobey (1990); Walter (1973); and Lopez (1992)]. Although comparisons of these studies are difficult due to different methodologies used, Dean (1992) has summarised three major results of these studies. First, on average environmental control costs[5] (ECC) are a smaller share of total costs of production. For example, average annual overall ECC for US exports was 1.75 per cent of the value of exports for 1968-70 while that for US imports is 1.52 per cent. However, it has been shown that some individual industries such as construction, mining and plastics could suffer from loss of competitiveness due to high ECC (Walter, 1973). Second, generally, reductions in output caused by abatement costs are insignificant although some individual sectors have been affected. For example, one study based on 14 US industrial sectors (Yezer and Philipson, 1974) found that the percentage decrease in output resulting from high ECC is less than one per cent. Third, the patterns of trade have not been affected significantly by the costs associated with environmental regulations.

Two recent studies [Sorsa, (1994); and Jaffe et al. (1995)] support the findings of the previous studies. Sorsa (1994) analyses trade flows in environmentally sensitive goods and ECC in seven industrial countries (Austria, Finland, Norway, Sweden, Germany, Japan and the United States). All these countries are claimed to have high environmental standards. First, Sorsa finds that there is no systematic relationship between higher ECC and competitiveness in environmentally sensitive industries. For Germany, Japan and the US the correlation coefficients between changes in export shares and ECC are not significant while that for Austria is positive. Second, in general, the countries under study have been able to maintain competitiveness in environmentally sensitive products all through the period covered. Despite similar environmental standards, the countries have shown remarkable differences in their export performance.

Jaffe et al. (1995) examine the issue of loss of competitiveness in the context of the US manufacturing industries and find no support to the hypothesis that environmental regulations have significant effect on competitiveness. One reason for this is that complying costs of regulations is a small portion of total costs of production, which is on average about two per cent although it may be high for some industries including electrical utilities, chemicals, petroleum refining and basic metal manufactures. These conclusions, however, subject to several caveats as admitted by the authors, in particular, difficulties in obtaining accurate data to measure relative stringency of environmental regulations[6].

All previous studies have been carried out either for the US or for other large industrial countries. Trade/environment relationship issues in respect of small open economies such as New Zealand have not been studied, mainly due to the unavailability of data, in particular on environmental aspects[7]. Second, with the exception of Tobey (1990) and Grossman and Krueger (1993), the previous studies have not attempted to analyse the relative role of environment stringency in explaining inter-industry differences in trade performance in the framework of trade models. Tobey specifies net exports as a function of country characteristics and estimates on a sample of 23 countries using 1975 data while Grossman and Krueger regress US imports from Mexico on factor shares on a sample of 135 industries using data for 1987. Both studies have not examined the role of industrial characteristics and trade policy induced variables in explaining trade flows between countries. Since international trade patterns are determined by many factors rather than factor endowments, it is important to specify environment stringency as a possible determinant of trade flows along with other industrial characteristics, factor intensities and trade policy measures. Third, the present study is an inter-industry analysis which uses industry level data while most previous studies have either used aggregate sectoral data or country level data. This paper attempts to fill the gap in the empirical literature by analysing the environment and competitiveness link in the context of New Zealand. In particular, it addresses the question "do environmental standards lead to loss of international competitiveness?".

In line with international literature, we focus on the manufacturing sector firstly because the competitiveness issue is more important in this sector than in the natural resource sector and also that is where most economic research has been carried out. Furthermore trade flows in manufactured goods are relatively less distorted by trade barriers than agriculture and other sectors. Finally, both trade data as well as data on environment in manufacturing are relatively more easily obtained.

The chapter is structured as follows. Section 2 compares New Zealand's environment with the rest of the world. Section 3 describes the measurements and sources of data. The link between environmental standards and international competitiveness is examined in section 4 using New Zealand's trade patterns and industry level estimates of revealed comparative advantage (RCA) of manufactured exports. This relationship is investigated econometrically in section 5. Major findings and concluding remarks are summarised in the final section.

New Zealand's Environment Compared With Other Countries

New Zealand is internationally known as a country endowed with clean and green natural heritage which contributes favourably to the development of agricultural, forestry and tourism industries. The human impact on environment is low because it has a relatively small and dispersed population compared with most other developed countries. The main purpose of the Resource Management Act of 1991 has been to protect this environmental heritage (MFAT, 1994). However, New Zealand's reputation for environmental cleanliness was challenged recently by an article titled "New Zealand's Poisoned Paradise" which appeared in *New Scientist* in July 1993, which expressed great concern about the pollution created by waste timber treatment sites in a number of places in New Zealand.

New Zealand was involved actively in international forums (eg. GATT, OECD, UNCTAD, FAO and UNEP) and treaties dealing with environmental concerns including the Earth Summit held in Rio de Janeiro, Brazil, organised by the U.N. Conference on Environment and Development (UNCED), Montreal Protocol on Substances, Framework Convention on Climate Change (FCCC) and Convention on Biological Diversity (CBD) and shown that it was a responsible member of the international community[8]. For example, New Zealand having shared the international concerns about the problem of climate change, signed FCCC in June 1992 and ratified the convention in September 1993. New Zealand's primary objective is to reduce net CO_2 emissions to their 1990 levels by 2000 and to maintain them at that rate thereafter.

The per capita CO_2 emissions for New Zealand in 1988 was 1.98 units compared with Canada (4.58), USA (5.34), Germany (5.36), and

Australia (4.02). New Zealand's per capita consumption of CFCs was 0.69 units compared with Canada (0.83), USA (1.37), Germany (0.95) and Australia (0.87)[9]. A study conducted by the UNCTAD calculated the degree of environmental stringency of a large number of countries and placed countries on a scale from one (tolerant) to seven (strict) (Walter and Ugelow, 1979). According to this survey, the mean score for developed countries is 6.1 while that of developing countries is 3.1. The environmental stringency index for New Zealand, Australia, Denmark, Germany and Netherlands was 5. The highest indices were recorded by USA, UK and Sweden (7).

Definitions, Measurements and Sources of Data

Many studies have used the concept of revealed comparative advantage (RCA) to measure a country's relative export performance in individual product categories. The RCA of country i in the export of product j is measured by the ratio of commodity j's share in the country's exports relative to the share of that commodity in world trade. The RCA index takes the form:

$$RCA_{ij} = (X_{ij} / X_i) / (X_{jw} / X_w)$$

where X_{ij} = country i's exports in commodity j; X_{jw} = world exports in commodity j; X_i = country i's total exports; and X_w = the world's total exports. When estimating New Zealand's RCA with a particular region, X_w and X_{jw} are replaced by regional flows.

This index is based on the assumption that trade patterns reflect intercountry differences in international competitiveness in terms of relative costs as well as non-price factors[10]. The index takes the values between zero and infinity. A RCA value greater than unity indicates that the country has a revealed comparative advantage in commodity j. A RCA value less than unity implies that the country has a revealed comparative disadvantage. The higher the value of RCA, the greater is the country's comparative advantage in the commodity concerned.

The RCA index is used to analyse trade patterns in section 4. However, it can not be used in the econometric analysis because of the difficulty in matching trade data with industry data. Therefore, an alternative widely used measure of trade performance, the net exports to total trade ratio, is used as follows:

$$NX_i = (X_j - M_j) / (X_j + M_j)$$

where X_j and M_j respectively give domestic exports and imports of commodity j.

Having defined a measure for international competitiveness, next question is to classify industries into environmentally sensitive (ES) and environmentally non-sensitive (NES) industries. In the absence of New Zealand data, we used a classification used by the US studies to classify our sample into ES and NES industries. According to the US classification, ES industries are those with highest levels of pollution abatement cost which is expressed as a percentage of value of output (Low and Yeats, 1992). The implicit assumption behind the use of the US classification for New Zealand is that both countries have similar environmental standards and preference for environmental quality.

The analysis is conducted on a sample of 109 manufacturing industries at the 3-digit level of the Standard International Trade Classification (SITC). As there are significant differences in the nature and levels of environmental standards followed by different countries, the analysis differentiates between exports to and imports from different country groups. We examine the impact of environment on trade using the data on New Zealand's trade with four different country groups: OECD, ASEAN, DCs and the world as a whole. In order to examine the changing patterns of comparative advantage over time, RCA estimates were obtained for each year beginning from 1980 to 1993. The data for econometric analysis was obtained from the Census of Manufacturing of the Department of Statistics. The construction of independent variables and data sources are give in Appendix 1.

International Competitiveness and Environmentally Sensitive Goods

We answer the question of whether environmental standards leads to loss of competitiveness in the context of New Zealand in two stages. First, we look at New Zealand's overall trade patterns in environmentally sensitive goods (ES) and environmentally non-sensitive goods (NES). Second, we analyse New Zealand's international competitiveness at industry level using the index of revealed comparative advantage (RCA).

Given New Zealand's reputation for clean and green environmental image and relatively high degree of environmental stringency as shown above, one would expect it to specialise in producing and exporting of NES goods[11]. This hypothesis can be tested using overall trade patterns summarised in Tables 3.1 and 3.2. Table 3.1 presents the composition of New Zealand's exports in terms of ES and NES to four different destinations: world, OECD, ASEAN and DCs. It shows that in 1980, ES shares of exports to all four destinations were higher than those of NES. The highest ES share was reported for ASEAN countries followed by DCs in the same year. By 1993, the picture has changed slightly. The NES shares of exports to OECD countries and DCs have increased over years and exceeded those of ES. However, no significant change can be observed in New Zealand's exports to ASEAN countries. Still a major portion of New Zealand's exports to these countries is originated from environmentally sensitive industries indicating that New Zealand's export penetration in ES goods is higher than that of NES goods in those markets.

Table 3.1: **ES and NES Shares in New Zealand's Total Exports by Country Groups (Percentage)**

	1980		1985		1993	
	ES	**NES**	**ES**	**NES**	**ES**	**NES**
OECD	51.9	48.1	50.2	49.8	49.6	50.4
ASEAN	61.6	38.4	57.7	42.3	60.9	39.1
DCs	58.6	41.4	33.4	66.6	46.4	53.6
WORLD	54.2	45.8	46.6	53.4	49.6	50.4

Table 3.2 looks at the same information from a different angle. It shows percentage shares of exports to different destinations under ES and NES sub-headings. In 1980, 66 per cent of ES goods were exported to OECD countries, 25 per cent to DCs and 8 per cent to ASEAN countries. Even by 1993, the major recipient of New Zealand's ES goods was OECD

countries (70.2 per cent) where environmental standards are expected to be high. However, these countries absorb almost the same share of NES exports from New Zealand (70.4) reflecting the overall export pattern.

Table 3.2:   Direction of New Zealand's Exports (Percentage)

	1980			1985			1993		
	ES	NES	Total	ES	NES	Total	ES	NES	Total
OECD	66.1	72.5	69.0	79.9	69.1	74.1	70.2	70.4	70.3
ASEAN	8.6	6.4	7.6	3.7	2.4	3.0	8.5	5.4	7.0
DCs	25.3	21.1	23.4	16.4	28.6	22.9	21.3	24.2	22.7

The composition of ES and NES imports to New Zealand by different country groups is given in Table 3.3. In 1980, 96 per cent of ES goods originated from OECD countries which declined to 86 per cent by 1993. During the same period, the share of ES goods accounted for by DCs increased from 3 per cent to 11 per cent. The share of DCs in NES goods increased from 9 per cent to 13 per cent over this period. The ES and NES shares of imports to New Zealand by major country groups are given in Table 3.4. It can be seen that 26 per cent of total imports from OECD countries in 1980 are environmentally sensitive compared with 11 and 10 per cent respectively from ASEAN and DCs. The OECD's share decreased over the years while those of the other two country groups increased.

Table 3.3:   Composition of New Zealand's Imports (Percentage)

	1980			1985			1993		
	ES	NES	All Goods	ES	NES	All Goods	ES	NES	All Goods
OECD	96.2	89.6	91.3	93.8	90.6	91.4	86.5	82.5	83.3
ASEAN	0.4	1.0	0.8	1.0	1.1	1.1	2.7	3.9	3.7
DCs	3.4	9.4	7.9	5.1	8.2	7.5	10.8	13.6	13.1

Table 3.4: ES and NES Shares in New Zealand's Imports (Percentage)

	1980		1985		1993	
	ES	**NES**	**ES**	**NES**	**ES**	**NES**
OECD	26.7	73.3	22.9	77.1	19.0	81.0
ASEAN	11.6	88.4	20.9	79.1	13.5	86.5
DCs	10.9	89.1	15.1	84.9	15.2	84.8

The RCA estimates of New Zealand's trade with the world as a whole at industry level are summarised in Table 3.5. In order to minimise any random factors which might influence RCA of a single year, three year averages are reported. The most interesting observation emerging from this information is that in terms of RCA, international competitiveness of environmentally sensitive (ES) goods has not changed significantly over the 13 year period under consideration. However, the number of ES products with RCA below unity has declined and the average RCA of such products increased over time indicating a slight improvement in New Zealand's international competitiveness. Similar observation can be made on New Zealand's trade with the OECD countries (Appendix Table 3.1). New Zealand's competitiveness in trade of ES products with ASEAN and DCs has declined slightly over the years (Appendix Tables 3.2, 3.3). On average, as shown by mean RCAs in 1992-93, New Zealand was slightly more competitive in ES goods than NES goods.

Although there is some evidence to suggest that New Zealand has increased its competitiveness of ES goods in OECD countries, detailed industry level analysis is needed to support such a proposition. This analysis is carried out in Tables 3.6 and 3.7.

Table 3.5: Frequency Distribution of RCA for New Zealand's Total Exports of Manufactures 1980-1993

RCA Range	Number of Products									
	1980-1982		1983-1985		1986-1988		1989-1991		1992-1993	
	ES	NES	ES	NES	ES	NES	ES	NES	ES	NES
0 and under 1	22	43	23	46	23	49	18	48	17	46
1 and under 2	4	13	5	8	8	7	11	10	11	10
2 and under 3	4	6	5	6	1	5	3	4	3	4
3 and under 4	1	2	0	3	1	1	0	0	1	1
4 and under 5	0	0	0	0	1	1	1	2	0	2
5 and under 6	1	0	1	0	1	0	1	0	2	0
6 and under 7	1	0	2	0	0	0	0	0	0	0
7 and under 8	0	2	0	1	1	3	0	0	0	0
8 and over 8	2	1	1	3	1	2	2	4	2	4
Total	35	67	37	67	37	68	36	68	36	67
Mean - RCA	1.73	1.24	1.58	1.35	1.51	1.34	1.62	1.70	1.77	1.60
S. Deviation	2.87	2.11	2.74	2.25	2.71	2.29	2.62	4.75	2.49	3.31

The top high performing 10 product categories in the RCA ranking for 1992-93 along with the RCA estimates for other periods are listed in Table 3.6. More than half of these commodities including the top two are non-environmentally sensitive. However, in 1980-82, the leading exporting product in terms of RCA was environmentally sensitive (aluminium). The second part of Table 3.6 shows that half of most low performing 10 product categories including the lowest two are environmentally sensitive. Overall, the numbers in this Table indicate that the most competitive exporting products from New Zealand are environmentally non-sensitive. A similar pattern can be seen in New Zealand's trade with the OECD countries (Appendix Table 3.4) while as with ASEAN countries and DCs, generally, it is environmentally sensitive commodities that are at the top in terms of competitiveness (Appendix Table 3.5 and 3.6).

Finally, we can look at the composition of ES goods and NES commodities at 2-digit level of SITC given in Table 3.7. Three product categories (non-ferrous metals, paper and paper boards and chemical materials) account for 72 per cent of total value of ES sensitive goods in 1980-82 and it declined only marginally during the period under consideration. Power generation equipment (15 per cent), machinery (15 per cent) and miscellaneous manufactured goods (10 per cent) dominated the NES category during the same period.

Table 3.6:   Highest and Lowest Values of RCA for New Zealand's Trade in Manufactured Exports

High Performing	Type of Product	1992-1993	1989-1991	1986-1988	1983-1985	1980-1982
613 - Fur Skins, Tanned, Dressed	NES	19.370	8.649	4.735	3.342	3.126
842 - Fur etc. Clothes, Prod.	NES	13.569	10.132	8.220	8.718	7.991
684 - Aluminium	ES	11.997	13.360	14.480	14.126	13.585
611 - Leather	NES	11.044	10.730	12.706	11.996	13.408
941 - Zoo Animals, Pets	NES	10.664	36.306	7.026	1.338	1.348
599 - Chemicals NES	ES	8.194	8.127	7.336	6.797	8.525
641 - Paper and Paperboard	ES	5.577	4.901	4.017	2.512	5.887
631 - Veneers, Plywood, etc.	ES	5.123	5.152	5.578	6.577	6.807
633 - Cork Manufactures	NES	4.417	4.812	7.196	7.365	3.625
657 - Floor Cover, Tapestry, etc.	NES	4.186	4.938	7.174	8.989	7.791
Low Performing						
862 - Photo, Cinema Supplies	NES	0.013	0.043	0.072	0.078	0.071
521 - Coal, Petroleum etc.	ES	0.013	0.055	0.172	0.022	0.013
667 - Pearl, Prec-, Semi-P Stone	NES	0.013	0.012	0.005	0.013	0.022
951 - War Firearms, Ammunition	NES	0.009	0.033	0.018	0.027	0.030
731 - Railway Vehicles	NES	0.008	0.400	0.054	0.245	0.213
683 - Nickel	ES	0.004	0.001	0.014	0.002	0.005
689 - Non-Fer Base Metals NES	ES	0.004	0.011	0.001	0.001	0.001
864 - Watches and Clocks	NES	0.003	0.005	0.007	0.007	0.018
515 - Radioactive etc Material	ES	0.001	0.002	0.002	0.000	-
671 - Pig Iron Etc	ES	0.001	0.000	0.003	0.000	-

In sum, by analysing the patterns of trade and revealed comparative advantage of New Zealand's trade with different country groups, we have shown above that despite relatively high environmental standards, New Zealand's international competitiveness of environmentally sensitive goods has not significantly changed over the years. We examine this observation econometrically in the following section.

An econometric analysis

In this section, first, we develop a model based on the theory of international trade to examine the role of environmental stringency in determining a country's comparative advantage and then estimate it using the data for the manufacturing sector of New Zealand.

Model specification

Most empirical studies explaining international trade between countries have been conducted within the framework of the Heckscher-Ohlin model (H-O) which explains trade patterns by differences in relative factor endowments of countries. The H-O model was based on a number of important assumptions including perfect competition in the goods and factor markets, constant returns to scale, identical technology and internationally immobile factors of production. According to this theory, a country exports (imports) that commodity which uses its relatively abundant (scarce) factor intensively (non-intensively).

Leontief (1954) by analysing the US input-output data, discovered that the US was a net exporter of labour services embodied goods. This was a paradoxical result given that the US was considered as a capital abundant country. Subsequently, others [eg. Leamer (1980); Leamer and Bowen (1981)] have shown that the Leontief results are based on a simple misunderstanding of data and mis-interpretation of factor abundance. The recent empirical testing of the H-O theorem was based on the analytical framework developed by this literature. According to this literature, a country is relatively labour abundant if:

$$L_X - L_M > 0 \text{ and } K_X - K_M > 0,$$

$$\frac{L_x - L_m}{K_x - K_m} > \frac{L_c}{K_c}$$

where L_X, L_M and L_C are labour services embodied in exports, imports and consumption respectively. Similarly, K_X, K_m and K_c are capital services embodied exports, imports and consumption.

Table 3.7: New Zealand's Exports: Percentage of Environmentally Sensitive and Non-Environmentally Sensitive Goods by 2 Digit SITC

Commodity – ES Goods	YEAR 1980-1982	1983-1985	1986-1988	1989-1991	1992-1993
51 - Organic Materials	0.69	1.99	4.91	5.06	5.71
52 - Inorganic Materials	0.01	0.01	0.02	0.01	0.00
56 - Fertiliser, except GRP 172	0.14	0.31	0.86	0.75	0.36
59 - Chemical Materials NES	22.69	20.36	19.70	19.89	21.02
63 - Wood, Cork Manufactures NES	8.10	7.52	5.75	4.62	5.76
64 - Paper, Paperboard and MFR	22.60	11.85	17.20	19.14	21.21
66 - Non-Metal Mineral Mfs NES	1.18	1.33	0.59	0.72	1.11
67 - Iron and Steel	5.96	7.06	7.29	11.36	11.64
68 - Non-Ferrous Metals	28.71	37.57	35.15	31.92	25.51
69 - Metal Manufactures NES	9.92	12.00	8.53	6.54	7.68
Commodity – Non-ES Goods					
53 - Dyes, Tanning, Colour Prod	1.03	0.86	0.61	0.65	0.99
54 - Medicinal, Pharm. Products	2.51	3.11	2.72	2.81	2.90
55 - Perfume, Cleaning etc Prod	2.44	2.77	3.28	3.10	4.34
57 - Plastics in Primary Form	0.18	0.04	0.06	0.06	0.05
58 - Plastics Materials etc	2.97	2.13	2.43	1.96	2.28
61 - Leather, Leather Goods	9.86	8.78	10.49	9.54	9.25

Table 3.7 *continued*

62 - Rubber Manufactures NES	2.45	1.01	1.71	2.16	2.31
63 - Wood, Cork Manufactures NES	0.21	0.33	0.37	0.31	0.25
65 - Textiles Yarn, Fabrics, etc	16.40	14.78	15.13	10.51	8.39
66 - Non-Metal Mineral Mfs NES	3.51	2.44	1.86	1.43	1.27
67 - Iron and Steel	0.00	0.00	0.00	0.00	0.00
71 - Power Generation Equipment	15.16	12.26	14.03	15.50	15.23
72 - Machs for Special Industries	11.79	9.99	12.69	12.85	14.96
73 - Metalworking Machinery	6.37	3.81	4.01	5.25	4.82
81 - Prefab Buildgs, Fttng etc	0.48	0.32	0.43	0.46	0.58
82 - Furniture, Cushions etc	3.26	3.12	3.18	2.44	2.55
83 - Trunk, Suitcases, Bag, etc	0.43	0.25	0.16	0.12	0.17
84 - Clothing and Accessories	7.05	5.37	4.73	4.98	6.67
85 - Footwear	0.87	0.72	0.51	0.98	0.92
86 - Instruments, Apparatus	1.04	1.25	1.89	2.93	4.05
89 - Misc Manufactured Goods NES	11.94	12.68	12.20	10.07	10.66
91 - Mail not Classified by Kind	0.00	0.00	0.00	0.00	0.00
93 - Spec. Transact. not Closed	0.00	13.92	7.38	11.05	7.14
94 - Zoo Animals, Pets	0.03	0.02	0.14	0.82	0.23
95 - War Firearms, Ammunition	0.02	0.02	0.01	0.02	0.00
96 - Coin, Nongold Noncurrent	0.00	0.00	0.00	0.01	0.00

In order to derive a testable model, suppose, T is a vector of net exports by country i and it is related to output (Q_i) and consumption (C_i) as:

$$T_i \equiv Q_i - C_i \qquad (1)$$

where

$$C_i = QS_i \qquad (2)$$

where $Q = \Sigma Q_i$ (world output) and $S_i = (GNP_i-B_i)/\Sigma GNP_i$. Here B is trade balance.

The factor endowments of country i is given by:

$$F_i = A_i \, Q_i \tag{3}$$

A is a vector comprising of a_{kj} components which give quantities of factor k embodied in a unit of output of commodity j in country i. Following Vanek (1968), factor services embodied in net exports (AT_i) can be derived as:

$$ATi = Fi - Si \, F \tag{4}$$

where F is a vector of factor endowment of the world. If trade is balanced, this says that a country relatively better endowed with a particular factor will be a net exporter (importer) of the services of that factor (the other factor) as embodied in trade. As shown by Vanek, equation 4 is a generalisation of factor proportion theory for a large number of factors (n) and commodities (m). If X_i is supplies of Home country factors and X_i^* is supplies of Foreign factors[12]:

$$\frac{X_1}{X_1^*} \geq \frac{X_2}{X_2^*} \cdot \geq \ldots \ldots \geq \frac{X_n}{X_n^*}$$

the Home country will be a net exporter of services of $X_1, X_2.....X_j$ and net importer of services of $X_{j+1}, X_{j+2}.......X_n$, where $j \neq n$.

In this setting, an equation regressing net exports on factor intensities can be written as:

$$Ti = A'\theta + U_i \tag{5}$$

θ is a vector of regression coefficients and U_i is a stochastic error term. These regression coefficients can be assigned to 2 groups of factor variables: W- factors of production derived from the traditional theory of factor proportions (H-O theorem) and X- new factors of production derived from modifications to H-O theorem (ie. neo-factor proportions and neo-technology). By adding a constant term (λ) to equation 5, we can obtain:

$$T_{ij} = \lambda + \alpha W_{ij} + \beta X_{ij} + U_{ij} \qquad (6)$$

where T_{ij} is net exports of commodity j from country i.

Firstly, in line with the factor proportions theory, in the context of manufactures, as a capital abundant developed country, New Zealand is expected to have comparative advantage in exporting commodities which are relatively intensive in physical capital (PCI) and human capital (HCI). Secondly, neo-technology theories emphasise the importance of inter-country differences in technological developments in the determination of trade flows. The hypothesis is that technological developments provide an opportunity for countries to export goods even if they do not have comparative advantage in terms of factor endowments. To the extent that New Zealand is likely to be relatively well endowed with technological know-how and skilled labour, it is expected to have comparative advantage in commodities which are relatively intensive in technology (RD).

The continued observation of intra-industry trade and the empirical failure of the H-O model to explain such trade patterns led to a large body of literature explaining the role of imperfect competition and economies of scale in international trade[13]. A well-known study by Helpman (1981) has incorporated these new theoretical developments into a H-O general equilibrium model and called it "the Chamberline-Hechscher-Ohlin approach". We modify equation 6 to incorporate variables representing imperfect competition and economies scale (Y) as follows:

$$T_{ij} = \lambda + \alpha W_{ij} + \beta X_{ij} + \gamma Y_{ij} + U_{ij} \qquad (7)$$

Following the literature on the role of imperfect market structures and IRS in determination of trade patterns [eg. Krugman (1979), Grossman (1993)], firstly, we hypothesise that economies of scale (ESC) will give rise to trade even if countries are identical in tastes, technologies and factor endowments. Secondly, it is believed that the firms achieving and maintaining the ability to differentiate products gain an additional basis for comparative advantage over the other firms. The expectation is that the industries with relatively high ability to differentiate products are more competitive than the other industries. Following the empirical literature in this area, we use advertising intensity (A/S) to represent product differentiation. Thirdly, industry concentration (CH) can exert influences on trade patterns in various ways.

First, the higher the concentration the greater will be the international competitiveness of manufacturing firms as the costs associated with production may fall through increased economies of scale when concentration increases. Second, Caves et al., (1980) have suggested the possibility that a monopolistic export industry may practise price discrimination against the domestic market and thereby export more than a competitive industry would. Both of these considerations suggest a positive relationship between seller concentration and trade performance. However, Helpman and Krugman (1985) who analysed the implications of oligopoly on trade patterns, have suggested that the less concentrated industries will be more competitive and perform better in international markets.

In addition, we include two variables representing industry structure and policy related aspects. Firstly, the widely-held view with regard to inward foreign direct investment (FDI) is that the multinational enterprises (MNEs) are powerful agents of export growth as they possess important requirements for growth such as technological leadership, product development skills, marketing and organisational skills and direct access to world markets. It can, however, be argued that the contribution of MNEs to export expansion depends crucially on the motives of their investment in host countries. If the dominant motive is to bypass tariffs and other trade barriers imposed on the imports to host countries, it is unlikely that such investments would be instrumental in promoting exports. Therefore, we cannot expect a priori that foreign ownership of industry (FO) is necessarily positively related to export intensity. Secondly, government interventions through tariffs and non-tariff barriers, by changing relative prices, may distort the trade patterns which are based on country's comparative advantage (Travis, 1972; Deardorff, 1984). For instance, the imposition of a tariff on imports may adversely affect exports in two ways. First, the increase in price resulting from the protection on intermediate inputs embodied in exports have to be absorbed entirely by exporters. Second, protection also raises the costs of labour for exporting industries. This happens when labour is attracted to high wage earning import-substituting sector (Clement and Sjaastad, 1984:2). We hypothesise that export intensity is negatively related to tariff and non-tariff barriers (NRP)[14].

As argued above, the stringency of environmental regulations seem to have important effects on trade patterns and therefore a variable to represent such regulations (Z) should be included in equation 7.

$$T_{ij} = \lambda + \alpha W_{ij} + \beta X_{ij} + \gamma Y_{ij} + \delta Z_{ij} + U_{ij} \qquad (8)$$

Since no data is available to measure Z_{ij} at industry level, we use a dummy variable (ENV) to represent environmentally sensitive commodities as explained before. Given that New Zealand is well known for her clean and green image and has undertaken a comprehensive environmental protection programme (ie. Resource Management Act of 1991), New Zealand is expected to specialise less in production and trade of environmentally sensitive goods and therefore the sign of ENV should be negative.

Regression results

As described in section 1, stringent environmental standards can impose significant costs on domestic firms and industries in countries where environmental standards are high, leading to the losses in international competitiveness. On the contrary, it has been argued that countries adjusting early and investing in environmentally friendly technology would be able to create comparative advantage in environmentally sensitive industries. In order to examine the impact of environmental standards, we tested this hypothesis econometrically in two ways.

First, we estimated equations using a dummy variable to represent environmental stringency. The regression results of this test are presented in Table 3.8. The standard tests for functional form mis-specification (RESET), heteroscedasticity (the White test) and multicollinearity were conducted and found that our results were free from such problems. Relatively low adjusted R^2 is not uncommon in cross-sectional regression analysis and it compares with previous studies linking trade with the environment (e.g. Grossman and Krueger). In the first four equations (Table 3.8), the model has been estimated without an environmental variable. As far as New Zealand's major trading partners (OECD) are concerned, physical capital intensity (PCI), human capital intensity (HCI) and industry concentration (CH) seem to exert positive influence on New Zealand's international competitiveness in manufactured exports while trade protection (NRP) and foreign ownership of industry (FO) provide a negative influence on her competitiveness in world markets. Almost similar results can be seen with New Zealand's trade with ASEAN. New Zealand seems to be less competitive in trade with developing countries

(DC) in capital and human capital intensive exports while again trade protection has been an impediment to international competitiveness.

In the second set of equations, we estimated the model with the environmental dummy (Table 3.8). In none of the equations, environmental dummy is significant indicating that environmental stringency is not a major determinant of New Zealand's international competitiveness in manufactured exports to any destination. This observation seems to be stronger in the cases of developing countries and the world as a whole where signs of the coefficient of ENV is negative. The coefficient has gained a positive sign for OECD and ASEAN equations although it is not statistically significant.

Second, we conducted a variable addition test to test the hypothesis that environmental stringency (ENV) has no effect on trade patterns. The results are presented in Table 3.9. The Chi-Square and F tests indicate again that environmental variable is not an important determinant of New Zealand's international competitiveness in exports to ASEAN, DCs and world as a whole. However, both tests are marginally significant under OECD.

Table 3.8: Determinants of International Competitiveness in Manufactured Exports

Independent Variable	Without Environment Variable				With Environment Variable			
	OECD	ASEAN	DC	WORLD	OECD	ASEAN	DC	WORLD
PCI	0.001 (2.497)[a]	0.006 (1.496)[c]	-0.005 (1.309)[c]	-0.006 (1.359)[c]	0.001 (2.160)[b]	0.001 (1.235)	-0.004 (1.123)	-0.001 (1.187)
HCI	0.002 (1.655)[b]	0.002 (1.297)[c]	-0.002 (1.756)[b]	-0.005 (0.301)	0.001 (1.266)	0.001 (0.982)	-0.001 (1.514)[c]	-0.001 (0.113)
RD	0.084 (0.939)	- -	-0.222 (1.745)[b]	-0.093 (0.647)	0.082 (0.924)	- -	-0.222 (1.732)[b]	-0.091 (0.632)
ESC	-0.004 (1.072)	0.005 (0.866)	-0.009 (1.436)[c]	0.002 (0.309)	-0.004 (0.961)	0.006 (0.952)	-0.008 (1.497)[c]	0.002 (0.244)
A/S	- -	- -	- -	-2.578 (1.280)[c]	- -	- -	- -	-2.482 (1.372)[c]
CH	0.542 (2.375)[b]	-0.727 (2.100)[b]	- -	0.102 (0.277)	0.562 (2.459)	-0.704 (2.026)[b]	- -	0.082 (0.224)
FO	-0.002 (1.866)[b]	-0.002 (0.972)	0.003 (1.904)[b]	-0.003 (0.122)	-0.002 (1.955)[b]	-0.002 (1.047)	0.003 (1.931)[b]	-0.137 (0.064)
NRP	-0.006 (1.804)[b]	0.006 (1.181)	-0.005 (1.275)[c]	-0.127 (2.408)[b]	-0.005 (1.487)[c]	0.007 (1.368)[c]	-0.006 (1.383)[c]	0.011 (2.211)[b]
ENV	- -	- -	- -	- -	0.107 (1.194)	0.132 (0.959)	-0.082 (0.645)	-0.099 (0.672)

Table 3.8: Determinants of International Competitiveness in Manufactured Exports *continued*

Independent Variable	Without Environment Variable				With Environment Variable			
	OECD	ASEAN	DC	WORLD	OECD	ASEAN	DC	WORLD
Constant	-0.723 (6.871)[a]	0.465 (2.912)[a]	0.221 (1.543)[c]	-0.477 (2.751)[a]	-0.749 (6.986)[a]	0.431 (2.642)[a]	0.240 (1.637)[b]	-0.447 (2.492)[a]
F	2.399	1.835	1.56	1.325	2.482	1.438	1.389	1.222
R^2	0.143	0.100	0.081	0.100	0.147	0.114	0.091	0.100

* t-ratios are given in parentheses, significant levels (2-tail test) one: a = 1%, b = 5%, c = 10%

Table 3.9:   Variable Addition Test

STATISTIC	OECD	ASEAN	DC	WORLD
Lagrange Multiplier [Chi-Sq (1)]	1.532	0.984	0.442	0.495
F (1, 100)	1.425	0.920	0.411	0.451

* Joint test of zero restrictions on the coefficients of additional variables.

Conclusion

In this chapter we have tested the hypothesis that environmental stringency leads to loss of international competitiveness in manufactured exports in three ways. Firstly, we analysed the changes in New Zealand's aggregate trade flows classified by environmentally sensitive (ES) goods and environmentally non-sensitive (NES) goods with three different country groups (OECD, ASEAN and DCs) over the last 13 years. Secondly, we examined the international competitiveness of 109 industries in terms of revealed comparative advantage of New Zealand's trade with those country groups over the same period. We found no evidence to suggest that New Zealand has lost its comparative advantage of environmentally sensitive (ES) goods during the period under consideration.

Finally, we analysed the role of environmental regulations in determining comparative advantage using two econometric methods and found that it was not an important determinant of New Zealand's international competitiveness. In terms of econometric results, there is no substantial evidence to suggest that environmental stringency leads to loss of international competitiveness.

The results give some support to the proposition that New Zealand has gained or increased comparative advantage in exporting some environmentally sensitive goods to some country groups, in particular, OECD. In the absence of information on pollution control at firm or industry level, it is not clear, however, whether this is due to the productivity improvements or new environmental control technologies as claimed by Porter and Linde. More indepth industry specific studies are needed before any strong conclusions are made regarding the impact of environmental stringency on international competitiveness.

Notes

1   Slightly different version of this paper has been published in *International Journal of the Economics of Business*, 5, 1, 77-96, 1998.

2   Two excellent surveys of the literature on this issue are found in Dean (1992) and Jaffe et al. (1995).

3   Pollution-intensive industries are defined in the literature as the ones with products whose direct and indirect abatement costs are equal or greater than 1.85 per cent of total cost of production in the US. These include iron and steel, ferrous and nonferrous metals, paper and paper products and wood and wood products [see Low and Yeats (1992)] for details.

4   This view, however, has been criticised by a number of economists including Oates et al. (1993) and Palmer et al (1995). Some others have analysed the link between pollution control and technological advance [see for instance, Magat (1978), Downing and White (1986), Millman and Prince (1989) and Barrett (1994)].

5   Environmental control costs include capital costs of environmental control equipment, depreciation on existing such equipment, operational costs associated with environmental management and research and development expenditure for compliance with environmental standards.

6   The issue of trade and environment has also been studied by a number of international organisations such as the World Bank (e.g. Low, 1992), OECD (e.g. OECD, 1993, OECD, 1994), GATT (e.g. GATT, 1992) and UNCTAD (e.g. Zarsky, 1993) which make a great contribution to the debate.

7   Although a number of government agencies including Ministry of Foreign Affairs and Trade (MFAT), Ministry of Agriculture and Fisheries (MAF) and Ministry for the Environment and researchers including Hewison (1995) have identified issues relevant for New Zealand, economic analysis on the subject of trade and environment in New Zealand is surprisingly limited. One noteworthy study was by MAF (1994) which examines the environmental effects of agricultural subsidies in New Zealand for the period of 1975 to 1990. The study finds that agricultural trade liberalisation, in particular removal of subsidies has had some positive effect on environment.

8   See Williams (1995) for details on New Zealand's contribution to international environmental matters.

9   These statistics are from UN Environmental Programme, Environmental Data Report, 1991-92.

10   As mentioned by Donges and Reidel (1977), this index has a number of limitations as a measure of trade performance. There are a number of alternative measures of RCA. See Balance et al. (1987) for details.

11   However, if clean and green environment is treated as a factor of production, New Zealand is expected to trade in ES goods rather than NES.
12   In addition to usual assumptions of H-O theory, Vanek assumed that two countries specialise in no more than m-n commodities.
13   See Grossman (1993) for a recent survey of this literature.
14   In the empirical model we represent protection by nominal rate of protection (NRP). However, in New Zealand's case, NRP is highly correlated with effective rate of protection (ERP).

References

Anderson, K. (1992), "The Standard Welfare Economics of Policies Affecting Trade and the Environment", in K. Anderson and R. Blackhurst (eds), *The Greening of World Trade Issues,* 25-48.

Anderson, K. and Blackhurst, R. (1992), *The Greening of World Trade Issues,* New York: Harvester-Wheatsheaf.

Barrett, S. (1994), "Strategic environmental policy and international trade", *Journal of Public Economics,* 54, 325-338.

Blackhurst, R. (1977), "International Trade and Domestic Environmental Policies in a Growing World Economy", in R. Blackhurst et al. (eds), *International Relations in a Changing World,* Geneva: Sythoff-Leiden, 35-52.

Copeland, B.R. (1994), "International Trade and the Environment: Policy Reform in a Polluted Small Open Economy", *Journal of Environmental Economics and Management,* 26, 44-65.

Dean, J. (1992), "Trade and the Environment: A Survey of Literature", in P. Low (ed), *International Trade and the Environment,* World Bank Discussion Papers, 159, 15-28.

Grossman, G. and Krueger, A. (1993), "Environmental Impacts of NAFTA" in P. Garber (ed), *The US-Mexico Free Trade Agreement.*

Helpman, E. (1981), "International trade in the presence of product differentiation, economies of scale and monopolistic competition", *Journal of International Economics,* 11, 305-340.

Jaffe, A.B., Peterson, S.R., Portney P.R. and Stavins, R.B. (1995), "Environmental Regulation and the Competitiveness of U.S. Manufacturing: What does the Evidence Tell Us?", *Journal of Economic Literature,* XXXIII, 132-163.

Leamer, E.E. (1980), "The Leontief Paradox, Reconsidered", *Journal of Political Economy,* 88, 495-503.

Leamer, E.E. and Bowen, H.P. (1981), "Cross-section Tests of the Heckscher-Ohlin Theorem: Comment", *American Economic Review,* 71, 1041-48.

Lopez, R. (1992), "The Environment as a Factor of Production", in P. Low (ed), *International Trade and the Environment*, World Bank Discussion Papers, 159, 137-156.

Low, P. (1992), *International Trade and the Environment*, World Bank Discussion Papers, 159, Washington DC: The World Bank.

Low, P. and Yeats, A. (1992), "Do 'Dirty' Industries Migrate?", in P. Low (ed), *International Trade and the Environment*, World Bank Discussion Papers, 159, 89-104.

Magat, W.A. (1978), "Pollution Control and Technological Advance: A Dynamic Model of the Firm", *Journal of Environmental Economics and Management*, 5, 1-125.

McGuire, M.C. (1982), "Regulation, Factor Rewards and International Trade", *Journal of Public Economics*, 17, 335-354.

MFTA (1994), "International Environment Issues: A New Zealand Perspective", Information Bulletin, 50, Wellington, New Zealand.

Millman, S.R. and Prince, R. (1989), "Firm Incentives to Promote Technological Change in Pollution Control", *Journal of Environmental Economics and Management*, 17, 247-65.

Oates, W.K., Palmer, K.L. and Portney, P. (1993), "Environmental Regulation and International Competitiveness: Thinking about the Porter Hypothesis", *Resources for Future Working Paper*, 94-02.

Palmer, K., Oates, W. and Portney, P. (1995), "Tightening Environmental Standards: The Benefit-cost or the No-cost Paradigm", *Journal of Economic Perspectives*, 9, 119-132.

Porter, M. (1991), "America's Green Strategy", *Science America*, 168.

Porter, M. and Linde, C.V.D (1995), "Towards a new conception of the environment-competitiveness relationship", *Journal of Economic Perspectives*, 9, 97-118.

Siebert, H. (1985), "Spatial Aspects of Environmental Economics", in A. Kneese and J. Sweeney (eds), *Handbook of Natural Resource and Energy Economics*, New York: North-Holland.

Sorsa, P. (1994), "Competitiveness and Environmental Standards: Some Exploratory Results", *Policy Research Working Paper*, Washington DC: The World Bank.

Tobey, J. (1990), "The Effects of Domestic Environmental Policies and Patterns of World Trade: An Empirical Test", *Kyklos*, 43, 191-209.

Vanek, J. (1968), "The Factor Proportions Theory: The N-factor Case", *Kyklos*, 21, 749-56.

Walter, I. and Ugelow, J. (1979), "Environmental Policies in Developing Countries", *Ambio*, 8, 102-109.

Williams, P. (1995), "The Environment", *New Zealand as an International Citizen*, Wellington: Ministry of Foreign Affairs and Trade.

Yezer, A. and Philipson, A. (1974), "Influence of Environmental Considerations on Agriculture and Industrial Decisions to Locate outside the Continental US", Public Interest Economics Center.

Appendix Table 3.1: Frequency Distribution of RCA for New Zealand's Trade in Manufactures with the OECD 1980, 1985 and 1993

| RCA Range | Number of Products | | | | | |
| | 1980 | | 1985 | | 1993 | |
	ES	NES	ES	NES	ES	NES
0 and under 1	23	44	22	47	16	45
1 and under 2	2	14	4	8	8	7
2 and under 3	3	4	2	4	4	6
3 and under 4	2	2	1	2	1	2
4 and under 5	0	1	0	2	1	2
5 and under 6	0	0	0	0	0	1
6 and under 7	0	0	0	0	0	1
7 and under 8	0	0	1	1	0	0
8 and over 8	3	3	3	4	3	3
Total	33	68	33	68	33	67
Mean - RCA	1.68	1.45	2.07	1.68	2.05	1.71
S. Deviation	3.14	3.09	4.01	3.23	2.86	3.28

Appendix Table 3.2: Frequency Distribution of RCA for New Zealand's Trade in Manufactures with ASEAN 1980, 1985 and 1993

| RCA Range | Number of Products | | | | | |
| | 1980 | | 1985 | | 1993 | |
	ES	NES	ES	NES	ES	NES
0 and under 1	9	38	10	34	12	41
1 and under 2	5	10	4	6	2	10
2 and under 3	1	4	2	5	4	6
3 and under 4	1	1	1	1	0	1
4 and under 5	2	1	0	2	0	1
5 and under 6	0	1	1	1	2	0
6 and under 7	0	0	0	0	1	1
7 and under 8	2	0	0	0	1	0
8 and over 8	6	5	6	8	4	4
Total	26	60	24	57	26	64
Mean - RCA	10.79	3.37	5.77	4.40	8.24	3.82
S. Deviation	24.75	13.85	11.35	13.27	17.43	18.42

Appendix Table 3.3:   Frequency Distribution of RCA for New Zealand's Trade in Manufactures with DCs 1980, 1985 and 1993

| RCA | Number of Products | | | | | |
| | 1980 | | 1985 | | 1993 | |
Range	ES	NES	ES	NES	ES	NES
0 and under 1	18	46	17	51	17	46
1 and under 2	1	12	8	6	6	11
2 and under 3	4	7	2	4	5	2
3 and under 4	4	2	3	1	1	0
4 and under 5	1	1	1	2	1	1
5 and under 6	2	0	1	2	2	3
6 and under 7	2	0	0	0	0	1
7 and under 8	0	0	1	0	0	0
8 and over 8	2	1	0	2	3	4
Total	34	69	33	68	35	68
Mean - RCA	2.75	0.99	1.52	1.51	2.31	1.92
S. Deviation	4.43	1.40	1.86	4.79	3.81	5.40

Appendix Table 3.4:   Highest and Lowest Values of RCA for New Zealand's Trade in Manufactured Exports with the OECD

	Type of Product	1993	1985	1980
High Performing				
842 - Fur etc Clothes, Prod	NES	19.302	15.248	12.678
611 - Leather	NES	14.973	14.214	19.328
684 - Aluminium	ES	11.348	17.376	12.261
631 - Veneers, Plywood etc	ES	10.727	11.831	10.191
613 - Furs skins Tanned, Dressed	NES	10.387	4.472	4.147
599 - Chemicals NES	ES	8.498	7.429	10.160
657 - Floor Covr, Tapestry etc	NES	6.101	14.461	12.189
941 - Zoo Animals, Pets	NES	5.598	2.013	1.203
656 - Textile etc Products NES	NES	4.894	7.857	1.908
633 - Cork Manufactures	NES	4.430	8.518	3.383
Low Performing				
667 - Pearl, Prec-, Semi-P Stone	NES	0.012	0.006	0.025
673 - Iron and Steel Shapes	ES	0.011	0.175	0.031
862 - Photo, Cinema Supplies	NES	0.010	0.073	0.061
951 - War Firearms, Ammunition	NES	0.008	0.028	0.077
513 - Inorg Elements, Oxides, etc	ES	0.007	0.041	0.014
671 - Pig Iron etc	ES	0.007	-	-
689 - Non-Fer Base Metals NES	ES	0.007	-	0.002
864 - Watches and Clocks	NES	0.003	0.010	0.045
515 - Radioactive etc Material	ES	0.001	0.000	-
911 - Mail Not Classed By Kind	NES	0.000	0.000	0.000

Appendix Table 3.5: Highest and Lowest Values of RCA for New Zealand's Trade in Manufactured Exports with ASEAN

	Type of Product	1993	1985	1980
High Performing				
633 - Cork Manufactures	NES	143.447	9.783	0.247
684 - Aluminium	ES	71.141	10.403	59.646
672 - Iron, Steel Primary Forms	ES	50.512	-	-
641 - Paper and Paperboard	ES	35.751	53.193	115.390
842 - Fur etc Clothes, Prod	NES	32.488	81.840	103.769
674 - Iron, Steel Univ, Plate, Sheet	ES	16.941	11.727	0.038
712 - Agricultural Machinery	NES	13.700	15.404	27.537
514 - Other Inorganic Chemicals	ES	7.389	3.196	0.417
695 - Tools	ES	6.363	0.216	0.209
896 - Works of Arts etc.	NES	6.021	0.323	0.274
Low Performing				
612 - Leather etc. Manufactures	NES	0.012	-	0.194
677 - Iron, Steel Wire Excl W Rod	ES	0.011	9.406	7.038
632 - Wood Manufactures NES	ES	0.009	0.181	0.110
661 - Cement etc Building Prod	ES	0.006	1.495	1.027
891 - Sound Recorders, , Producrs	NES	0.006	0.011	0.090
666 - Pottery	NES	0.004	-	0.169
731 - Railway Vehicles	NES	0.004	-	-
864 - Watches and Clocks	NES	0.004	-	-
851 - Footwear	NES	0.003	0.007	-
911 - Mail Not Classed by Kind	NES	0.000	0.000	0.000

Appendix Table 3.6:   Highest and Lowest Values of RCA for New Zealand's Trade in Manufactured Exports with DCs

	Type of Product	1993	1985	1980
High Performing				
613 - Fur Skins Tanned, Dressed	NES	41.909	1.747	1.319
641 - Paper and Paperboard	ES	18.711	7.371	21.908
599 - Chemicals NES	ES	11.284	3.399	5.518
633 - Cork Manufactures	NES	9.955	4.954	1.375
554 - Soaps, Cleaning etc Preps	NES	8.702	5.005	2.457
553 - Perfume, Cosmetics, etc	NES	8.552	2.348	2.108
684 - Aluminium	ES	8.550	4.309	13.441
842 - Fur etc Clothes, Prod	NES	6.094	0.584	0.446
611 - Leather	NES	5.691	4.247	9.236
712 - Agricultural Machinery	NES	5.395	0.711	1.449
Low Performing				
851 - Footwear	NES	0.017	0.070	0.121
831 - Travel Goods, Handbags	NES	0.014	0.031	0.117
731 - Railway Vehicles	NES	0.007	0.013	0.114
667 - Pearl, Prec-, Semi-P Stone	NES	0.004	0.004	0.001
515 - Radioactive etc Material	ES	0.003	0.000	-
864 - Watches and Clocks	NES	0.002	0.002	0.004
681 - Silver, Platinum, etc	ES	0.001	0.002	-
671 - Pig Iron etc	ES	0.000	-	-
689 - Non-Fer Base Metals NES	ES	0.000	-	0.001
911 - Mail Not Classed By Kind	NES	0.000	0.000	0.000

Appendix 3.1: Variable Definitions and Data Sources

Variable	Definition
PCI	Capital intensity computed as the book value of fixed capital divided by number of employees, 1986-87, Department of Statistics.
HCI	Wage value added, divided by number of employees, 1986-87, Department of Statistics.
RD	The ratio of research and development expenditure to sales, 1986-87, Department of Statistics.
ESC	Value added per person of the class containing 50th percentile of industry value added, divided by the total value added per person of the industry.
A/S	Advertising expenditure as a percentage of industry sales. In the absence of data for advertising, value given in the item no: 83 (data processing fees, legal and advertising) of the questionnaire for economy-wide census of manufacturing has been used to represent advertising expenditure, Department of Statistics.
CH	Industry concentration represented by Herfindhal Index, 1986-87, Department of Statistics.
FO	Industry sales accounted for by foreign owned firms divided by total industry sales.
NRP	Nominal rate of protection, Industry Assistance Reform, Treasury, Wellington.

4 Agri-Environmental Policy and Market Developments in the EU and Their Potential Impact on New Zealand Trade

CAROLINE SAUNDERS

The developments in the European Union (EU) and its environmental policy have important implications for New Zealand. While the importance of the EU as a market for New Zealand produce has diminished, it is still significant accounting for 17 per cent of exports (6 per cent of which are to the UK) especially as a high value market and in commodities such as sheepmeat, fruit and dairy. It is because of the importance of primary products in New Zealand trade with the EU and the fact that much EU environmental policy intervention and market changes are in the primary products sector that this chapter will concentrate upon EU environmental policy and its impact on agriculture.

The implications of changes in the EU on New Zealand are both indirect and direct. Indirect impacts include the influence the EU has in the outcome of WTO negotiations, particularly in relation to agricultural trade, which of course is of vital importance for New Zealand. Policy and market changes in the EU also affect New Zealand indirectly by impacting on other potential New Zealand export markets. Direct impacts of changes in the EU include the rise in demand for produce produced in an environmental friendly manner (henceforth referred to as "green" produce) particularly at the high value end of the market. Other important factors include the continuing access for New Zealand exports to the EU market especially under preferential arrangements.

CAP Policy and Reform

The basic system of support in the EU was, and to some extent still is, based upon the fixing of target prices, that is, the ideal price for producers. From this the intervention and threshold prices are derived. The intervention price is effectively a minimum price at which supplies are removed from the market by Government agencies. The threshold price is the price at which imports are allowed into the domestic market and is maintained by a system of import levies. These common prices were, in the case of most commodities, set well above world market prices. This led to increases in production within the Community, aided by increases in productivity through technological change. Thus self-sufficiency increased and the EU became a major exporter of temperate zone products, disrupting world markets, especially for traditional food exporters like New Zealand.

This CAP policy led to a number of well-documented problems and therefore pressures for reform the main ones being the rising cost of the CAP, the deterioration of international relations, as well as environmental degradation. There have been various reforms to the CAP, generally on a piece meal basis, especially over the 1980s, but the McSharry reforms in 1992 were the most comprehensive. Whilst these left the basic price structure in place they have reduced fixed prices to, or closer to, world market levels and compensated producers by direct payments based upon past production patterns.

The level of support given to agricultural commodities is still however considerable in New Zealand at $68.5 billion in 1997, that is 44 per cent of the EU budget. In particular since the CAP reforms, the level of public exchequer support in the form of direct payments has risen. For example in the UK in 1991/2 72 per cent of this expenditure was on market support and 27 per cent on headage/area payments (most of which were for sheep producers). In 1995/6 these percentages were reversed with only 20 per cent for market support and 80 per cent for headage/area payments (most of which was for arable area payments) (MAFF 1996).

To show the impact of this, and the degree of agricultural support, the financial/private returns, public exchequer cost, and social value of agricultural output have been calculated for the UK (Saunders 1996 and 1997).

The social value of agricultural output has been measured by removing the impact of intervention policies using an adaptation of Corden's Theory of Effective Protection, revaluing agricultural output at world market prices and deducting from this the world market value of the inputs, (Corden 1966). The results of these analysis for financial, social and public exchequer impacts, for a selected number of commodities in the UK, as reported in Table 4.1.

Table 4.1: **Financial, Public Exchequer and Social Value of Livestock Output £ per Livestock Unit**

	Dairy	**Beef**			**Sheep**	
		Single Suckler	18 month	Intensive	Hill	Lowland
Private Financial Cost	485.3	206	380	98	213	230
Social Opportunity Cost	-164.8	-95	-401	-558	153	155
Public Exchequer Cost	770	255	191	0	517	179

Source: Saunders (1996)

Therefore the level of support, to UK agriculture is still large despite recent reforms. The reforms did at least start the process of moving away from support which distorted markets towards direct payments. However, Table 4.3 does illustrate that under current market conditions the dairy and beef sectors would certainly not survive without support in their current form in the UK. Given the objective of maintaining populations in rural areas support would therefore have to continue in some form or another.

Agri-Environmental Policy

In parallel with, and additional to, these changes, recognising the environmental and social problems with conventional agriculture, the EU has introduced measures to encourage the development and continuation of measures/policies to encourage low input (including organic) farming. These measures are specific to member states and generally relate to designated areas (Environmentally Sensitive Areas (ESA)). They were first recognised in EU policy in 1987 with regulation 760/87 and were strengthened in 1992 as part of the McSharry reforms. The extent of these measures are illustrated in Table 4.2.

Table 4.2:   Extent of Measures Related to Environmentally Friendly Farming

	Percentage of agricultural area	Cost Million ECU per year
Belgium	4.6	7.75
Denmark	7.5	18.58
Germany	25.0	426.00
Spain	15.0	139.65
France	21.0	325.50
Ireland	8.0	69.00
Italy	8.4	10.40
Luxembourg	12.0	2.63
Netherlands	3.3	9.75
Austria	91.0	335.30
Portugal	19.0	47.50
UK	16.0	94.40

Source: Whitby, (ed) (1996); Putter (1995)

As Table 4.2 shows the area covered by the schemes varies across member state from 3.3 per cent in the Netherlands to 25 per cent in Germany, and to the exceptional 91 per cent in Austria. It is significant that Germany's area under environmental schemes is high given Germany's influence in EU policy making.

The level of EU expenditure on these schemes however is relatively small as a percentage of its budget on agriculture, but given that member states contribute a major proportion of spending, (typically 75 per cent), actual spending is much higher. This expenditure has risen from 0.76 per cent of guaranteed agricultural spending in 1994 to 4 per cent in 1995 and 4.4 per cent in 1997 and 5.3 per cent in 1998 (*Agra Europe*, 1996).

Table 4.3: MAFF (UK) Expenditure on Agri-Environmental Schemes

	£,000			
	95/6	**96/7**	**97/8**	**98/9**
ESA	39.5	40.4	45.7	50.4
Countryside Stewardship		16.9	21.5	27.0
Nitrate Sensitive Areas	5.4	6.9	8.9	9.9
Habitat Scheme	1.7	2.2	3.8	3.8
Moorland Scheme	0.4	0.7	1.4	1.8
Organic Scheme	0.5	0.6	1.2	1.2
Total	**47.5**	**67.7**	**82.5**	**94.1**

Source: MAFF

In the UK the level of expenditure by scheme administered by MAFF is illustrated in Table 4.3. This shows the level of expenditure nearly doubling over the last few years. Add to this other conservation schemes in the UK, which compensate farmers for low input farming, such as National Parks, and Sites of Special Scientific Interest (SSSI) the actual level of expenditure is higher.

Generic Policy Developments

In addition to the above there are general policy measures, both at the EU level and by member states, encouraging low-input farming, such as the nitrate directive which limits the amount of nitrate run-off. Other measures have been adopted by member countries to reduce fertiliser and pesticide use. For example, the Netherlands and Denmark, both of which have undertaken to reduce pesticides by 50 per cent.

In the Netherlands their target is to reduce pesticide use by 2000 and also that fertiliser application does not exceed absorption capacity of the environment.

Denmark has introduced a number of action plans relating to agriculture and farming practice. In 1987 the plan on the aquatic environment set targets of reductions in discharges of nitrogen by 50 per cent and of phosphorous by 80 per cent. This was reiterated in the action plan for agriculture in 1991 which aimed to reduce use of nitrogen and pesticides by 50 per cent by 1997. Moreover, the Danish government has an organic action plan to have 7 per cent of the land farmed organically by 2000.

The European Market for "Green" Produce

Another factor of importance to New Zealand is the development of the market for "green" produce in the EU, that is products produced to minimise chemical and other inputs for both food safety and environmental reasons. This rise in demand for "green" produce is a result of changing consumer attitudes in the EU and rising awareness of the potential threat of intensive farming. Thus, for example, Europe is the world's largest consumer of organic produce, a considerable amount of which is imported (Lampkin and Padel 1994). Current estimates of the present and forecasted size of the European organic industry are difficult to obtain. Lampkin and Padel (1994) estimated that in 1990 the market was approximately £900m, this figure was predicted to grow to £2700m by 1995 and £8200m by the year 2000. Growth is predicted to be especially strong for meat and dairy products. The organic meat market is estimated to be $400 million in 1996 of which $311 million is beef. In addition it is predicted that meat and dairy products will grow by 190 per cent between 1996-2002 to $1 billion. The main reasons given for this are the BSE scare, and loss of confidence in hygiene standards (Saunders et al., 1997 a and b).

Price premiums do exist for green products although they vary considerably, with 20 per cent being the most common for organic produce. However, price premiums are being removed with major supermarket chains in the UK such as Tesco removing price premiums presumably to increase market share. This is also seen in Denmark where the rise in consumption of organic milk has been stimulated via marketing campaigns and the removal of price premiums (Saunders et al., 1997 a and b).

This is an opportunity to New Zealand in that it can capitalise upon its clean green image and target higher value market niches. This has been seen with the rapid rise in the export sector of green produce over the last few years. In 1994 exports of organic produce were estimated at NZ$23.5 million and this is predicted to rise to NZ$65 million by 2002 (OPEG, 1997). However there are areas where the trend towards environmentally friendly production systems may threaten New Zealand producers. New Zealand has one of the OECD's highest application of phosphate fertilisers at 2.56 tonnes per square kilometre compared to 2.36 in Europe and 0.9 in the OECD; and whilst application of nitrogen fertilisers is low nationally compared with other OECD countries it varies considerably regionally in New Zealand (OECD, 1996). In New Zealand application rates of both fertilisers are growing, with a threefold increase in the use of nitrogen from 1990/1 to 1995/6 (MOE, 1997). The use of chemicals in New Zealand is also significant at 0.43 tonnes per kilometre square of crop land compared to 0.22 in the OECD and 0.42 in Europe.

New Zealand producers may therefore have to alter production techniques to meet the new demand for "green" products, as has already been seen in the development of Integrated Pest Management programmes in New Zealand particularly in the fruit sector.

Future Reforms of the CAP

It is generally recognised that the 1992 McSharry reforms were just the first stage in the reform of the EU agricultural policy, expectations are that the next reform round, coinciding with the round of WTO negotiations, will lead to further radical change. The switch from market to headage/area payments initiated in the 1992 reforms (which are additional to the environmental schemes outlined above) is expected to increase. However, recent changes in US policy mean that these payments as they currently stand will not be acceptable under the next WTO round of negotiations as they are based on production and therefore other criteria for their payment will have to be devised, the most likely of which will be environmental enhancement, as described in more detail below (*Agra Europe*, 1998).

The US Fair Act 1996 decoupled direct payments from production and thus removed them from the "blue box" in to the "green box". This is likely to put pressure on the EU in the next round of WTO negotiations to similarly decouple its direct payments to farmers. Under the Uruguay agreement the most likely justification for these, over the long-term, is direct payments for environmental reasons as defined in Annex 2 of the agreement. That is payments to farmers will have to be based upon extra costs, or loss of income involved, from environmentally friendly farming methods, the current basis for payments under the ESA schemes. This would meet a number of EU policy objectives such as maintaining farm incomes at present levels, reducing environmental damage and increasing positive externalities from agriculture, as well as meeting international obligations.

In the EU this could imply that the current agricultural budget on market support and area/headage payments of over 40 billion ecus could be diverted into headage/area payments based upon low-input environmentally sensitive farming, which is a radical change when compared to the 2 billion ecus expenditure on these schemes in the EU at present (*Agra Europe*, 1997).

This could transform the output from EU agriculture. It would also have the benefit of reducing output, therefore exports; and reducing competition for New Zealand in international markets. However it is likely to increase the demand for "green" products and could increase the threat of restrictions on imports of food based upon production and process methods.

The McSharry reforms have not been successful in meeting their objectives of reducing output and distortions to markets. The EU commission has admitted not only that the intention of the arable area payments was a transitional arrangement whilst the cereal sector adjusted to lower prices but also that these payments have failed. This is partly due to the fact that cereal prices in member states did not fall as much as expected and coupled with arable area payments mean that the EU commission predicts that farmers were overcompensated by 8.5 billion ecu, (UK MAFF argues this was actually 14 billion ecu) (*Agra Europe*, 1997).

The scheme has not, as the commission expected, reduced output, nor improved the social and environmental acceptability of the CAP. The rise in output due to increased productivity is expected to continue with conservative estimates at 12 per cent between 1992 and 2000. The high costs of the regime (42 per cent of the guaranteed budget in 1996) and the concentration of subsidies to the large farmers.

As under the GATT agreement the level of subsidised exports from the EU is limited making disposal of any increase in cereal output difficult. This will be exasperated by the relaxation of the set-aside rules preventing significant reduction in output due to lower arable area. Whilst the cereal sector is not of direct importance to New Zealand, it is important as it is the base of the CAP and will be crucial in the development of the next WTO reform round.

Further CAP Reform and the Next Round - Agenda 2000

The EU, under Agenda 2000, has put forward initial proposals for further reform to the CAP. These in general are cautious and build on the McSharry reforms. Price cuts for cereals and beef are proposed and are to be compensated by greater direct subsides, with a maximum ceiling. It is proposed to drop the cereal price by 20 per cent, from the current 119.19 ecu per tonnes to 95.35 ecus. Compensation would be 66 ecus per tonne, (a rise from the current 54.34 ecu per tonne) converted into area payments using the 1992 regional reference yield, an average payment of around 370 ecu per hectare. However the proposed changes would be subject to review if cereal prices rose. Compulsory set-aside would be abolished, which would not help to address over supply problems. Only half of the fall in cereal prices would be accounted for by the rise in arable area payments.

The prices in the beef regime would be cut by 30 per cent to 1950 ecu per tonne by 2003, from its current level of 2780 per tonne. This would be compensated for by higher premium payments as illustrated in Table 4.4, these premium payments can be supplemented by member states up to a certain maximum.

Table 4.4: Current and Proposed Prices and Subsidies in the Cereal, Dairy, and Beef Regimes

	Current level	**Proposed level**
Cereal prices	119.19 ecu/t	95.35 ecu/t
Arable area payments	54.34 ecu/t	66 ecu/t
Beef prices	2780 ecu/t	1950 ecu/t
Suckler cow premium	145 ecu/ha	180 ecu/head
Special beef premium		
Bulls	135 ecu/ha	220 ecu/head
Steers	109 ecu/ha	170 ecu/head
Dairy cow premium		35 ecu/ head

Source: *Agra Europe*, (1998); MAFF

In the case of dairy the quota regime is proposed to be continued until 2006, but increased by 2 per cent in four stages. Prices will be cut by 15 per cent and a new dairy premium to compensate for the price fall.

This does not seem to address the problems outlined above with the existing cereal regime. The ceiling may address the problem of the policy favouring large farms but in practice this will be hard to pass the EU Council of Ministers which was the cause of the failure to reduce the support to larger farms in the original proposed 1992 reform package.

As with the 1992 reform, the reforms will increase the cost of the CAP further with savings in export refunds offset by rises in direct and other subsides by an expected 6 billion ecus.

It is proposed to increase the agri-environmental measures with greater subsidies for organic farming, habitat protection as under the ESA scheme, and link current payments in LFA to low-input systems. These changes alone are minimal and do not address many of the concerns with the current policy especially in relation to agriculture and the environment.

However of potentially more importance is the proposal to allow member states to reduce direct payments by up to 20 per cent if national environmental requirements are not met. Further proposals allow member states to alter payments based upon, yet to be determined, employment criteria on farms.

However the reforms have not been well received, including by the French and German governments and by environmental groups. Moreover they do not address the problems likely to be encountered in the 1999 trade negotiations with the likely removal of the blue box in which current direct payments fit.

CAP Reform and the Next WTO Round

The link between trade and the environment is set to play an increasing role in the next WTO round. In general it is hypothesised that free trade is bad for the environment with production moving to areas with relatively low environmental controls. However liberalising agricultural trade may well have the opposite effect due to the distortionary policies in this sector. So liberalising agricultural trade may actually improve the environment.

However there are indications that environmental reasons may be used to restrict agricultural trade further. The EU has an interest in restricting trade on environmental grounds and the US has also restricted trade on environmental criteria.

For example, Franz Fischler has commented that the EU should take a hard line approach to the coming round of negotiations and in particular defend the model of EU agriculture and protect food safety. The Austrian Minister of Agriculture argued that the next WTO round of negotiations should amend agreements to allow countries to use ecological and social standards in regulation of trade. He argued that there should be "more flexibility in trade rules to account for consumers desire for higher environmental and animal welfare standards for farming" (*Agra Europe*, 1997).

Other proposals include extending the existing product liability clause to make importers of farm goods (as well as farmers) responsible for any damage caused by unsafe products.

Under GATT/WTO rules at present there are a number of clauses which could be used to restrict trade on environmental grounds, in particular clauses b and g from article XX as given below:-
  - necessary to protect human, animal or plant life or health
and
  - relating to the conservation of exhaustible natural resources if such measures are made in conjunction with restrictions on domestic consumption or production.

Application of these clauses allows exemption from the MFN clause as well as the clause requiring countries to give similar treatment to imports and products produced domestically.

These clauses were the basis of the agreements on Technical Barriers to Trade (TBT) and Phytosanitary (SPS) in the Uruguay round. The TBT aims to establish international standards but where these would be ineffective or inappropriate it allows countries to have as more stringent environmental requirement. Under the SPS agreement countries are allowed to enforce measures to protect human, animal, or plant life and health so long as they are not discriminatory. However these restrictions on trade should be based upon scientific criteria.

Both TBT and SPS provide a new regime of multi lateral trading system which is not just restricted to the quality of the product itself but the way it has been produced. However the interpretation of these clauses has caused, and continues to cause, considerable controversy (as currently seen with the ruling on beef produced with hormones in the US which the EU wished to ban but failed to under ruling). It could be expected that these agreements will come under pressure in the next round of negotiations.

In addition to the SPS and TBT agreements environmental issues were significant in the Uruguay round not least in the establishment of the WTO which states that the relations should allow "for the optimal use of resources in accordance with sustainable development seeking both to protect and preserve the environment and enhance the means of doing so". Moreover a special committee on trade and the environment (CTE) was established in 1995.

Relevant to this is the relationship between Multi-Lateral Environmental Agreements (MEAs) and GATT/WTO rules. Around 20 MEAs contain trade restrictions which are potentially against the rules, these have not yet been challenged, but it is recognised that they need clarification.

Also the ISO14000, which established the Environmental Management System (EMS), provides a vehicle by which environmental factors can be included in trade mainly by the private sector.

However under current rules restricting trade purely on production and process methods is limited. So a WTO member cannot unilaterally restrict trade because of the environmental effects of its production in the exporting country. However some argue this is contrary to Principle 2 of the Rio declaration which is "to ensure that activities within their jurisdiction do not cause damage to the environment of other states or of areas beyond the limits of national jurisdiction".

Conclusion

The support for agriculture in the CAP has changed, switching from market based support to direct payments. However these payments are largely based on historical production patterns and have done little to reduce the output and market distortions caused by the policy. The next round is likely to ban such payments (currently in the blue box) unless they are decoupled from production.

The estimates of social value of agricultural output in the UK above show that the change in support for cereals has removed much of the market distortion. Thus cereals have a positive social value in the UK However both dairy and beef production have negative social value in the UK, both sectors continuing to receive a high degree of protection both from the public exchequer and through the market. Sheep production has positive opportunity cost of output which is similar whether produced on the hill or in the lowlands. Thus further removal of production based support systems in the UK will have the greatest impact on the dairy and beef sectors.

The next round of CAP reforms will further reduce market distortions. This will have the impact on New Zealand of freeing up both EU and international markets although the negative effect on some sectors of reducing the quota rent currently earned from preferential access, a factor not discussed in this paper.

However it is not politically feasible for the total removal of agricultural support from the EU so direct payments are expected to increase further in importance. These direct payments will likely be conditional on low-input farming schemes. The threat, or opportunity, to New Zealand is that these policies will be used as a basis for restricting trade in products not produced under similar conditions and therefore may well mean New Zealand may have to alter its production methods to obtain continued access to the EU market.

References

Agra Europe: various issues. London.

Corden, W.M. (1966), "The structure of a tariff system and the Effective Protection Rate", *Journal of Political Economy*, 74, 221-237.

Lampkin, N.H. and Padel, S. (1994), *The Economics of Organic Farming: An International Perspective*, Wallingford, UK: CAB International.

MAFF (1996), *Agriculture in the UK*, London: HMSO.

MOE (1997), *The State of the Environment*, Wellington: Ministry for the Environment.

OECD (1996), *Environmental Performance Reviews*, Paris: OECD.

OPEG (1997), pers comm.

Primdahl, J. (1996), "Denmark", in Whitby, M.C. (ed) (1996), *The European Environment and CAP reform*, Wallingford, UK: CAB International.

Putter, J. (1995), *Greening of Europe's Agricultural Policy*, Netherlands: MAF.

Saunders. C. (1996), "Resource cost of agricultural output", *Working Paper No. 13*, University of Newcastle-upon-Tyne: Centre for Rural Economy, Department of Agricultural Economics and Food Marketing.

Saunders, C.M. (1997), "Current and future developments in agri-environmental policies and the CAP in the EU and their implications for New Zealand", Paper presented at the New Zealand ARES Conference, July.

Saunders, C.M., Manhire, J., Campbell, H. and Fairweather, J. (1997a), "Organic Farming in New Zealand: An evaluation of the current and future prospects including an assessment of research needs", *MAF Policy Technical Report*, 97/14.

Saunders, C.M., Manhire, J., Campbell, H. and Fairweather, J. (1997b), "Organic Farming in New Zealand: An evaluation of the current and future prospects including an assessment of research needs", Comprehensive report, *MAF Policy Technical Report*, 97/13.

Whitby, M. (ed) (1996), *The European Environment and CAP reform. Policies and Prospects for Conservation,* Wallingford, UK: CAB International.

5 Foreign Direct Investment and the Environmental Regulatory Regimes of the Countries of the APEC Region: Where Does New Zealand Stand?

MICHAEL WYDEVELD

Abstract

The APEC region is one of the most dynamic regions of the world, with rapidly accumulating material wealth. The maintenance of such growth requires that countries adopt sustainable management of resources as one of their key policy objectives. An appropriate conception of sustainable management includes both aspects of efficiency and sustainability. It is the argument of this paper that the current concerns raised in some quarters as to the anti-competitive nature of many environmental regulations does not stem from legitimate differences between countries over what levels of pollution are sustainable, but rather from the failure of domestic governments to introduce sufficiently adaptive environmental regulatory regimes. It is the hypothesis of this paper that such adaptiveness would reduce many of the apparent conflicts between sustainability and efficiency, thus, helping to retain the competitiveness of certain pollutive, or resource intensive, sectors as international economic integration proceeds. There is evidence that some APEC countries have been particularly more adept at mitigating efficiency and sustainability conflicts than others. New Zealand stands out as a country which has been particularly successful in this regard.

Introduction

The Asia Pacific Economic Co-operation (APEC) grouping, which at the beginning of 1996 comprised 18 member states, is the most dynamic grouping of countries in the world[1]. The APEC region embraces over 2 billion people, more than half the world's population, and together the countries of APEC account for more than half of the world's output, trade, and foreign direct investment (FDI). These are already impressive figures, yet most commentators also expect the region's importance to continue to advance into the future. As a member of this APEC group, New Zealand is in a unique position to benefit from the regions dynamism.

To maximise the benefits of global integration New Zealand has undergone significant economic reforms in the past 10 years or so. Reforms which have permeated all sectors of the economy. This reform of how New Zealand conducts her business has lead to a general embrace of the goal of efficiency. To reduce inefficiency New Zealand has opened her economy to international competition, deregulated many sectors of the economy and privatised many previously state owned monopolies. New Zealand's moves in these regards are not dissimilar from some of the other APEC countries.

The strive for efficiency has also extended to the area of management of environmental resources. However, the goal of efficiency is not the only new objective to be adopted. The sustainable management of resources and environments has also become an equally important goal[2]. Sustainability in its "weak form" requires that eco-systems which can reproduce themselves, and which provide life-supporting functions, are not so overburdened that they lose such capacities. Efficiency for its part implies that current opportunity costs are minimised in the production and consumption of goods and services. The efficient management and the sustainable management of resources are not equivalent, yet they are related, with efficiency being a prerequisite, but not sufficient condition, for sustainability. Therefore, the environmental concerns in New Zealand and other APEC countries extend beyond the efficient management of resources to the sustainable management of entire eco-systems[3].

The relationship between efficiency and sustainability could further be evaluated over a time period. The goal of efficiency and sustainability may be in direct conflict in the short run, as in the case of an observed business entity discharging excessive (i.e., beyond the environments carrying capacity) noxious effluent into the environment. The conflict stems from the presumption that such degradation if allowed to continue would do so indefinitely and due to possible cumulative effects would ultimately prove unsustainable.

However, there is no a priori reason to believe that such an observed conflict need necessarily remain so. Time frames and the adaptiveness of business and environmental policy are now recognised as an important factor in reconciling efficiency and sustainability conflicts. It is argued that if a more long term and integrated perspective is taken, and if policies designed to protect the environment were sufficiently adaptive, then this apparent conflict could be transitive in nature. In the case mentioned above the business entity could be encouraged, for example, to change its production technique over time, reducing its effluent discharge each period.

Viewed in this light, efficient environmental policy could then be reinterpreted as any policy that induces agents to change their behaviour with the least economic costs, in order to meet specified environmental objectives. Environmental objectives which have been established by an assessment of what level of resource use and effluent discharge from production and consumption are sustainable[4]. There is evidence that across the APEC region some countries have been significantly more apt at mitigating efficiency and sustainability conflicts than others.

Despite the increasing recognition of the importance of sustainable management, across the APEC countries the concept has received varying levels of support. Some countries, usually the more materially developed, have adopted more stringent environmental standards than others in the region, i.e., the developed countries have set a lower limit on the level of effluent discharge from production and consumption processes that they perceive as sustainable. This has raised some concerns in these same countries that the international competitiveness of their businesses may be perversely affected by the instigation of such high environmental standards. This would then result in trade being perversely effected and may even prompt the relocation of production capacity, which in-turn has implications for welfare and employment in any particular country.

It is this concern with the possible loss of competitiveness that I aim to address in this chapter. The validity of such concerns will be evaluated for the APEC region as a whole and from the perspective of New Zealand businesses operating in this region. The chapter will attempt to evaluate how apt APEC governments have been in mitigating environment protection and competitiveness conflicts. Legitimate differences in environmental standards between countries which stem from either differences in environmental carrying capacities, or preferences (resultant from countries being at various levels of material wealth), are false causes of concern. It is the hypothesis of this essay that the more apt governments are at mitigating efficiency and sustainability conflicts, the less important international competitiveness issues become and that their success depends very much on the adaptiveness of their environmental regulatory regime (ERR).

Ideally I would seek to substantiate my hypothesis by asking two related questions. The first is whether the flows of FDI are likely to be affected by environmental policies? While the second would ask; if so, does this stem from legitimate differences in sustainability standards, or is this largely a result of failure on the part of governments to mitigate environment and competitiveness conflicts where there was potential to do so?

The first question has been empirically dealt with by numerous writers. For most studies environmental regulations represent an insignificant determinant in FDI flows, though in limited instances as in the case of particularly pollutive industries it may be significant[5]. This chapter does not wish to repeat such empirical work for New Zealand and the APEC countries, nor could it hope to, due to the general lack of data. Instead, I seek to qualitatively determine New Zealand's place in the APEC group with regard to the significance of FDI for its economy, the stringency of its environmental regulations and the adaptiveness of its ERR. Similar information will be presented for the other APEC countries. These issues discerned, the substance of my hypothesis can be more fully evaluated.

This chapter proceeds as follows; section 2 examines the links between trade and FDI and seeks to determine the significance of FDI across the APEC countries, thus providing an indication of which countries are most likely to be effected by environmental policies which may influence FDI flows. In section 3 I evaluate New Zealand's recent experience with FDI and its reforms, including those in the area of environmental law. Section 4 presents theoretical considerations with regard to environmental regulations determining the amount of inward and outward FDI. In particular it focuses on the barriers to entry of inward FDI and an evaluation of the adaptiveness (pro-competitive nature) of environmental regulations in the APEC region. In section 5, I present the results of a survey of Auckland based manufacturing firms, evaluating the influence of environmental regulations and the ERR on their costs, investment decisions and export competitiveness. It also questions them on their perceived scope for input into the development of environmental policy. Section 6 then presents a summary and some concluding remarks.

The Trends and Significance of FDI in the APEC Region[6]

In economic theory, trade and FDI can act as both substitutes or complements for one another under alternative conditions. In the past, when the APEC region was characterised by high protective barriers such as tariff and quotas, FDI and trade were largely substitutes. Multinational corporations (MNCs) would establish behind protective walls to serve the host market. Over the past 15 years barriers to trade have been dismantled and a dynamism in the APEC region has been unleashed. With a relative lack of capital - particularly in the Asian newly industrialised countries (NICs) - the conditions in the APEC region have encouraged both trade and FDI. Thus, across the APEC region FDI and trade are now generally viewed as complements[7].

Correlations between trade and FDI are high and range in 1992 from 0.7681 for the US to 0.9947 for Mexico. After the US, New Zealand showed the weakest correlation between trade and FDI with a percentage of 0.7832 in 1992[8]. As a subgrouping the NICs, which comprises the Republic of Korea (ROK), Hong Kong, Taiwan, and Singapore, show the strongest correlation at 0.9928. These figures tend to suggest that if environmental regulations effect FDI then trade will likewise be effected. Together these effects on trade and FDI then have implications for welfare and employment. However, to evaluate these welfare and employment effects, we must begin by establishing the significance of FDI in the economies of the APEC countries.

The significance of FDI can be measured by the shares of FDI stock to GDP. The share of APEC inward FDI stock in APEC GDP averaged about 7.4 per cent in 1992, yet the importance of inward FDI stock across individual APEC countries varied markedly. In 1992 the share of inward FDI stock in GDP ranged from a meagre 0.7 per cent in Japan to 75 per cent for Singapore. In New Zealand the figure for the same period was 22.8 per cent. For the same year, the share of APEC outward FDI stock in APEC GDP averaged about 8.7 per cent and as in the case of inward FDI stock, the importance of outward FDI stock across individual APEC countries varied markedly. In 1992 the share of inward FDI stock in GDP ranged from a low of 0.3 per cent for China to 45 per cent for Hong Kong. In New Zealand the figure for the same period was 10.5 per cent.

Table 5.1: Trade Correlations and the Share of Inward and Outward FDI in GDP for the APEC Countries, 1992

Country	Correlation Trade & FDI	Inward FDI share in GDP	Outward FDI share in GDP
Australia	0.8056	24.7	14.7
Brunei	n/a	n/a	n/a
Canada	0.9905	19.2	14.7
Chile	n/a	n/a	n/a
China	0.9900	8.8	0.3
Hong Kong	0.9885	30.2	44.9
Indonesia	0.8705	55.7	1.9
Japan	0.9186	0.7	10.6
Korea	0.9811	2.9	1.9
Malaysia	0.9767	39.2	3.7
Mexico	0.9947	11.2	0.4
New Zealand	0.7832	22.8	10.5
Papua New Guinea	n/a	n/a	n/a
Philippines	0.9722	7.6	9.3
Singapore	0.9622	74.8	23.4
Taiwan	0.9804	8.0	2.7
Thailand	0.9743	11.8	0.7
USA	0.7681	7.0	8.3

Source: APEC Economic Committee (1995)

These figures tend to indicate that the significance of the effects environmental standards may have on FDI, and subsequently welfare and employment, will vary across the APEC countries. For New Zealand the effects are expected to be significant due to its dependence on FDI. This is important to know as the current significance of the stock of FDI in an economy will help determine the potential gains and losses this same country may realise from altering its environmental standards as measured against this status quo.

However, what is difficult to establish is the lines of causality. In other words, a low significance for some countries, as indicated by a current low share of inward and/or outward FDI to GDP, need not imply that the significance could not be greater in the future. Nor is it unfathomable to suggest that environmental regulations have themselves influenced the significance of these shares, or that they will do so in the future. To establish causality would require a review of the general policies of individual governments affecting the degree of capital mobility in the APEC region and a review of the particular environmental protection regimes of each country. In other words, what are the determinants of FDI flows, and how do we separate out the influence of environmental regulations from those of other variables? The enormity of such a task has required that I henceforth proceed by focusing on New Zealand's situation, while drawing broad observations and contrasts to other APEC countries from various sources[9].

New Zealand's Reforms

In New Zealand the flows of FDI have been dramatically effected by the recent restructuring of the economy[10]. As a result of excessive overseas borrowing in the late 1970s and early 1980s New Zealand's overseas debt in 1986 had reached 70 per cent of GDP, while servicing costs were absorbing 50 per cent of New Zealand's total export income. Liberalisation and deregulation was adopted as the only means to avoid New Zealand developing an unsustainable debt situation[11].

Policies relating to FDI under went significant change as New Zealand has established a very liberal FDI regime and although FDI has been encouraged in rhetoric, few direct incentives have been provided to entice overseas investors. The New Zealand government relies on economic fundamentals to attract FDI and promotes policies to stimulate favourable conditions. A strong anti-inflation policy has been adopted, labour markets have been deregulated and New Zealand has entered into a Closer Economic Relationship (CER) with its largest trading partner, Australia. Access to primary resources have also been allowed for overseas investors[12]. In fact it would be fair to say that in general, overseas investors are now treated similarly to New Zealand investors. MNCs are required to comply with all New Zealand legislative and regulatory requirements as New Zealand businesses do[13]. One such area of compliance is environmental policy. It would therefore be poignant timing to highlight some of the major recent changes in New Zealand's environmental policy and what implications this may hold for FDI.

Without question environmental policy, as with many policies in New Zealand, has made significant changes in the past 10 years. The major legislative change in this regard has been the passing of the Resource Management Act 1991 (RMA). Whereas previous legislation emphasised the regulation of land use activities, the RMA's main emphasis is on evaluation of environmental effects[14]. Further, this new legislation has prompted changes in both the planning and decision-making processes of those who administer the Act.

In the area of planning Montz and Dixon (1993) argue that the purpose of planning had become in the 1980s a process in its own right. The RMA has shifted focus to where planning is viewed as a means to achieving outcomes. The pair also suggest that previous legislation encouraged decision-making which was site-specific and discipline-specific. The RMA on the other hand encourages a more integrated and interdisciplinary approach[15]. This has allowed those businesses considering investment in certain sectors latitude in how they met their environmental responsibilities. This is in stark contrast to the situation found in many other APEC countries.

Benidickson (1994) argues: "Canadian environmental controls have been described as - and criticised for - tending to be prescriptive rather than results oriented...If this characterisation is valid, the investor's concern may well be directed to the costs of procedures that either fail to accomplish their stated objectives or achieve their purposes at costs greater that the cost of prohibited alternatives." Australian environmental policy has also been criticised in some of their domestic quarters for policies which aim at regulation by zoning and include requirements that particular production pollution control technologies be applied without further regard being given to individual business' discretion in choice of environmental protection means. Similar observations have been made of the environmental regulatory systems in the US and Taiwan[16].

New Zealand's current approach benefits from the use of an environmental impact assessment report to achieve integration, as it allows all groups with a significant interest to express their views. In fact the onus is on businesses, environmental groups, and consumers to all have their input, with executive power ultimately resting with local councils who will make decisions on the best information available. In cases where scientific evaluations are lacking a cautious approach has been taken by many local authorities. If some groups are unable to take on the responsibility of scientifically evaluating the likely impacts of the activities in question, then an adaptable ERR will not achieve its full potential. This may suggest a role for some further government resources being committed to undertake such research. Currently there is also no government body keeping track of the prosecutions under the RMA. This is an area which must be addressed if a truly integrated approach at the national level, not just the regional level, is to be achieved[17].

FDI Flows and Environmental Regulatory Regimes

There are numerous determinants of FDI flows[18]. However, in this section I wish to focus on environmental considerations. Three broad areas of consideration must be given with regard to environmental policy and the flows of FDI. These areas include: the ability and desirability of entering the New Zealand market, the ability and desirability of continuing to operate within the market after the operation has been established, and the ability to exit an industry. These considerations include elements which are themselves of course not mutually exclusive, but reflect the differences in transparency of different areas of the ERR.

In establishing an operation in New Zealand foreign MNCs will have to give regard to any initial environmental abatement equipment they will need to purchase to comply with current laws[19] and whether they will have access to certain environmental resources which may be required by their operation. Whether a firm continues to operate in a market will depend on the marginal profit effects of rising or lowering environmental standards and whether investment certainty is maintained, i.e., if a MNC has been given access to an environmental resource, whether access will be continued in the future with due consideration as to the capital investments of the business. A major consideration for a business seeking to exit a sector will be its liability for any environmental problems it has caused[20].

In New Zealand access to resources has been liberalised significantly in the early 1990s, although in certain sectors barriers to access persist. These barriers do not differentiate between domestic and foreign operations, but have obvious implications for inward FDI where limited access is allotted on a historical basis and as a push factor to outward FDI where expansion is limited by the domestic pool of resources[21]. However, recently concerns have gravitated to the long-term security of access to resources, with some businesses fearing a reversal on the policies of liberalised access to resources[22].

In the areas of entry the APEC countries still have restrictions on inward FDI in certain environmentally sensitive sectors. These are barriers which are generally outside the fold of environmental management, but could have significant impact on the flow of FDI into pollutive sectors. Table 5.2 highlights some of the barriers to inward FDI in these sectors. Taiwan stands out in the group as the only country that explicitly prevents FDI in sectors which create significant pollution or environmental damage.

Table 5.2: Restrictions/Prohibitions on Inward FDI with Possible Environmental Impact, 1994

Australia	New projects in the uranium sector.
Brunei	None.
Canada	Large part of the nuclear sector, transportation, fishing and energy.
	Provincial governments restrict ownership of certain agricultural land.
Chile	Fishing.
China	Various sectors in developing and processing precious mineral resources.
	Projects producing native products or traditional export products.
Hong Kong	None.
Indonesia	Foreign logging.
Japan	None.
Korea	185 sectors are specified in Korea's negative list of exceptions. Some of these may include environmentally sensitive sectors. Permission is granted on a case by case basis.
Malaysia	None.
Mexico	Petroleum extraction and refining, coal mining and fishing.
New Zealand	Transportation, electricity generation and supply, and the use of rural land.
Papua New Guinea	None.
Philippines	Engineering, rice and corn production.
Singapore	Electricity, gas and water.
Taiwan	Explicitly any sectors causing high pollution including: mining and natural gas drilling, cigarette and liquor manufacturing; petroleum refining and electricity generation.
Thailand	Fishing, agriculture, mining and manufacturing.
USA	Atomic energy and transportation (aviation, shipping).

Source: Adapted from PECC (1995)

In considering whether to continue to participate in a given market, businesses will have to give regard to the competitiveness effects of rising environmental standards[23]. As mentioned earlier these effects are likely to depend on the structure of the regulatory system. It could be speculated that regimes which currently employ the use of strict process standards would have the most adverse effect on competitiveness should they be tightened. A short-term reaction of a business to the imposition of tighter environmental standards could be a reduction in output, or a change in the input mix. Whereas the long-run reaction could be for the business to take on new technology or to relocate its plants.

Table 5.3 highlights how adaptive existing environmental laws were to maintaining business competitiveness in the countries of the APEC region in 1994[24]. The poor performance of the US, a country with the most extensive ERR, stands out. This is because of the tendency for new environmental regulations in the US to take the form of strict standards in the production process rather than by setting standards on the final environmental outcomes. Thus firms have typically been required to purchase specific environmental abatement equipment rather than paying a tax on emissions levels, or actual output volumes. In contrast Singapore and Hong Kong, those two countries with the highest dependence on FDI in the APEC grouping, have the most adaptive of ERRs.

Table 5.3: Environmental Laws and Corporate Competitiveness, 1992

Rank	Country	(0 - 10)[25]
1	Singapore	8.17
2	Hong Kong	7.35
3	New Zealand	7.31
4	Malaysia	7.05
5	China	6.92
6	Mexico	6.86
7	Indonesia	6.65
8	Chile	6.59
9	Japan	6.41
10	Thailand	6.34
11	Canada	6.30
12	Philippines	6.03
13	USA	5.66
14	Australia	5.44
15	Korea	5.36
16	Taiwan	4.72

Source: World Competitiveness Report 1994

In New Zealand it would seem a fair conclusion to suggest that the environmental regulatory regime is quite adaptive to the need for maintaining business competitiveness. Yet, in certain sectors there remain arguments that adaptiveness could be further encouraged. Recently the fishing industry has charged proposed environmental regulations, as planned by the Ministry of Fisheries, with creating an extra $21 million annual expense. They argue that "[i]f the components of fisheries management were analysed on a commercial basis - recognising that the minister had to be satisfied with the sustainability of key stocks and to ensure a high degree of compliance" - total environmental compliance costs (ECCs) should still be significantly lower[26].

On the question of exit barriers information is scarce with liability seeming to be enforced on a case by case basis. A recent New Zealand official discussion paper on the Cleanup of Contaminated Sites would make polluters responsible for historical contamination. Already a major paint company is spending some $4m to remediate such a site[27].

The Survey[28]

The survey consisted of 21 firms across a variety of manufacturing categories[29]. Those firms with the greatest potential environmental impact were identified[30]. Due to the small size of the sample it was imperative that sectors with significant environmental impacts were targeted. Table 5.4 presents the firms and industries.

Tables 5.5, 5.6 and 5.7 reveal the results of the survey. Besides this data some specific comments from individual firms was also obtained. The numbers in brackets at the end of some statements refer to those firms who shared such an opinion.

Table 5.4: Categories of Industries Surveyed

	No. of Firms	**No. of Firms**
Auto Parts & Accessories	3	1-3
Aluminium Products	2	4, 5
Cement	1	6
Chemicals & Oil Refinery	4	7-10
Whiteware	1	11
Health & Beauty	2	12, 13
Machinery	2	14, 15
Plastics & Paint	4	16-19
Pulp and Paper & Furniture	2	20, 21

Source: Auckland Manufacturers Association Yearbook 1993/94[31]

Despite pollutive firms being targeted most firms freely added that they believed their operations had very limited environmental impacts. This perception stemmed in part from a distinction between environmental effects which accrued on the consumption side and those which occurred on the production side. The former largely being dismissed as being beyond the firms responsibility (15).

There was a general perception that good environmental practices brought a positive business image which then benefited the firm. However, two firms did express some concern over the inability to quantify these intangible benefits (6, 12).

Table 5.5: Results of the Survey

Firm Number	1	2	3	4	5	6	7
Sales	$45m	$10m	$12m	n/a	$71m	$100m	$8.5m
Ownership	Canada	Aus	Japan	NZ	NZ	NZ	UK
Outward FDI	No	No	No	No	Aus 50% NZ 50%	No	No
Inputs ($ or %TC)[i]	Yes	$5.5m	70%	No	10%	$5m	40-45%
Source	n/a[ii]	Aus (50%) Jap (20%) US (20%)	Aus, US, Italy	n/a	US	Mexico, Germany	Aus, US, UK
Exports (% Sales)	100%	5%	43%	5-10%	15%	15-20%	5%
Destination	US (90%), Can (10%)	Pac.Isl.	Aus	Aus, Pac.Isl.	Aus, Sth. Pac.	PNG, Tahiti (80%)	Pac.Isl.
Operating an EMS	Yes	Yes	No	No	No	Under devel.	No
Total Costs	n/a	$9m	$10.5m	n/a	n/a	$50m	n/a
ECCs ($ or %TC)	2-3%	$50,000 or 0.6%	10%	n/a	<2%	$250,000 or 0.5%	<2%
Significance of ECCs[iii]	Significant	Moderate	Significant	None	None	Significant	Significant
Adaptiveness of ERR[iv]	Acceptable	V.Good	Poorly	n/a	V.Good	Good	n/a

i   Problems were encountered in identifying sources for inputs as many of the manufacturers suppliers could source from outside New Zealand. For example, firm 17 suggested its share of imported material could range from 20%, if calculated by the firms direct imports, but may be as high as 80% once suppliers are included.

ii n/a - either means; not applicable, not available, or confidential. It is this writer's opinion that the reader should, from the other questions answered and the comments presented herein, be able to discern which is applicable.

iii This was ascertained by use of a five point scale; Very Significant, Significant, Moderate, Little, None.

iv This was ascertained by use of a five point scale; Very Good, Good, Acceptable, Poor, Very Poor.

A precise quantification of ECCs was difficult. This can be traced largely to the failure of many firms to operate an environmental management system (EMS). When ECCs are recorded they tend to be segmented to various areas of the financial accounts making aggregate ECCs difficult to determine (4, 7, 9, 16). Despite this quantification problem the majority of firms still perceived ECCs as insignificant cost. However, some managers made mention that significance depended to a great degree on the ferocity of competition (3, 17). One also alluded to the possibility of cross-subsidisation of environmental costs from sales in markets were competition is a little less fierce (3). As industry groups it appears that only the Auto Parts and Accessories, and the Pulp and Paper and Furniture found ECCs to be a significant cost. The majority of firms in other groups finding them insignificant.

Given this information, it could be speculated that ECCs are unlikely to be a significant determinant in investment decisions or overseas competitiveness. However, this must be qualified, as there were several firms who suggested that the capitalisation costs of environmental regulations were a significant cost and influenced decisions as to whether new plants would be constructed or older plants upgraded (3, 5, 17). Further, the uncertainty surrounding the ability to gain ongoing resource consents also have affected the level of investment (6, 20).

Of the four firms surveyed who undertook outward FDI, the greater number when questioned on their motivation highlighted greater market access, including access to retail and wholesale outlets, as an overriding factor (5, 11, 15). Firm 20 suggested greater access to resources was its primary motivation. All saw environmental regulations as an insignificant determinant in their decision. However, two firms raised the possibility that it may become more important in the future (5, 20).

Table 5.6: Results of the Survey

Firm Number	8	9	10	11	12	13	14
Sales	$1m	$7m	n/a	$800m	$20m	$22m	n/a
Ownership	French	NZ	NZ	Publicly listed	US	NZ	Swiss
Outward FDI	No	No	No	Aus (15%)	No	No	No
Inputs ($ or % TC)	50%	No	5%	66%	80%	$10m	20%
Source	Aus, US, China, Korea	n/a	Aus	Aus, Japan	US, UK	China, Aus, Japan	Japan, Switz.
Exports (% Sales)	No	20%	No	46%	5%	5%	100%
Destination	n/a	Aus.	n/a	Aus, US, Japan	Pac.Isl.	Aus, Malaysia	Europe, Aus, US, Thailand
Operating an EMS	Yes	No	Yes	Yes	No	Yes	No
Total Costs	n/a	n/a	n/a	n/a	n/a	$19m	n/a
ECCs ($ or %TC)	<$5000	n/a	5-10%	<1%	<0.1%	1%	0%
Significance of ECCs	None	n/a	Significant	Moderate	None	None	None
Adaptiveness of ERR	n/a	n/a	Poorly	Acceptable	V.Good	Good	V.Good

There was general consensus among managers that the New Zealand ERR was very well adapted when compared to overseas ERRs, with several managers drawing direct comparison to Australia and the US who they felt had much more authoritarian regimes (1, 8, 13, 14, 20). A few firms perceived that in New Zealand local Council gave only lip service to the needs of business and were authoritarian (3, 10, 20, 21). Numerous firms mentioned that under the RMA the onus had now gone on business to voluntarily set standards and undertake more research as the environmental impact of their operations (1, 5, 6, 17, 20). For at-least one foreign owned firm the impetus for improving environmental standards was coming from the foreign parent company (17). A couple of firms also believed their industrial associations had some influence in the setting of environmental standards (4, 20). While one beauty and health care firm felt their standards would be driven by the consumer (12).

Questioned on the level, rather than the form of environmental standards, all firms concurred that New Zealand generally had lower standards than Western Europe, the US and Australia. New Zealand was perceived to have higher standards than the less developed countries of Asia and the South Pacific, with Malaysia, South Korea and Fiji being singled out in particular (1, 21).

Table 5.7: Results of the Survey

Firm Number	15	16	17	18	19	20	21
Sales	n/a	$2m	$22m	$38m	$1.5m	n/a	$1m
Ownership	NZ	NZ	UK	Aus	NZ	US (50%) Public	NZ
Outward FDI	Yes Dist.-Australia	No	No	No	No	Yes Aus, Canada, Chile	No
Inputs	2%	No	20%	Yes	60-70%	Yes	No
Source	Italy	n/a	UK	Canada, US, Japan	China, Taiwan, Germany	n/a	n/a
Exports	Yes	2-3%	No	25%	2%	Yes	30%
Destination	Aus, US Pac.Isl.	Aus	n/a	Aus	Aus	n/a	Aus, Japan
EMS	No	No	Yes	No	No	Yes	No
Total Costs	n/a	n/a	n/a	n/a	n/a	n/a	n/a
ECCs ($ or %TC)	5%	0.5%	5%	<1%	$200 or <0.1%	n/a	1%
Significance of ECCs	Little	None	Significant	None	None	Significant	Moderate
Adaptiveness of ERR	V.Good	V.Good	Good	V.Good	n/a	n/a	Poorly

Questioned on the future prospects for environmental regulatory regime, all firms expected standards to rise with the majority believing that their firms could take an active role in developing these standards. However, a few firms feared that they would become more draconian (3, 6, 21). Several firms questioned future levels of environmental standards asking whether New Zealand standards really had to rise as high as the US, for example, given New Zealand's relatively low industrial density (1, 20). They also questioned the scientific basis for some environmental standards, suggesting there is still a significant void in hard scientific evidence (7, 11, 17, 20).

A couple of firms also made mention of the possibility of overseas environmental regulations, or the harmonisation of world standards as a possible barrier to trade and investment (13, 20).

Concluding Remarks

If governments can mitigate the conflicts between the sustainable and efficient management of resources to a greater degree, then the significance of differing environmental standards between countries is greatly reduced. As developed countries typically have the more stringent environmental standards it would seem imperative they adopt adaptive solutions. Some quarters in the US have recently been quite vocal in their condemnation of the anti-competitiveness effects of their domestic environmental regulations. This has resulted in attention being diverted to the supposed unfair practices of other developing countries.

Similarly those countries with significant dependence on FDI as a source for investment could benefit from a more adaptive ERR. New Zealand, Singapore and Hong Kong are examples of more developed countries which have successfully met this challenge, while Australia and Canada represent developed countries where much progress could still be made. Taiwan's policy of explicitly preventing FDI into environmentally sensitive sectors must also be concluded to be of both dubious economical and environmental worth.

In New Zealand the challenge exits in certain sectors for greater scientific research into the sustainability effects of certain substances, or harvesting techniques. This current void in research has created the scope for introducing ad hoc and excessively high environmental standards where scientific data is deficient and the worst case environmental scenario adopted. Similarly, the failure of any government authority to monitor prosecutions under the act, or undertake greater research, also indicates that other sector's standards may be in fear of slipping to the lowest common denominator regardless of the sustainability issues at stake.

Thus, in short, the adoption of an adaptive regime although providing greater potential to mitigate efficiency and sustainability conflicts, also creates an added responsibility for all interested parties; charging businesses, environmental groups, consumers and government alike with taking an active role in the setting and monitoring of standards. Some of these aspects need further addressing in New Zealand. How well they are met will determine both the attractiveness of New Zealand as a place to invest and as a place to live.

Notes

1   The APEC countries are: Canada, US, Mexico, Japan, Republic of Korea, Taiwan, Hong Kong, Singapore, Indonesia, Thailand, China, Philippines, Malaysia, Brunei, Papua New Guinea, Chile, Australia, and New Zealand.

2   Section 5(2) of the Resource Management Act 1991 (NZ) defines *sustainable management* to mean – *"[M]anaging the use, development, and protection of natural and physical resources in a way, or at a rate, which enables people and communities to provide for their social, economic, and cultural well being and their health and safety while - (a) Sustaining the potential of natural and physical resources (excluding minerals) to meet the reasonably foreseeable needs of future generations; and (b) Safeguarding the life-supporting capacity of air, water, soil, and ecosystems; and (c) Avoiding, remedying, or mitigating any adverse effects of activities on the environment."*

3   Medeiros (1992) in a study of Taiwan argues that the Taiwanese government has pursued quick-fix environmental policies, such as requiring industrial firms to increase the height of their smokestacks to alleviate local pollution, which have worked only in the short run and have in fact resulted in increased regional problems, such as acid rain. He therefore argues for a long run and more integrated approach to environmental policy formulation.

4   If we employ such a conception of efficiency then the dichotomy between sustainability and efficiency can largely be ignored. In other instances, such as the conservation of particularly fragile eco-systems and those eco-

systems with particular spiritual or identity values for the community, the conflict between sustainability and efficiency will be of a more permanent nature and a reinterpretation of efficiency less meaningful.

5   Jaffe et al. (1995), Low and Yeats (1992), Tobey (1990).

6   Figures presented in this section are from APEC (1995), PECC (1992). Note also that in this section FDI refers to total FDI, i.e., it includes both inward and outward flows.

7   Colgate and Featherstone (1992).

8   However, this is a much higher percentage than was found prior to the reforms New Zealand undertook in the mid 1980s. In 1980 the correlation between trade and FDI in New Zealand was a mere 0.6897, the lowest correlation in the APEC region at the time.

9   Appendix A includes some simple aggregate data analysis to evaluate the validity of the notion that environmental regulations will influence FDI flows across the APEC countries as a whole. However, such aggregate approaches suffer from a general lack of data and were therefore abandoned as a course of inquiry.

10   After significant disinvestments in the initial stage of economic reform, New Zealand has attracted positive net FDI flows for the past 6 years. The low ebb in FDI came in 1987-88 as the FDI which had originally been established to serve a protected domestic market no longer was competitive and as overseas investors recalled funds in the aftermath of the stockmarket crash. The sector most hurt during this period was the wholesale and retail trade sector. Though, in the textile, clothing and footwear sectors there was also significant disinvestments. Colgate & Featherstone (1992).

11   Colgate and Featherstone (1992).

12   In contrast Taiwan's government has created a negative list of activities now closed to FDI as they believe greater FDI in these sectors will only exacerbate environmental problems. Among others the sectors included on the list are mining and natural gas drilling, cigarette and liquor manufacturing, petroleum refining, and the generation of electricity. Medeiros (1992).

13   Under the Overseas Investment Regulation (1985) administered by the Overseas Investment Commission, only investments of over $10 million require approval. Exceptions, however, include broadcasting, commercial fishing within the Exclusive Economic Zone, and use of rural land.

14   Prior to the RMA the Town and Country Planning Act 1977 was the major piece of legislation governing the environmental obligations of regional and territorial authorities.

15   On this point Dormer (1994) suggests – *"[t]he joint hearing procedure provides decision makers with the opportunity to adopt an integrated approach to environmental considerations and makes it possible to obtain*

development approvals for major projects within time frames that could rarely have been achieved in days gone by. The requirement to provide an environmental assessment report is assisting in this regard."

16   Smith (1993), Krugman (1994), Medeiros (1992).

17   In the future greater use of economic instruments is contemplated for some sectors. As the instruments used in each sector are likely to vary markedly, it remains to be seen whether this results in a loss of integration. Dormer (1994) states – *"The greater use of economic instruments to allocate resources more efficiently was seen by some as likely to emerge from the resource management debate. The Act, however, makes very limited provision in this area and the procedures it contains are unlikely to be widely adopted."*

18   Refer to Dunning (1981) for a comprehensive study of these determinants.

19   Waikato's Waitoa factory of New Zealand Dairy Group - fifth and latest factory opened in early 1995. The milk powder plant cost $100 million to build. Ten percent, or $10 million, was tagged for environmental controls such as filters and other emission controls for driers and boilers, *Consumer* (May 1995). One firm in my survey had earmarked $350,000 to update its plants facilities.

20   E.g., The US Multinational Union Carbide's liability for the environmental damage it caused in Bhopal, India, stopped it from exiting immediately. However, enforcement of Union Carbide's responsibility has required the US government to support the Indian government's pursuit for compensation.

21   Akoorie and Enderwick (1996) on the issue of outward FDI argue that motivations for New Zealand businesses as first time investors overseas appears to fall into two categories; resource seeking and market seeking investment. The Resource seeking businesses included Fletcher Challenge and Carter Holt Harvey in the forestry sector. A major motivation to invest overseas was the uncertainty with regard to long term access to then State-owned forestry resources.

22   In New Zealand it is a requirement that the Ministry for the Environment (MfE) monitor the implementation of the RMA to ensure that it does not give rise to unnecessary costs or uncertainty for investors, while district Councils are charged with giving regard to the costs of environmental protection and to the efficiency and effectiveness of the methods used. Further in dealing with resource consents that have expired, Councils should continue to have regard to the existing capital investment and infrastructure and consider if this needs to be made explicit in policies and plans, MfE (1994).

23   Olewiler (1994) argues environmental regulations effect costs, productivity, output, prices, the size and distribution of plants, profits, market shares,

locational decisions and investment activity. Each of these could be examined in isolation, as indeed many studies have attempted to do, yet for the purpose of brevity I wish to discuss these issues in the unifying theme of competitiveness. Competitiveness for its part being maintained when a business chooses to continue to operate in a market while retaining profitability and an economically viable marketshare, i.e., a share that allows it to retain comparable economies of scale and employment levels.

24   It is important to note that this index is very aggregate, for countries with federal structures the adaptiveness of the ERR is likely to vary across states. Walter (1982) notes this for the US. Similarly one of my survey respondents suggested that in Australia, South Australia stood out as a state with a more adaptive ERR than those of NSW, Victoria, or Queensland.

25   0 = The ERR is poorly adapted to maintaining corporate competitiveness, 10 = The ERR is excellently adapted to maintaining corporate competitiveness.

26   *New Zealand Herald* (15/6/1996), "Fishing Fee Attacked: Industry fears it may become enviable". Mr Goodfellow, chairman of Sanford Ltd, suggested compliance costs should not exceed $24 million for the 1996-97 fishing year, whereas under the planned scheme a figure of $45 million was reported.

27   p.27, *NZ Engineering News* (December 1995).

28   While completing this survey a common remark made by business executives was that with the restructuring and staff downsizing of the past ten years came an inability to devote time to completing external questionnaires. During work on an earlier project I encountered similar problems with Statistic New Zealand who suggested that the removal of trade and FDI barriers over that last ten years had also made trade and FDI data more difficult to obtain. It appears that with efficiency in internal organisation has come a loss of data for external sources to evaluate macro impacts of these micro changes. This may yet prove to be a temporary situation, but does suggest the possible need for future action on the part of government to develop integrated programmes of action.

29   The Survey was conducted by telephone and worked from a standard questionnaire. However, the telephone survey had advantages in that I was able to explore tangent issues which were of particular significance for the firm. It also allowed me to qualify answers or pose further questions.

30   Pollutive industries were identified by Walter (1982), Tobey (1992), and Low and Yeats (1992). 25 firms were targeted in all, with 21 providing responses. Of the firms surveyed only two had less than 60 per cent of the operation engaged in manufacturing, with the lowest having only 30 per cent of it operation devoted to manufacturing and the remainder engaged in distributing other related products.

31   I thank Mr Ian Robertson, Executive Officer of the Auckland Manufacturers Association, for supplying me with this publication.
32   Figures were calculated from data contained in UN (1992, 1994), OECD (1995). The data covered the ten years between 1983-93.
33   Pollutive industries were identified by Walter (1982), Tobey (1992), and Low and Yeats (1992).
34   The more suspect results, i.e. results for which data was missing, included: Singapore: 0.50 (0.716); Korea: 0.495 (0.555); Canada: 0.726 (0.751); Taiwan: 0.743 (0.870); Malaysia: 0.786 (0.582); Hong Kong: 1.495 (1.495); China: 0.055 (0.065); Japan: 0.429(0.604).

References

Akoorie, M. and Enderwick, P. (1996), "Foreign Direct Investment at the Level of the Firm. Presentation to Symposium on FDI", APEC Study Centre, University of Auckland (14 March).

APEC Economic Committee (June 1995*), Foreign Direct Investment and APEC Economic Integration* , Singapore: APEC Secretariat.

Benidickson, J. (1994), "Canadian Environmental Law and Policy: Considerations from the Investment Perspective", *Getting the Green Light: Environmental Regulation and Investment in Canada*, Ottawa: C.D. Howe Institute.

Clegg. J. (1987), *Multinational Enterprise and World Competition*, London: Macmillan.

Colgate, P. and Featherstone, K. (1992), "Changing Pattern of FDI in the Pacific Region: New Zealand", *Changing Pattern of Foreign Direct Investment in the Pacific Region,* 2, 216-30, New Zealand Institute of Economic Research, Pacific Economic Cooperation Council.

Consumer (1995), "The Green Green Grass of Home", *Consumer Magazine*, 337, May.

Dormer, A. (1994), "The Resource Management Act 1991: The Transition and Business", Report prepared for the New Zealand Business Roundtable, August.

Dunning, J. (1981), *International Production and the Multinational Enterprise,* First edition, Sydney: George Allen & Unwin.

Hewison, G. (1995), "Reconciling Trade and the Environment: Issues for New Zealand", Victoria University of Wellington: Institute of Political Studies.

Jaffe, A., et al. (1995), "Environmental Regulations and the Competitiveness of U.S. Manufacturing: What does the evidence tell us?", *Journal of Economic Literature*, 132-163, March.

Krugman, P. (1994), *Peddling Prosperity*, New York: W W Norton and Co.

Low, P. and Yeats, A. (1992), "Do 'Dirty' Industries Migrate?", in P. Low (ed), *International Trade and the Environment*, World Bank Discussion Papers, 159, 89-103.

Medeiros, F. (1992), "Cooperative Alliances and FDI: US-Taiwan Implications for Trade", in Abbas, A. (ed), *How to Manage International Competitiveness, International Business Press*.

Ministry for the Environment (1994), "Investment Certainty Under the Resource Management Act 1991: A Discussion Paper", March.

Montz, B. and Dixon, J. (1993), "From Law to Practice: EIA in New Zealand", *Environmental Impact Assessment Review*, 13.

OECD (1995), *International Direct Investment Statistics Yearbook*.

_____ (1996), *Implementation Strategies for Environmental Taxes*, Paris.

Olewiler, N. (1994), "The Impact of Environmental Regulations on Investment Decisions", *Getting the Green Light: Environmental Regulation and Investment in Canada*, Ottawa: C.D. Howe Institute.

PECC (1995), "Impediments to Foreign Direct Investment and Technology Flows", Section 6, *Survey of Impediments to Trade and Investment in the APEC Region*.

Smith, B. (1993), "Natural Resource Use and Environmental Policy", in King, S. and Lloyd, P. (eds), *Economic Rationalism: Dead end or way forward?* George Allen & Unwin.

Tobey, J. (1990), "The Effects of Domestic Environmental Policies on the Pattern of World Trade: An Empirical Test", *Kyklos*, 43, Fasc.2, 191-209.

United Nations (1992), *World Investment Directory: Vol. 1, Asia and the Pacific*.

_____ (1994), *World Investment Directory: Vol. 4, Latin America and the Caribbean*.

Walter, I. (1982), "Environmentally Induced Industrial Relocation to Developing Countries", in Rubin, S. and Graham, T. (eds), *Environment and Trade*, Allanheld: Osmun & Co.

Appendix 5.1: Some Aggregate Data on FDI Flows in Pollutive Industries

The pollution haven hypothesis suggests that the developing countries will accrue a disproportionate share of FDI flows in the pollution intensive industries because of their lower environmental standards. In this appendix I present some figures which compare the flows of aggregate inward FDI to those flows in the pollution intensive industries[32]. The aggregate data was broken down into 3 sectors - primary, secondary and tertiary - and then in 21 industries of which 6 were categorised as pollution intensive[33].

I proceed by calculating a ratio for the percentage increase in the FDI flows to the pollutive sectors compared to the percentage increase in aggregate flows. If the pollution haven hypothesis is to have any substance we would expect the ratios calculated to be greater than one for the LDCs and less than one for the developed countries, while assuming developed countries do have relatively more stringent environmental regulations.

I have included only those results in which I'm confident, i.e., calculations made with no data missing. I also calculated the ratio of the rate of growth in pollution industries' FDI stock to the rate of growth in the primary plus the secondary sectors, i.e., I dropped the tertiary sector from the calculations as no pollutive industries were included under this sector. These figures are presented in parentheses.

**Table 5.8: Growth of Inward FDI in Pollutive Industries /
Growth of Total Inward FDI**

Country	Growth of Inward FDI in Pollutive Industries	Growth of Total Inward FDI
Indonesia	1.218	(1.188)
Philippines	1.118	(0.960)
Thailand	1.010	(0.859)
Australia	0.984	(1.095)
USA	0.731	(0.806)

If we examine these results, which include two developed countries (Australia and US) and three LDCs (Thailand, Philippines and Indonesia), we discover that the LDCs indeed have a ratio greater than one. This indicates that the rate of increase in the stock of FDI in the pollutive sectors has been greater than the rate of increase in the aggregate stock of FDI, while the ratios for Australia and the US are less than one. This adds support to the validity of pollution haven hypothesis. However, once we adjust the figures by removing from the aggregate flows the flows to tertiary sector this dichotomy between LDCs and developed countries no longer holds[34].

PART II:

SECTORAL STUDIES

6 Trade and Environmental Linkages in New Zealand Fisheries

BASIL SHARP

Introduction

The development and utilisation of New Zealand's wild fish stocks provides an outstanding example of the outcomes of two different governance structures. Until 1986 New Zealand fisheries were managed on the basis of input controls *viz.* licensing, controlled access, and so on. Within this period there were episodes of open entry spurred on by government subsidy. Although resource development and export growth occurred in response to these initiatives they did not occur within a legislative framework that promoted economic and biological sustainability. In the early 1980s firms could barely make a profit and valuable fish stocks showed signs of over-fishing.

By the mid-1980s proposals to reform fisheries management were well advanced. It was no coincidence that the rights-based based system of management was introduced during a wave of economy-wide reforms that progressively exposed the public sector to market forces and removed government producer subsidies. The new quota management system (QMS) incorporated the notion of tradeable rights working within the constraints of a sustainable harvest. New Zealand was the world's laboratory for the use of transferable rights to manage commercial fisheries. Under the QMS for-profit fishers operate within a regulatory environment aimed at satisfying sustainability.

The purpose of this chapter is to illustrate the linkages between property rights, trade and sustainable resource use. Most of harvest from New Zealand's exclusive economic zone (EEZ) is exported and so the links between trade and sustainability are transparent. The chapter proceeds as follows. First, a simple model of fisheries policy provides a framework for discussing the outcomes observed under regulated access. The second section describes trade within the context of the rights-based QMS. Again, a simple model is used to illustrate the economic implications of an unsubsidised producer competing with a subsidised producer. Performance of the New Zealand fishing industry is described and offered as evidence of the successful adjustment of government policy away from subsidies to rights-based sustainable fisheries management.

Fisheries Policy

The basic economic model of a fishery illustrated in Figure 6.1 incorporates open-access and sole-ownership as two alternative systems of governance (Gordon, 1954). Spurred on by competition, open entry is shown to dissipate economic surplus (S^o) and result in low stock levels. In contrast, a profit-seeking owner has the incentive to maximise economic surplus (S^*) which, in turn, results in relatively higher stock levels. Open-access and sole-ownership are, of course, analytical conveniences for policy analysis. In this model the fictional agency has to discover the optimal level of effort E*. In contrast, policy aimed at controlling output focuses on harvest and the fictional manager must discover Q*.

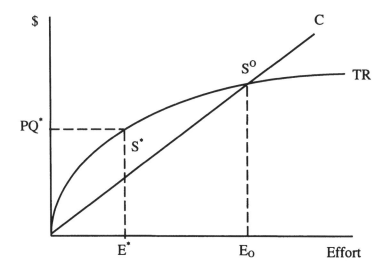

Figure 6.1: Simple model of optimal fisheries management

We can use this simple model to illustrate the economic impact of input subsidies and output incentives. Figure 6.2 shows input subsidies – such as low interest loans and fuel tax rebates – to lower the cost of harvest from C to C_s and encourage greater harvesting effort in the fishery. If subsidies are applied in combination with open access then effort will increase to $E_{os} > E_o$, real economic surplus is negative ($S^{OS} < 0$) and stocks are further depleted. Output incentives – such as export subsidies – would work positively to shift harvest revenue per unit of effort upwards. If output incentives are applied in combination with open access then effort will increase, real economic surplus will be negative and stocks are reduced.

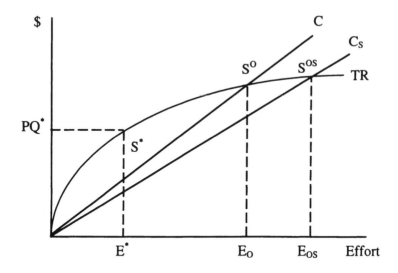

Figure 6.2: Impact of subsidies on economic surplus

Figures 6.1 and 6.2 illustrate two dimensions of fisheries policy vis-à-vis economic efficiency. First, the structure of property rights is a significant determinant of efficiency. If a country's fisheries policy has attributes of relatively open access then resources – including scarce fish stocks – are not being used efficiently. Put another way, the economy is forgoing economic wealth. Scarce fish stocks are under-priced and combined inefficiently with other factors of production. Furthermore, the supply price of fish products to the market does not equal the opportunity cost of supply. In effect, this is a subsidy on production arising from poorly defined property rights. The second dimension of fisheries policy has to do with government incentives and their impact on resource allocation. Fiscal incentives lead to dead-weight losses in the economy and a loss of welfare by individuals who pay for the incentives through the taxation system.

Resource development

Maori were the first to harvest and trade fish in New Zealand waters. Harvest was controlled through tribal-based institutions. New commercial opportunities were created with the arrival of European whalers and settlers. Maori adapted to changes in the relative price of fish products and the new technologies available. They soon became very proficient traders. At the time of early settlement access to fishery resources was essentially open. An expanding population created market opportunities for products harvested from proximate fisheries, especially from easily accessible shell fisheries. Early legislation aimed at limiting harvest was piecemeal and it was not until 1908 that government established a statutory framework for fisheries management. Thus began a remarkably long regulatory regime, lasting until 1963, aimed at achieving biological conservation. Throughout this period catching, wholesaling, and retailing were licensed. In the 1950s it became evident that the cumulative effect of technological change had made the licensing system ineffective. The presence of foreign vessels fishing just beyond New Zealand's three-mile limit was further evidence of the need to reform fisheries policy. Even though there was potential to better utilise the resource, the economic benefits of increased production clearly depended on improved processing and marketing arrangements to meet the needs of consumers. Economic development of the fishery required technology, processing and marketing arrangements, different from those to which the industry was geared.

During the 1950s most of the harvest was consumed locally, the balance of around 25 per cent was exported to Australia. However, access to the Australian market was hampered by unpredictable import restrictions. Government appointed a Select Committee to report on the state of the fishing industry and advise on economic development. The Committee concluded that licensing was not an effective instrument for achieving biological conservation and that it had resulted in an industry that was stinted and lacking in the ingredients necessary for growth and competition. Most of the catch was taken beyond the three-mile limit in an area where foreign vessels could operate outside the existing regulatory regime. The Committee recommended that the existing licensing and one-port landing system be abolished, government ensure alternative sources of finance were available for investment, and fisheries research be expanded.

Government moved quickly to implement the recommendations of the Select Committee. The early 1960s marked the beginning of a period of relatively unconstrained entry. In contrast to earlier periods, when biological conservation was the dominant goal of fisheries management, fishery policy encompassed fiscal and regulatory instruments aimed at stimulating development. Beginning in 1965 government guaranteed mortgages for the purchase of new fishing vessels and equipment. Assistance was reserved for the purchase of new vessels with the objective of increasing the quantity and quality of fish for the local and export market. With the 1977 declaration of the 200-mile fishing management zone, industry required additional investment for larger deep-water trawlers and purse seiners, and onshore infrastructure. Government's package of development incentives was soon expanded to include the removal of import duties and suspensory loans, at concessional interest rates.

Data from this period reflect the structure of property rights and the policy of successive governments to encourage fisheries development (Sharp, 1997). For example, in 1963 there were 1,727 registered vessels, 10 years later the number of vessels had more than doubled to 5,178. The composition of the fishing fleet also changed with a relatively large increase in the number of small vessels that worked the inshore fishery. These smaller vessels landed less than 10 per cent of the catch. The combination of more vessels, and greater catching capacity per vessel, resulted in quite dramatic increases in total catch. Growth in reported landings was about 6-7 per cent per annum. Domestic markets for fishery products could not satisfy the increase in landings and provide an economic return to fishing and processing firms. As numerous government committees had already indicated, export markets had to be developed. Export growth began to accelerate in 1979 about four years after the beginning of growth in recorded wet fish landings. The value of exports increased by a factor of five over the 1979-83 period.

The economic state of the inshore fishery in the early-1980s accords well with the outcomes predicted by Figure 6.2. Vessels larger than 18 metres landed 42 per cent of the catch. These vessels were unable to produce a positive net income before taxation over the 1981-83 period. Smaller trawling vessels, long-lining, and Danish Seining vessels, reported positive net incomes over this period. However these latter vessels landed a smaller percentage of the harvest. Thus, although the growth in landings and exports was quite remarkable, the economic signs of overfishing were apparent.

Foreign fishing effort in the deepwater fisheries increased with overseas' consumer acceptance of New Zealand's deep-water species. Between 1972 and 1977 the catch of foreign vessels increased from 75 per cent to almost 90 per cent of the known total demersal catch of 475,600 tonnes (Campbell, 1979). In contrast, New Zealand vessels could only expand their catch by 39 per cent over this period. Expansion was hampered by an inadequate stock of capital, limited experience with deep water fishing, relatively little knowledge of the resource and poor access to international markets.

The Territorial Sea and Exclusive Economic Zone Act 1977 established an area of 4.1 million square kilometres of ocean over which the Fisheries Act 1908 applied. The Law of the Sea Convention gave New Zealand an internationally recognised right to set an annual total allowable catch (TAC) for species in the zone. A share of the TAC was allocated to New Zealand industry which, at the time, comprised domestic companies, foreign chartered vessels, and joint-ventures. The share that could not be harvested by local interests was allocated to foreign countries under licence for an annual fee. Government also negotiated bilateral agreements that established foreign licensed fishing allocations with Japan, Korea and the Soviet Union. Once the quota had been allocated, each nation submitted a fishing plan describing the number of vessels, method and approximate timing of harvest. Foreign vessels were required to submit catch logs so that quota limits could be monitored.

Beginning in the late 1970s, two policy instruments were used to encourage expansion of the domestic fishing fleet into the exclusive economic zone (EEZ). First, a package of financial incentives was offered to domestic industry, including duty free vessel importation, concessionary interest and suspensory loans, investment allowances and tax incentives. Joint ventures were the second, and probably most significant, policy initiative. Joint ventures enabled domestic fishing companies to acquire technology and expertise, gain access to international markets, supply on-shore processing facilities, and evaluate the economics of deep water fishing. Foreign partners usually contributed equity to the joint venture, provided capital for plant and equipment, and assisted with access to international markets. Alternatively, New Zealand companies could charter foreign vessels. Although the benefits to New Zealand were considered to be lower than joint ventures, chartered foreign vessels were used to the supply raw material necessary to establish on-shore processing and distribution facilities.

It is generally recognised that the industry's rapid expansion into the deepwater fishery is largely attributable to joint ventures. Exports of deepwater trawl fin fish increased from 4,000 tonnes in 1978 to 26,000 tonnes in 1982, producing a 400 per cent increase in export earnings (Duncan, 1983). Throughput in onshore processing plants of deepwater trawl species increased from 7,000 tonnes to 42,000 tonnes, and onshore processing employment increased from 1,500 to 3,500, over the same period.

Rights based fishing

The Fisheries Act 1908 had provided the legal basis for fisheries management for 75 years. Biological conservation was a primary goal and government management rights were used to control access, harvesting technology and, in some instances, catch levels. This structure of rights, the incentives that attached to these rights, and the policies of government, produced unsustainable outcomes. In 1986 a new structure of property rights was introduced by an amendment to the 1983 Fisheries Act. The 1983 Act was the product of a government still focused on regulations as a solution to economic and biological problems. In contrast, the 1986 Amendment Act enabled an economic mechanism to operate within the constraints of sustainable harvest. The notion of a TAC, based on that contained in the United Nations Conference of the Law of the Sea (Article 61) is set for each commercial species. Individual fishers hold transferable harvesting rights. Fish stocks outside the QMS are managed by a system of non-transferable permits and administrative allocations.

New Zealand's QMS is a leading example of how the theory of rights-based fisheries management has been implemented (Sharp, 1997; Batstone and Sharp, 1999). The QMS has two key structural pillars. First, a TAC is set for each species in each fishery management area. The TAC, which is set annually, is based on estimates of sustainable harvest - the TAC may be adjusted according to economic and social conditions. A portion of the TAC is then allocated to commercial fishers as a total allowable commercial catch (TACC) after allowances have been made for non-commercial interests. The second component is a set of individual transferable quota (ITQ) rights - defined as a proportion of the TACC.

Economic efficiency requires setting an optimal harvest (TAC = Q^*) and an allocation of rights to Q^* in a way that maximises net present value. Provided rights are well defined and transferable the market mechanism will determine who gets the rights to fish. Firms buy (sell) quota as long as the additional value to the firm is greater than (less than) market price. Two important results follow. First, the more efficient firms will harvest fish. Second, the market value of quota provides summary information about current and future conditions - biological and economic - in the fishery. Returning to the New Zealand model, if the TAC is set at Q^+ then claims about the economic efficiency of the QMS hinge on whether $Q^+ = Q^*$. For any given Q^+ we can say that relatively more profitable firms will hold the rights to fish.

In the New Zealand model, efficiency can be further compromised when allocating the TAC between commercial and non-commercial fishers (Batstone and Sharp, 1999). Let's assume that the net benefit to the two groups is NB_C and NB_{NC} respectively and that the marginal cost of supplying a harvesting right to either group is the same. Figure 6.3 shows that the TAC should be allocated in such a way that net benefits are equalised. If the right to harvest is not differentiated, then competition will result in a uniform price P^+. Commercial fishers will harvest Q_c^+ and the non-commercial Q_{NC}^+.

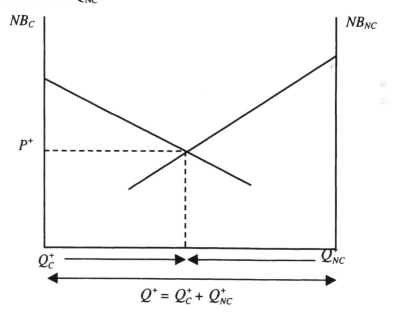

Figure 6.3: Optimal allocation of the total allowable catch

Trade from Sustainable Fisheries

In many fisheries throughout the world government policy combines input subsidies with inefficient management systems which is a lethal combination for the efficient use of scarce resources. In 1993, the Food and Agriculture Organisation (FAO) estimated total cost and total revenue for the world's fisheries. The FAO study concluded that total costs, including operating and capital costs, exceed revenues by US$54 billion and inferred that a substantial share of the deficit was explicitly financed by subsidies. A more recent study by Milazzo (1996) estimated global subsidisation at about US$8 billion, significantly less than the FAO estimate. Subsidies come in various forms and include direct government payments of the construction of vessels, loan guarantees, income support programmes and fuel subsidies. Subsidies are seen to contribute to the depletion of fish stocks in most coastal states throughout the world (FAO, 1993). Without proper adjustment to achieve a sustainable rate of harvest, the ability of a fishery to provide a sustainable source of food and opportunities for economic wealth will be jeopardised.

In this section a simple model is used to provide a framework for viewing the distortions created by subsidies. The traditional view of subsidies can be extended to cover the economic distortions created by relatively inefficient systems of fisheries governance.

Model

The structure of property rights underpinning fisheries management in New Zealand prices access to a regulated harvest. The significance of tradeable rights can be established in terms of a simple general equilibrium model. One equilibrium condition for efficiency requires the product price ratio to equal the ratio of marginal costs. The problem created by government subsidies is that they drive a wedge between the price ratios seen by producers of fisheries products and consumers. As is well known, subsidies upset the conditions required for efficiency and the economy delivers too much of the subsidised product and too little of the unsubsidised. This result can be extended to the issue of property rights. If we view open-access as a subsidy – the right of access is not priced – then the earlier conclusion about inefficiency holds. Under open-access too much capital and labour is being applied to under-priced access to fish stocks.

The implications that subsidies have for trade are illustrated in Figure 4. Panel 4a shows domestic demand D_A and supply S_A for an unsubsidised trading nation A – such as New Zealand. World price is P_W. The fishing sector produces Q_{AS}, Q_{AD} is consumed locally and (Q_{AS} - Q_{AD}) is exported. Panel 4b shows the demand and supply conditions in another country B supplying subsidised products from its fisheries to the world market. Domestic demand is D_B and supply is S_B. The subsidy is measured by the vertical distance between S_B and S_{BS}. Given a world price of P_W country produces Q_{BS}, Q_{BD} is consumed locally and (Q_{BS}, - Q_{BD}) is exported. Holding the world price constant, if subsidies were removed then B's domestic production and exports would fall to Q_{bs} and Q_{bx}. The impact on country A would depend on world supply and demand. If B is a significant producer then the world price could increase and A's export earnings increase.

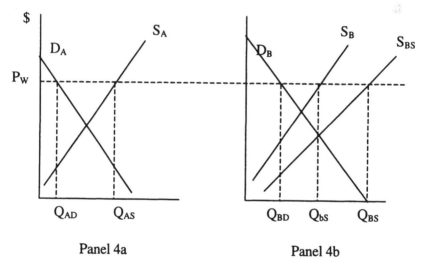

Panel 4a   Panel 4b

Figure 6.4: Subsidies and trade flows

The above model shows how government policy can affect trade flows. First, seafood trade can be influenced through incentives offered to domestic industry. Second, trade patterns can be affected through the management structure used to govern access to stocks. For the purpose of further discussion these two aspects of fisheries policy are combined and referred in terms of their impact on the relative cost of production. Returning to the above example where B's output can impact price, a decision by B to use a cheaper production process (e.g. poorly defined property rights) will keep the world price of seafood down. This will be true as long as the supply curves have positive slopes. World demand for seafood products will be higher as a result of the lower price. Country B will certainly produce more seafood if it doesn't adopt the relatively more expensive production policy because the lower price will increase both domestic demand and foreign import demand. Thus the total world production of seafood is likely to increase as a result of B not eliminating subsidies and/or adopting more efficient fisheries governance structures.

The magnitude of the economic impact of adjusting the fisheries policy in country B will depend on the relative slopes of the alternative supply curves and the distance between them. If domestic demand and foreign import demand are price inelastic, then total expenditures on output in B will fall. Employment in B's seafood industry may fall because the input of labour per unit of output falls. A decision by country B to eliminate subsidies and adopt a relatively efficient governance structure may produce a deterioration in its balance of payments and an increase in unemployment – but it depends on price elasticity. In the long run if country B does not reform its fisheries policy, when other countries do, then it will enjoy a comparative advantage in the production of seafood at the expense of economic distortions introduced into its economy and the global economy. Furthermore, B's inaction will threaten the productive sustainability of its natural capital.

New Zealand's Seafood Trade

New Zealand's seafood trade is dealt with at two levels. The first section discusses resource development and seafood exports within the context of the TACC. The second section contrasts industry profitability before and after introduction of the QMS.

Sustainable Exports

The commercial harvest of seafood from wild stocks in New Zealand's EEZ is limited by the annual TACC set by the Ministry of Fisheries. The

TACC is a management instrument guided by sustainability criteria. Figure 6.5 shows the TACC as an upper bound on the volume of seafood exported. It should be noted that the TACC is based on "green weight" whereas export weights are derived from an aggregation over a range of seafood products. Nevertheless, Figure 6.5 illustrates the physical constraint imposed on an output regulated industry. Since 1986 the industry-wide TACC has ranged from approximately 560,000 tonnes to peak 670,000 tonnes in 1990. The TACC for individual species within the QMS has been adjusted over time. For example, the coefficient of variation (a ratio of the standard deviation over the average) for orange roughy is 32.14 and rock lobster 19.81. Confronted with harvesting limits industry must look for adding value to the raw material it harvests.

By the late-1970s most of the deepwater vessels fishing the EEZ were foreign owned and temporarily registered in New Zealand, where they were chartered by local fishing companies or authorised co-operative fishing ventures. Joint ventures required government approval, and the guidelines established by government were aimed at securing maximum domestic benefit, including technology transfer, export orientation and local on-shore processing. Under the Law of the Sea Convention, New Zealand was entitled to exclude foreign vessels if it did not have the capacity to harvest sustainably the stocks within its EEZ. Since the 1970s the foreign licensed fleet's share of total production has consistently fallen. This fleet, predominantly from Japan, only has a significant presence in the tuna fishery. Charter vessels are still used by New Zealand companies who target hoki, squid and southern blue whiting.

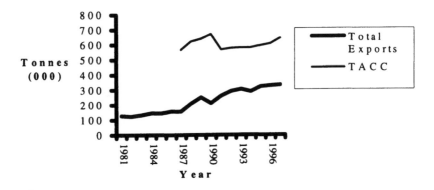

Figure 6.5: Export growth in an output constrained fishery

Figure 6.6 shows that the share of annual harvest landed by domestic boats has increased from 37 per cent in 1988 to 56 per cent in 1995. In 1990 the domestic fleet accounted for most of the inshore and shell fishery landings, and by 1995 its landings exceeded that of the charter fleet. The increase in landings by the domestic fleet is the result of investment in large deep-water vessels aimed at replacing charter effort. Since 1991 seven large vessels, with an average length of 55 metres, have been added to the harvesting capacity of the domestic fleet. In the hoki fishery - which was the largest charter fishery - the total landed by New Zealand vessels increased from 9 per cent in 1991 to 54 per cent in 1995 (New Zealand Fishing Industry Board, 1996). Similar developments have occurred in the ling fishery where landings by domestic vessels increased from 35 per cent in 1990 to 56 per cent in 1993.

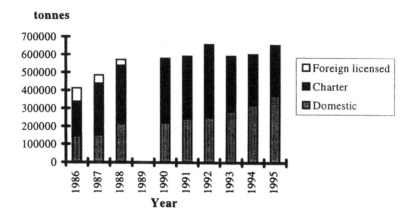

Figure 6.6: Harvesting New Zealand's exclusive economic zone

Figure 6.7 shows growth in the nominal value of seafood exports, beginning in 1981 when fisheries were managed under a command and control regime coupled with government incentives. In 1997 the value of seafood exports – in the absence of subsidy and managed under a rights-based system - increased by about 600 per cent. Over the period 1986-95 exports, as a percentage of the total value of production from the EEZ, increased from 83 per cent to 91 per cent (New Zealand Fishing Industry Board, 1996). In 1986 five major species - orange roughy, squid, rock lobster, snapper and hoki - accounted for 88 per cent of the exports by value. Significant export growth occurred in 1991. A 23 per cent increase in the volume coupled with a 4 per cent increase in the average value of exports resulted in the total value of exports increasing by 28 per cent to $961 million. This large rise was attributed to larger volumes, further processing, and depreciation of the New Zealand dollar (New Zealand Fishing Industry Board, 1991). The same five species - orange roughy, hoki, rock lobster, squid and snapper - remained the industry's main export earners, accounting for 51 per cent of the total value. Hoki has become a top export earner, with one of the main factors being the switch from whole frozen hoki to frozen fillets. Hoki proved to be an acceptable substitute for cod in North American white fish markets. Although Japan, the US and Australia remained New Zealand's main export markets, Figure 6.8 shows the increasing share of exports to "other countries" such as Korea, Hong Kong, Singapore and Europe.

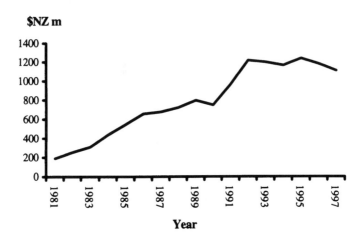

Figure 6.7: Growth in the total value of seafood exports, 1981-97

Figure 6.8 shows Japan, North America and Australia to have been major markets for New Zealand seafood. Economic conditions in these countries - as influenced by their fisheries governance structures, fiscal and monetary policies - have significant impacts on industry profitability. In 1986 trading was buoyant in the Japanese and North American markets. The increased value of exports to North America was the combined result of volume increases and firm prices for species such as rock lobster and orange roughy. The US generated $263 million of export receipts, or 40 per cent of the total, with Japan being the next largest, accounting for $232 million or 35 per cent of the total. Unfavourable export opportunities in Australia resulted in a modest increase in the volume of exports and a fall in their value. At this time secondary markets were emerging in Hong Kong, Singapore, Korea and Europe.

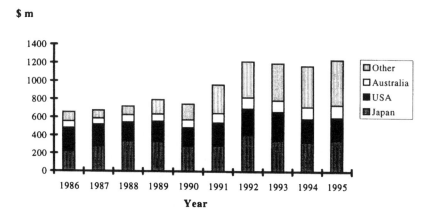

Figure 6.8: Destination of fishing industry exports, 1986-95

Because harvest from wild stocks is limited there is an incentive to add value through processing. Figure 6.9 shows changes in the composition of fin fish exports by volume. From 1988 the percentage of the total catch from the EEZ landed in New Zealand for further processing or distribution has increased. In 1993 alone that percentage increased by 13.7 per cent. The increase was largely attributable to the greater volumes of hoki landed, which rose from 37.2 per cent in 1990 to 70.6 per cent in 1993. Unlike transhipping - where processed fish are exported directly from factory trawlers - the landing of product involves the use of unloading facilities, cold storage plants, transport and shipping companies. The extent to which landed seafood is further processed depends on relative prices in foreign markets. Increases in landings, processing employment and changes in export statistics suggest that the amount of further processed product has increased. Export data show a decline in volumes of processed product and an increase in the export volumes of fillet, value-added and by-product forms (New Zealand Fishing Industry Board, 1994). These trends in harvesting and processing are consistent with the growth in employment in fish processing.

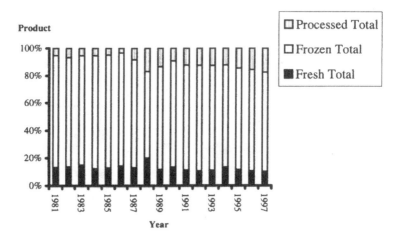

Figure 6.9: Changes in the composition of the value of fin fish exports

Profitability

In the early-1980s many firms operating in the inshore fishery were not profitable. Trawlers larger than 18 metres landed about 25 per cent of the inshore harvest. These vessels were unable to produce a positive net income before taxation over the 1981-83 period. Smaller trawling vessels, long-lining, and Danish Seining vessels, reported positive net incomes over this period. The economic signs of over-fishing were apparent. Under rights-based management, access is priced and harvesting rights are exercised if it is profitable to land fish. Information on the expected economic surplus attaches to the property right. Therefore quota prices signal expectations about profitability, stock availability and changes to government's fisheries management policy (Batstone and Sharp, 1998). The financial results of 18 major quota holders (who controlled 65 per cent of the available quota) for the year ended 1992 shows a return on assets 17.7 per cent before interest and tax (New Zealand Fishing Industry Board, 1994). For non-major quota holders, who harvest mainly inshore species, including high-value species such as snapper and rock lobster, the return before interest and tax was 11.9 per cent and 7.7 per cent.

Data obtained from the Annual Enterprise Survey provides evidence of the relative performance of activities within the fishing industry.

Trawling, which accounts for the largest share of the volume harvested in New Zealand's EEZ, has the lowest return on assets. Costs per full-time-equivalent (FTE) unit of labour are the highest, reflecting the relatively high capital-intensity and operating costs. Potting - primarily rock lobster - is more labour-intensive and operating costs per FTE are relatively low. This cost structure coupled with high unit revenue results in a relatively high return on assets. The performance of line fishing is similar to potting. Processing is a large employer and posts a return on assets of 14.2 per cent. These data present a limited view of performance within the industry at a given point in time.

Conclusions

This case study clearly illustrates the linkages between governance, incentives, bio-economic outcomes, and trade. Subsidies aimed at stimulating production and exports were successful in achieving these limited goals. But the management regime of regulated access coupled with subsidies contributed to serious depletion of high value fish stocks and minimal economic surplus in the fishing industry. Subsidies and non-transferable property rights had combined to produce unsustainable outcomes.

The transition from an unsustainable and unprofitable fishing industry to a dynamic profitable industry was accomplished within the framework of rights-based fishing. In the context of comparative analysis it is proper to compare real with real. In terms of biological sustainability and economic wealth in the fishery, the QMS easily out-performs regulated access. Industry is profitable because a positive quota price attaches to most harvesting rights. In New Zealand's case, the sustainability criterion takes the form of maximum sustainable yield adjusted according to economic and social conditions. This criterion does not sit-well with economists and many biologists.

The issue of sustainability is being successfully addressed within the framework of the QMS. Because the TACC is a binding constraint on harvest in many fisheries, additional wealth creation will depend on the extent to which additional value can be added to the harvest of scarce natural capital. New Zealand exports most of its harvest into highly competitive markets. Therefore the economic challenge facing the New

Zealand seafood industry is to discover lower cost harvesting and processing technologies, and the production of new products that can successfully compete in international seafood markets. There is evidence of greater value-added processing occurring. As a relatively small player in the global market, the profitability of investment depends to a very large extent on market access and the removal of subsidies. The extent to which the removal of subsidies can contribute to further growth is an empirical issue.

References

Batstone, C.J. and Sharp, B.M.H. (1998), "Minimum Information Systems and Fisheries Management", paper presented to the New Zealand Association of Economists Conference, Wellington, August.

Batstone, C.J. and Sharp, B.M.H. (1999), "New Zealand's Quota Management System: the First Ten Years", *Marine Policy*, 23(2), 177-190.

Campbell, J.S. (1979), Keynote Address, 7-14, "Proceedings of the Demersal Fisheries Conference", October 1978, Fisheries research division, *Occasional Publication No. 19*, Wellington: Ministry of Agriculture and Fisheries.

Duncan, A.J. (1983,) "Economics of the Deepwater Fishery" , 94-99, in Taylor, J.L. and G.G. Baird (eds), *New Zealand Finfish Fisheries: The Resources and Their Management*, Auckland: Trade Publications Ltd.

Food and Agriculture Organization (1993), *Marine Fisheries and the Law of the Sea: A Decade of Change*, Rome: FAO Fisheries Department.

Gordon, H.S. (1954), "The Economic Theory of a Common-Property Resource: The Fishery", *Journal of Political Economy*, 62(2), 124-142.

Milazzo, M.J. (1996), "Re-examining Subsidies in World Fisheries", Office of Sustainable Fisheries, National Marine Fisheries Service, NOAA, Department of Commerce.

New Zealand Fishing Industry Board (1994), *New Zealand Fishing Industry Economic Review*, Wellington.

New Zealand Fishing Industry Board (1996), *New Zealand Seafood Industry Economic Review*, Wellington.

Sharp, B.M.H. (1997), "From Regulated Access to Transferable Harvesting Rights: Policy Insights From New Zealand", *Marine Policy*, 21(6), 501-517.

7 Agricultural Trade and Environment: Exploring the Linkages

MIA MIKIC

Introduction and Overview

Agricultural trade was addressed directly for the first time in the history of the GATT/WTO trading system by the Uruguay Round Agreement on Agriculture (URAA) concluded in 1994. This agreement provides new rules and commitments in market access, domestic support and export competition. It requires for all non-tariff barriers to agricultural imports (except quarantine) to be tariffed and bound; these bound tariffs to be reduced in scheduled phases, and subsidies to production and exports of agricultural goods to be reduced. Since this was the first attempt of introducing order and discipline into the world of agricultural trade, URAA allowed for many exceptions (packaged in the variously coloured boxes - green, blue and red box). Although the intent of the URAA was to facilitate freer trade in agricultural goods, the average tariffs on agricultural goods (currently above 40 per cent) were not nearly as reduced as those on manufacturing goods (admittedly, manufactures have been through eight rounds of trade talks over a period of fifty years). In addition, tariff escalation in agriculture has still not been tackled seriously. With these large differences in the level and structure of tariff protection between agricultural and manufacturing goods now revealed, it is expected that further agricultural trade liberalisation will maintain a high priority in the next trade round (scheduled to begin by the end of 1999).

Other factors which will secure a top priority for agriculture in future rounds relate to the relevance of agriculture for the "non-trade" issues such as: environment; food safety and development of biotechnology; food security or viability of rural areas. Agriculture is a sector where governments, of both rich and poor countries alike, are least ready to commit to free trade. One of the reasons for this is perhaps due to confusion between free trade in agricultural goods and laissez-faire in the agriculture sector. While there is scope for government intervention whenever there are environmental externalities involved, and agriculture is a prime sector for that, it does not follow that intervention should be in the area of trade policy. However, given a history of governments' readiness to give in to the protectionist demands, it is easy to see how trade policy might get to be used for environmental goals, particularly in the agriculture sector. This is made even more likely by the fact that scope for ordinary border trade measures, such as tariffs, has been significantly narrowed and that environment presents itself as one of the most acceptable escape routes. Thus it is easy to foresee how the relationship between agriculture and environment might be used by interest groups as they lobby for more protection.

This chapter explores two linkages between agricultural trade and environment. Section 2 reviews mechanisms and evidence for the impact of agricultural trade liberalisation on environmental quality, while section 3 looks into the impact of environmental policies on agricultural trade. Section 4 provides a brief review on how the concerns of agriculture and environment are being handled in New Zealand, a leading country among the OECD members when it comes to elimination of assistance to agriculture. A final section derives conclusions.

Effects of Agricultural Trade Liberalisation on Environmental Quality: Mechanisms and Evidence

Trade is an economic activity whose task is to bring together supply and demand in different ways: interpersonally, internationally or intertemporally. Trade *per se* may cause only negligible environmental problems. Therefore, any policy that directly affects volume and/or composition of trade (such as tariffs, quantitative trade barriers, etc.), and is applied with a sole intention to eliminate environmental problems is likely to produce only n^{th}-best ($n>1$) results. This has been known ever since Meade's, Johnson's and Bhagwati's work on trade policy under domestic distortions (Corden, 1997). As any trade economist would agree, the relationship between trade and environment is not a direct one. It is the effects of trade on production and consumption that might affect environment and so it is production and/or consumption activity where all (if any) policy intervention should aim at. When trade is reduced (say by introduction of new trade barriers) or expanded (by reducing some trade barriers), the relative prices of goods and services are changed. The new prices signal to producers and consumers that they ought to be changing their decisions on production and consumption. These new decisions on production and/or consumption will then have an impact, positive and/or negative, on environment. For example, a decision to produce more of an agricultural good after its relative price has been artificially increased by a tariff may have a positive externality in terms of improving the landscape. Negative externalities from such a decision may include one or more of the following: noise, air, soil, surface water and groundwater pollution, food safety risk, or deforestation (see also Table 7.1). The net effect depends, of course, on the strengths of the positive and negative effects and is ultimately an empirical issue.

Table 7.1:   Potential   Negative   Environmental   Consequences   of Agricultural Production (selected examples)

Practice	*Consequences*
Irrigation	Salinisation of water and soil
	Increased potential for nitrate pollution of ground water
	Depletion of water supplies
	Water logging
	Soil erosion
	Landscape degradation
	Reduction of ecological diversity
Fertiliser use	Nitrate leaching into soils and water
	Eutrophication
	Reduced soil fertility
Pesticide use	Food contamination
	Farmworker exposure to chemicals
	Water and soil contamination
	Loss or extinction of plant, animal, and insect species
Land conversion	Deforestation
	Habitat loss
	Degradation of water systems
	Erosion
Machinery use	Compaction of soil
	Reduced soil productivity
	Soil and landscape degradation
	Disturbance of soil ecosystems

Source: Adapted from Krissoff et al. (1996, Table 3, p.17)

To conceptualise the agri-environment link it is best to turn to the basic microeconomic tools of analysis, such as Figure 7.1. It illustrates some of the mechanisms through which trade liberalisation and policy reforms may affect environmental quality in a stylised economy (Krissoff et al., 1996). The upper right-hand quadrant demonstrates the producer's choices on the usage of two inputs, land and fertilisers, to produce wheat.

Isoquants $Q_A...Q_E$ show different levels of output achieved by using different combinations of these two inputs.

The upper left-hand and lower right-hand quadrants show the relationships between the use of inputs and environmental effect on land. The curve CD in the upper left-hand quadrant illustrates the adverse effect of an increasing use of fertilisers on land degradation (so-called fertiliser run-off): the more a fertiliser is used in the production of wheat, the more extensive is the chemical degradation. Similarly, in the lower right-hand quadrant, curve LD shows that an increase in the production of wheat requires more and more land to be cleared resulting in excessive deforestation or soil erosion, both indicating worsening of the environmental quality. Finally, the lower left-hand quadrant illustrates total degradation by plotting a map of degradation trade-off curves, D_i. Each trade-off curve is associated with one of the isoquants for wheat. Although the level of total degradation is constant along the degradation trade-off curve, different points along the curve show different combinations of chemical and land degradations. Of course, the further away from the origin the curve is, the larger total degradation is.

Let us first consider the case of trade liberalisation from an import-substituting perspective. Suppose that prior to trade liberalisation production of wheat is given by point A at Q_A, which is chosen by farmers who minimise the cost of producing Q_A given the prices for land and fertilisers. Note that the domestic wheat price is distorted by an import tariff. The combination of fertilisers and land chosen to produce Q_A of wheat is associated with total land degradation of A_d. If now the tariff on imported wheat is reduced (i.e. an example of trade liberalisation), farmers will face competition from more efficient overseas producers and the price of wheat will fall. This new signalling is reflected in the farmer's choice to produce less; we illustrate this with a shift to the lower isoquant, say Q_B. Assuming that in a short run prices of inputs do not change, input combination at point B leads to a smaller total degradation consistent with a better quality of environment (B_d). This result is very simple and shows that the smaller volume of agricultural production, *ceteris paribus*, leads to a higher environmental quality.

If, on the other hand, tariffs were initially imposed only on imported fertilisers, reduction of those tariffs will change relative prices of inputs and with fertilisers now being cheaper compared to land, farmers will opt to substitute fertilisers for land, resulting in a higher degradation (not

shown in diagram). Another scenario might combine the trade
liberalisation and domestic agricultural policy reform. Assume that in
addition to elimination of import tariffs on imported wheat, subsidies to
fertilisers are also eliminated. This again pushes farmers on to the lower
isoquant (because of the lower wheat price) but because of the change in
the relative input price their budget constraint becomes flatter leading them
to reduce the production of wheat even further. This is illustrated by point
E on isoquant Q_E. The effect on total environmental quality (at point E_d) is
welfare improving due to a smaller total degradation due to a reduction of
production of wheat and additional positive effect induced by a change in
input prices. At the new equilibrium the combination of types of
degradation is different too with a relatively less chemical degradation.

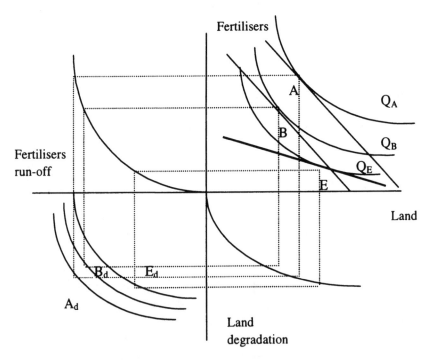

Figure 7.1: Trade liberalisation and environmental quality

Source: Adapted from Krissoff et al. (1996, p.18, Figure 7)

Another possibility is to look at the production of wheat as being export oriented. Say that the original pre-URAA equilibrium is depicted by point E. With the URAA induced price increase (or a better access to export markets), farmers will produce a larger quantity of wheat (Q_A). With that increased production there will be larger use of both fertilisers and land at the constant input prices, and the total degradation level is given by A_d. If we again assume a simultaneous agricultural reform so that the relative price of fertilisers faced by farmers goes up (due to elimination of subsidies), an increase in production will not be that large and the level of total degradation will end up between E_d and A_d. There are several other scenarios that could be illustrated by the help of Figure 7.1. However, it is not essential to capture all possible policy changes in our diagram to realise that it is not simple to identify the net effect of trade liberalisation on environmental quality. It is clear however that the effects of trade liberalisation on the environmental quality are modified by the simultaneous implementation of reform in the domestic agricultural policy. When trade liberalisation has a positive effect on environment, a domestic reform enhances such an effect; when trade liberalisation has a negative effect, a domestic reform dampens it. Just how important it is to use domestic agricultural reform (and environmental policies) to fight against environmental degradation caused by agricultural production? This is answered by the discussion below which focuses more closely on the mechanisms through which agricultural trade liberalisation may affect environment.

Runge (1998) provides a detailed description of different linkages between agricultural trade liberalisation and environmental quality. There are several mechanisms at work linking agricultural trade liberalisation and environmental quality (they can be trailed in Figure 7.2).

The first mechanism works through allocative efficiency. Increased specialisation in accordance with a country's comparative advantage which is a consequence of trade liberalisation allows for more efficient allocation and utilisation of natural resources than it is possible under protectionist or autarkic policies. Thus New Zealand with comparative advantage in the production of butter relative to olive oil is much better off by reallocating its resources into butter production and trading butter for olive oil from Spain. The gains of such an exchange would be positive even under restricted trade, but freer trade would certainly bring a country closer to optimal allocation of resources assuming no other distortions are present.

However this does not say much about the effect on environment apart from implicitly assuming that more efficient allocation of resources and higher income is associated with improvement of environmental quality. We show later that this is not necessarily so.

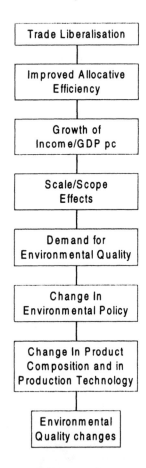

Figure 7.2: Mechanisms of linkages between agricultural trade liberalisation and the environment

Source: Runge (1998, Figure 2, p.4)

The next mechanism refers to the effect of agricultural trade liberalisation on the scale (and scope) of agricultural production. It is common to argue that freer trade may lead to an excessive scale of production or consumption with a potentially negative consequence for environment. This is true if such expansion of scale is allowed without compensation in terms of developments of parallel products, technology and alternative policies put in place to neutralise possible negative effects of scale. Thus it is plausible to expect positive environmental effects from an increased scale if increased trade also induces adaptation of better environmental policies, which stimulate changes in technology and consumption patterns amiable to environmental quality.

The third mechanism describes the link between increased agricultural trade and sectoral or intersectoral composition of output. The issue here is whether trade induces changes in the national production mix or within the agricultural sector which is more agreeable with environment. For example, if a country has a comparative advantage in a relatively high polluting crop such as cotton, wouldn't trade liberalisation then induce a change in a production mix even further in favour of this crop resulting in an environmental stress? Again, this effect of trade liberalisation ought to be neutralised by more specifically designed environmental policies, which will encourage the development of different production methods to exploit a country's comparative advantage.

This is related to the fourth mechanism described by Runge as the effect trade may have on technological innovation and transfers of agricultural technology. We are all aware of negative (even disastrous) environmental consequences of the technology transfers in the past. The risk of this happening in the long run is hopefully reduced by much larger environmental awareness of consumers world-wide who may be able to influence production. In addition increased governments' readiness to adopt regulations amiable to the development of sustainable agriculture should make a positive impact in the long run. In other words, we should not be witnesses of "pollution havens" mushrooming all over the globe. In the short run it is sure that we will see examples of increased trade inducing transfers of both "good" and "bad" technologies.

The last mechanism in the chain connecting agricultural trade liberalisation and environment refers to the significance of policy or politics. Whether trade liberalisation, by improving allocative efficiency and inducing actions capable of protecting and improving environmental quality, would in fact produce such effects ultimately depends on public choice and political process. In case of government failure the opportunity to use trade liberalisation to improve environment will most probably not be used. Agriculture is one of those sectors where government failure is more prevalent, and this is so in the case of both rich and poor countries. The lack of regulatory response to possible damaging environmental effects is more common in this sector than in any other sector of the economy (Ervin, 1997).

To sum up, agricultural trade liberalisation improves allocative efficiency which increases income growth and GDP p.c. but may also produce some negative scale and scope effects. Whether the effect on environmental quality will then be positive or negative depends heavily on the further links in the chain. This initial positive effect on the level and growth of income will be reflected in the protected and improved environmental quality if it is successful in increasing demand for better environmental protection and if such demand is being responded to by improvements in environmental policies, technological and structural changes. If, however, due to government failure there is no response to market failures (that is no response to the existence of externalities in agriculture) trade liberalisation may very well cause further degradation of environmental quality.

The overall environmental effects of liberalised trade in agricultural goods depend upon the country, the extent of trade liberalisation and the volume of trade, the production response, and the policy response. Above all, they depend on the responsiveness of the environmental services (including technological and structural changes) to the increase in income. If environmental services are treated as normal or superior goods, then an increase in income should result in an increase in demand for such goods by the same percentage or by a greater percentage than the rise in income, respectively. This assumption has been at the heart of much of the work done so far on the link between economic growth and environmental quality.

Ever since Grossman and Krueger (1995) introduced the environmental Kuznets curve, it was argued that the solution to environmental degradation (such as pollution) is automatic and given by income growth. More specifically, they hypothesised that environmental consumption first rises and then falls after a certain level of income (GDP p.c.) has been reached. The curve reflecting such a functional relationship has got an inverted U-shape (or a "hump"). Unfortunately there are many methodological and empirical problems[1] with this hypothesis, which make it much less universally applicable. Notwithstanding that, two important conclusions could be derived from the empirical work. Firstly, despite many exceptions there is a general thrust supporting Kuznets curve shaped relationship between environmental quality and per capita income level. Attention should be paid to the fact, however, that this relationship is not uniform for all environmental indicators (Ervin, 1997; Runge, 1998). Secondly, it seems that export orientation improves environmental protection, in particular for smaller countries. This result is independently supported by studies on the factors that help in the determination of which firms could become good exporters. For example Richardson et al. (1996) indicates that such firms would typically invest more in the research and development in general, and also in environmentally friendly technology. However much more work needs to be done to provide reliable data on the relationship between trade liberalisation induced increase in income and environmental quality. At the moment, with empirical evidence being so inconclusive, it is safer to go along with a conclusion such as made by Arrow et al. (1995) stating that trade liberalisation and other policies introduced to induce economic growth could not be substitutes for environmental policy. At the least, taking into account our conclusions on the importance of the political process and collective decision making, would shift the downward-sloping portion of the curve closer to or further away from the origin reflecting the fact that solutions are not automatic. Thus the "economic growth-environmental quality" hypothesis should be re-phrased in an "if-then" way: "if an increase of income brings about the changes in remedial environmental policies, then an improvement in the environmental degradation would be directly associated with the higher levels of income, and economic growth and environmental quality might be mutually reinforcing." However, there is more empirical work needed to present reliable data in support of this statement on the link between growth and environment.

Effects of Environmental Policies on Agricultural Trade: Mechanisms and Evidence

The conclusion from the previous section is that there is a definite place for environmental policies in the agriculture sector. Most of the OECD countries are already engaged in a number of policies to help develop so-called sustainable agriculture. Examples of such policies include changes in agricultural practices (such as rotation, agri-forestry, integrated pest management, etc.), stricter environmental regulations including the banning of certain chemicals, land set-aside programmes, or the application of the polluter-pays-principle (PPP). The further concerns arising then are related to the impact that such environmental policies may have on volume and composition of agricultural trade, as well as on the prospects for further liberalisation.

As a way of illustrating the link between environmental policy and agricultural trade we will discuss two simple cases. In both of them we will have a negative externality (pollution) occurring in the production of the exporting good. In the first case a country-exporter is a small country and externality is localised within national borders. In the second case we allow an exporter to influence world prices and we also allow for pollution to cross borders.

Let us thus assume a small country where pollution occurs in the production process of the exporting goods, say potatoes, but the pollution is contained within national borders. This externality is illustrated in Figure 3 by the difference between social and private marginal cost of supplying potatoes ($MC_S > MC_P$). Because private producers do not realise there is a cost of pollution, at any given price they will tend to overproduce potatoes. For example, if a world price is at the level p^*, the producers will choose to produce Q_S (as long as they do not have to internalise the costs of externality). At that price, domestic demand is only at the level of Q_D so the country exports the difference $Q_S Q_D$. If the government now imposes a Pigovian tax at the specific rate T to cover fully for the difference between social and private marginal costs, the price domestic producers receive falls to p^*-T. This is a signal to produce less and supply falls to Q_S^1. Since domestic consumers are not taxed, their demand is not changed, leaving exports to absorb the whole change in production. Thus exports fall. Welfare changes could be summarised as follows: producers lose area a+b+c+d+e; domestic consumers' welfare is not changed; and government collects revenue equal to area a+b+c+d. The improvement in environmental quality is equal to a sum of areas e and f. The net welfare effect then is positive and equal to area f. Hence, despite the fact that this equilibrium was reached at a smaller volume of exports, the imposition of the optimal Pigovian tax is Pareto-efficient. This is more clear if it is presented in the following way. The amount of export fall is worth to the farmers a sum of areas e+h. At the same time, society values that quantity of reduction in exports at e+h+f. Thus the net gain is equal to area f.

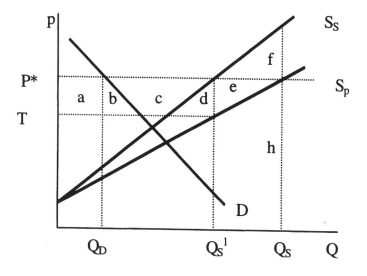

Figure 7.3: Trade and welfare effects of a Pigovian tax in a small exporting country

Let us look now at the second illustration on how environmental policy may influence agricultural trade. Assume as in Corden (1997) two countries, Home and Foreign, each having two sectors, polluting agriculture (say wheat) and non-polluting services, but we focus only on the agriculture sector. Pollution is related to the production process. We also assume that Home is a large country (i.e. able to influence world prices). We want to study the effects of the optimal Pigovian tax imposed on agriculture in Home country. Figure 7.4 illustrates this case.

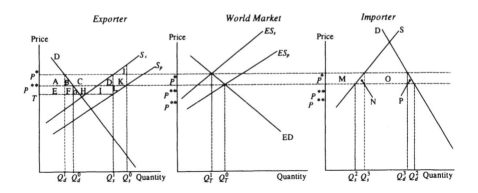

Figure 7.4: Trade and welfare effects of an optimal Pigovian tax in a large exporting country

In Home country initially the cost of pollution caused by production of wheat is not internalised and farmers are overproducing wheat at price P*. When then the optimal Pigovian tax is introduced at a specific rate T, farmers reduce production along the societal cost of production curve and supply to the world market (panel b) falls. Given stable demand in the world market, this shortage of wheat at price p* causes price to rise and the market clears again at price P**. This increase in price is felt in both Home and Foreign country and participants in both countries are affected. In Home country, farmers incur welfare losses equal to a sum of E+F+G+H+I+L, and consumers lose area A+B. Revenue collection is equal to A+B+C+D+E+F+G+H+I, so that net effect resulting from a tax amount to a gain of J+K+L. However, being a large country, Home also benefits from terms of trade gains which amount to C+D. In Foreign, the importing country, consumers lose M+N+O+P. Only the amount equal to area M goes back to farmers in Foreign, area O is redistributed to Home, and the net loss is N+P. Thus the burden of fixing environmental externality in a large country also falls on Foreign consumers. The effects on trade are similar to the previous case: volume of exports is reduced, but in this case also the competitiveness of farmers is weakened. This could be counteracted only if farmers in Foreign are also required to internalise externality similarly to Home's exporters. If Foreign has got larger tolerance to pollution, its farmers will definitely be at advantage to Home's farmers. This is at the root of a situation known as "eco-dumping" which is the cause of many renewed demands for increased protection. However, protection cannot be justified if a sector's competitiveness is weakened by an appropriate environmental policy (Corden, 1997).

Empirical studies for non-agricultural industries find little adverse effect of environmental policies on trade (Krissoff et al., 1996). These studies mostly focus on identifying the impact of pollution abatement costs (PAC) in industrial sectors on their trade. It seems that PAC are sufficiently small as a share of industry's costs without much effect on output or trade. There is also a concern about the importance of the difference in the PAC among countries and the impact of that on firms' migration. Again, empirical evidence does not support the claim that differences in PAC will affect industrial location decisions in any major way[2].

Much less empirical work exists on the impact of environmental policies on agricultural trade in the OECD countries. It seems that the impact of environmental policies on the competitiveness of the agricultural sector was a non-issue due to the existence of generous subsidies that prevented full internalisation of costs of environmental policies. In other words, farmers did not have strong enough incentive to change their decisions on output and trade. If anything, because subsidies were larger than the minimum amount needed to compensate for environmental compliance, the effects were such to attract resources in those activities and worsen the problems. The effect of many environmental programmes in the past (such as land retirement payments, cost-sharing for wetland drainage, below-market financing costs for irrigation etc) was to reallocate resources from other sectors into agriculture, boosting production and trade. This was of course aggravated with production and export subsidies.

The evidence that environmental policies have not significantly affected trade in the past cannot be necessarily projected into the future (Ervin, 1997, p.19). There are indications that an increasing number of instruments applied in environmental programmes may increase cumulative costs significantly. The effect of that is not known until we have information on what is happening in other countries. If all countries follow the same route, competitiveness should not be affected much.

Another concern here of course is that in view of increased environmental protection costs faced by farmers, government may be inclined to give in to their protectionist demands, which would be a major factor in distorting agricultural trade.

In summary, there are two most important findings on the link between environmental policy and agricultural trade in the OECD countries. Firstly, environmental programmes that have been run so far have had negligible trade effects. Secondly, the programmes that may be run in future may have much stronger effects on trade. This is so because new programmes are relying on the application of the polluter-pay-principles, introduction of eco-labelling, land set-asides and other policies that all may increase costs of agricultural production and thus have potentially stronger effects on trade.

Agriculture, Trade and Environment in New Zealand

New Zealand is one of few original OECD members where agriculture contributes close to 5 per cent to the GPD and 9.5 per cent to the total employment in 1996 (OECD, 1997b). Contribution to total merchandise exports, although declining steadily, is still high for an OECD country (51 per cent in 1996). Not surprisingly, New Zealand is one of the most engaged players in the world negotiations on liberalisation of agricultural trade.

Although New Zealand's present position regarding the world agricultural trade has been conditioned by a country being a party to bilateral, regional and multilateral liberalisation of agricultural trade, the biggest environmental impact ought to be associated with the unilateral trade liberalisation and agricultural reforms that the agricultural sector was exposed to since the mid 1980s (see Table 7.2).

Unilateral liberalisation (Reforms 1984)

New Zealand's agricultural sector was not a recipient of significant government assistance until the early 1980s. By that time the economy was in stagnation and unemployment was rising. Inflation, the current account deficit and fiscal deficit became so severe that government of the day chose to fix the problems by increasing its intervention in the economy. This was reflected in a significant increase in assistance to the agriculture sector until 1984 when it was acknowledged that such levels of support were not sustainable. When the new government thus announced an almost complete and instantaneous withdrawal of assistance, the reform did not come as a surprise but still farmers did not accept it without protest. The reforms included the ending of output price assistance, farm subsidies, fertiliser and other input subsidies, as well as termination of investment and land development concessions. This led to New Zealand providing the lowest assistance to the agriculture sector (in terms of producer subsidy equivalents) among all the OECD countries in 1995 (see Table 7.3). What was left of assistance to the agriculture sector was decoupled from production and initially consisted of research, disaster relief and exit grants. Changes during the 1990s saw disaster relief being virtually eliminated.

Table 7.2: Agricultural Reforms / Agricultural Trade Liberalisations and Potential Effects on Environment in New Zealand since 1984

Type of reform/ liberalisation	Example	Potential net environmental effects
Unilateral	Reforms of 1984 Resource Management Act 1991	+ (Ervin, 1997)
Bilateral / Regional	CER APEC	+ (Lloyd, 1997) + (Scollay and Gilbert, 1998)
Multilateral	Uruguay Round Agreement on Agriculture	+ (Martin and Winters, 1995)

In addition to the reforms of 1984, the agriculture sector was greatly affected by the Resource Management Act (1991). The Act's main goal was to promote the sustainable management of the country's natural and physical resources so that future generations as well as the present generation benefit (MAF, 1996). Consequently, *sustainable agriculture* policy is formulated with the objective to encourage farmers to adopt more sustainable forms of agricultural production.

The environmental consequences of the agricultural reforms of 1984 and of the Act could be separated into the short-term and long-term consequences. The immediate effects of the removal of subsidies to agricultural production, such as a reduction in volume of production, had a positive impact on the environment because of:

- Reduction in fertiliser use
- Reduction in land clearing
- Reduced pesticide use
- Reduced total livestock
- Increased diversification.

Namely, as subsidies were withdrawn, and with the world commodity prices suffering a downturn at the same time, farmers opted to reduce production which affected the usage of inputs such as fertilisers, pesticides, and their use of marginal land. All of that helped to reduce negative environmental externalities from agriculture. Farmers also reduced sheep numbers and diversified into deer, goats, horticulture and forestry. This not only had beneficial environmental effects but also helped farmers increase their earnings.

Table 7.3: **Producer Subsidy Equivalents 1996 (estimate)**

Country	Absolute amounts US$ bill	% of farm production, including price support and direct payments
EU	85.0	43
Japan	40.5	71
USA	23.5	16
Switzerland	5.5	78
Canada	3.8	22
Australia	11.9	9
New Zealand	0.1	3

Source: OECD (1997b)

However, due to the prolonged economic downturn, farmers were facing reduced incomes for some time and that affected the way they managed land. Most of the negative effects for the environment came thus through:

- Reduced soil conservation
- Lower level of risk management for climatic events
- Lower investment in agricultural and forestry sector.

In the long run, environmental effects stemming from agricultural reform and agricultural trade liberalisation depend also on general performance of the economy and its macroeconomic policies, as well as on the outcome of further global agricultural liberalisation affecting world commodity prices. According to Reynolds et al. (1993, p.18) growth inducing policies "would favour agriculture, and contribute positively to farm incomes. Better farm incomes would in turn, when combined with greater environmental institutional controls, give beneficial environmental impact". Of course, such growth is easier to achieve if other countries follow the same sort of growth inducing policies including the agricultural policy reform à la New Zealand.

Bilateral and regional liberalisation

At the bilateral and regional level, New Zealand is a party to Closer Economic Relations between Australia and New Zealand (CER) and the Asia-Pacific Economic Council (APEC), respectively. CER has not been overly concerned with trade in agricultural goods except in the area of harmonisation of food standards. The Agreement on Joint Food Standards was signed in 1996 envisaging the setting up of the common Australia - New Zealand Food Authority and the common food standards code. The importance of this agreement is not so much in breaking the technical barriers to trade in agricultural goods, but in achieving progress in harmonisation methods relative to the WTO practice (Lloyd, 1997). It is not possible to say anything about the possible welfare effects arising from this single achievement, although it is clear that welfare effects from liberalising trade through the CER have been positive in terms of environmental quality improvements.

APEC was not very successful in achieving progress in trade liberalisation in general, and even less so in agricultural trade liberalisation. On the basis of the various voluntary commitments of the APEC members, there are various estimations of the welfare effects of region-wide trade liberalisation. There are also estimations of the welfare effects from the liberalisation in trade of agricultural goods (Scollay and Gilbert, 1998; Anderson et al., 1997). It turns out that 50-70 per cent of the total welfare gains from APEC liberalisation for the total region comes from the agricultural liberalisation. Estimates for New Zealand's welfare effects are equally favourable, meaning that there is a lot of scope for welfare improvement via agricultural trade liberalisation in the APEC. Although there are no separate studies on the environmental effects of such liberalisation, it is possible to deduct from the change in social welfare that environment will probably not be hurt.

Multilateral liberalisation (URAA)

Finally, New Zealand is a signatory to the URAA. It was expected that this agreement would affect commodity prices, some of them significantly. The upward movements in most of the prices (such as the prices of dairy products or beef) is seen as having a favourable effect on New Zealand agriculture and thus on environment too. However, the commentators are critical about the extent of liberalisation as expressed in average tariff equivalents of non-tariff measures in agriculture. According to them, global implementation of the URAA appears to be at the level of managing trade more than really liberalising trade in agriculture. Thus the prices have not changed as dramatically as expected and the changes in output and trade have not materialised yet.

In sum, it is evident that agricultural policy reforms and agricultural trade liberalisation, helped with a specific macroeconomic environment at the time of reform, have produced mixed environmental consequences. The net effect of policy changes is seen as positive (Ervin, 1997, p.11). Notwithstanding this it has also become clear that not all negative externalities from agriculture could be solved by reforming agricultural policies only. Specific environmental policies are called for as the first-best policy option to address these environmental externalities.

New Zealand has already moved in the right direction with its environmental policies. For example, the government no longer provides disaster relief payments. Farmers are instead required to manage their land by internalising the risks of natural disasters. According to the report by the MAF (1996, p.226) the user-pays and the polluter-pays principles are well established in New Zealand. For example, all users of agricultural inspection services pay for them themselves, while levies or special property taxes on landlords who mostly benefit from such controls largely fund the pest management.

Furthermore, farmers themselves are taking initiatives to address environmental externalities more directly. Among the initiatives already producing effects are the codes of practice for farmers or landcare groups. Thus the process of internalisation of negative environmental externalities resulting from agricultural production has already begun. The remaining question relates to the effects of such a process on the competitiveness of New Zealand farming. Although there is no hard evidence to substantiate comments on this issue, plenty of anecdotal evidence supports the view about minimal or no adverse effects of the environmental policies on the competitiveness of the agricultural sector. On the contrary, given the interest of consumers in the production processes for food (organic food is only one example), the establishment of environmental policies principles gives New Zealand farmers an additional advantage.

Summary

Two most important linkages between agricultural trade and environment were explored in this paper: the impact of trade liberalisation on environment, and the impact of environmental policies on trade in agriculture. With respect to the first of those links, it has been concluded that trade liberalisation in general as well as in agricultural goods results in improved economic efficiency and economic growth. These effects may be fed into improved environmental quality, but that outcome is not automatic and an increased efficiency is a necessary but not sufficient condition. What is required for the improvement in environmental quality is that environmental policies are put in place as first-best instruments to deal with environmental degradation. In short, trade liberalisation cannot be used as a substitute for environmental policies although it could be used as a remedial policy or as a second-best instrument in a limited number of cases.

Regarding the impact of environmental policies on competitiveness and further trade liberalisation, it has been found that it is possible for such policies to weaken competitiveness and thus invoke renewed demand for protection. However, it has been shown too that there is no reason based in economic theory to respond to such demands by increasing levels of protection. Although some sectors, or some activities within sectors, may be faced with higher costs of production (due to internalisation of environmental costs), societal benefits more than offset those increased costs. Moreover, this could induce some of the producers to invest in development of new products and processes which may improve their competitiveness in the long run.

Ultimately, the welfare superiority of liberalised trade will depend upon the existence of mechanisms to internalise the external environmental costs and benefits. Furthermore, as Corden (1997, p.242) puts it, although trade policy may have environmental effects, and environmental policy may have trade effects, it is essential to keep these two policies separated. While environmental policies justify departures from lassiez-faire, which does not automatically imply that a departure from free trade is also justified. Trade policy simply should not be used for environmental objectives. Corden selects two plausible cases when an exception could be made: a) in case of transborder pollution, and b) as threat instruments to enforce international environmental agreements if other diplomatic and political channels are not working.

Notes

1 Some of the problems mentioned in the literature include: ignoring dynamic comparative advantage and economic stagnation; importance of environmental policy as instrumental force in initiating environmental solutions; curves tend to differ over geographical and cultural boundaries; shape of curve depends on the type of econometric model and data used; or existence of secondary turning points for some pollutants. Furthermore, this hypothesis does not take into account the possibility of irreversible environmental effects.

2 But the studies also showed that differences in PAC among OECD countries have been declining. It is not clear if that was due to an upward movement in PAC in countries with lower environmental standards. If so, there is even less support for "pollution havens" concerns.

References

Anderson, K. (1992), "Agricultural Trade Liberalisation and the Environment: A Global Perspective", *The World Economy*, 15(1), 153-71, January.

Anderson, K. (1998a), "Domestic Agricultural Policy Objectives and Trade Liberalisation: Synergies and Trade-offs", *Policy Discussion Paper*, 98/08, University of Adelaide: Centre for International Economic Studies.

Anderson, K. (1998b), "Agricultural Trade Reforms, Research Incentives, and the Environment", *Policy Discussion Paper*, 98/04, University of Adelaide: Centre for International Economic Studies.

Anderson, K. and Strutt, A. (1996), "On Measuring the Environmental Impacts of Agricultural Trade Liberalisation", in Bredahl, M., Ballenger, N., Dunmore, J. and Roe, T. (eds), *Agriculture, Trade, and the Environment: Discovering and Measuring the Critical Linkages*, 151-72, Boulder, CO: Westview Press.

Arrow, K., et al. (1995), "Economic Growth, Carrying Capacity, and the Environment", *Science*, 268, 520-21, April.

Bredahl, M., Ballenger, N., Dunmore, J. and Roe, T. (eds), *Agriculture, Trade, and the Environment: Discovering and Measuring the Critical Linkages*, Boulder, CO: Westview Press.

Corden, W.M. (1997), *Trade Policy and Economic Welfare*, 2nd edition, Oxford: Clarendon Press.

Ervin, D. (1997), *Agriculture, Trade and the Environment: Anticipating the Policy Challenges*, OECD/GD(97)171, Paris: OECD.

Grossman, G. and Krueger, A. (1995), "Economic Growth and the Environment", *Quarterly Journal of Economics*, 110(2), 353-77, (May).

Josling, T. (1998), *Agricultural Trade Policy - Completing the Reform*, Washington, DC: IIE.

Krissoff, B., Ballenger, N., Dunmore, J. and Gray, D. (1996), "Exploring Linkages Among Agriculture, Trade, and the Environment: Issues for the Next Century" *Agricultural Economic Report No. 738*, Natural Resources and Environment Division, Economic Research Service, US Department of Agriculture.

Lloyd, P. (1997), "Unilateral and regional trade policies of the CER countries, 1970-96", in Piggott, J. and Woodland, A. (eds), *International Trade Policy and the Pacific Rim*, Basingstoke: Macmillan.

MAF (1996), "New Zealand: The Environmental Effects of Removing Agricultural Subsidies", *MAF Policy Papers*, Wellington.

Martin, W. and Winters, L.A. (1995), *The Uruguay Round - Widening and Deepening of World Trading System*, Washington, DC: The World Bank.

OECD (1997a), *Environmental Benefits from Agriculture: Issues and Policies (The Helsinki Seminar)*, Paris: OECD.

OECD (1997b), *Agricultural Policies in OECD Countries, Measurement of Support and Background Information*, Paris: OECD.

OECD (1998a), "Agricultural Policy Reform: Stocktaking of Achievements", *Discussion Paper AGR/CA/MIN* (98) 1, March.

OECD (1998b), *Agriculture and the Environment: Issues and Policies*, Paris: OECD.

Reynolds, R. et al. (1993), "Impacts on the Environment of Reduced Agricultural Subsidies: A Case Study of New Zealand", *MAF Policy Technical Paper*, 93/12, Wellington: MAF, July.

Runge, C.F. (1994), "The Environmental Effects of Trade in the Agricultural Sector", *The Environmental Effects of Trade*, 19-54, Paris: OECD.

Runge, C.F. (1998), "Emerging Issues in Agricultural Trade and the Environment", OECD Workshop on Emerging Trade Issues in Agriculture, COM/AGR/CA/TD/TC/WS, (98) 103, Paris: OECD.

Scollay, R. and Gilbert, J. (1998), "Measuring the Gains from APEC Trade Liberalisation: An Overview of CGE Assessments", mimeo.

Sumner, D.A. (1995), *Agricultural Trade Policy-Letting Markets Work*, Washington, DC: The AEI Press.

8 Trade and Environmental Linkages in Manufacturing Industries

RAVI RATNAYAKE[1]

Introduction

The concerns for environmental protection are widespread in New Zealand which has been undergoing a lengthy period of trade liberalisation multilaterally, bilaterally and unilaterally over the last two decades. Trade barriers including tariffs and quantitative restrictions have been eliminated or lowered on exports as well as imports, making significant changes in the patterns of trade. The purpose of this chapter is to examine some selected trade/environment linkages at the industry level focusing on New Zealand's manufacturing industries. We examine these linkages in three environmentally sensitive manufacturing industries: plastics and synthetics, steel, and paper industry. Our investigation is based on a sample survey conducted in these three industries.

Major Issues/Linkages

In this chapter we concentrate on three major issues relating to the linkages between trade and environment and test them using the survey data obtained from some selected manufacturing industries.

Environmental standards and international competitiveness

It is claimed that stringent environmental regulations impose significant costs on domestic firms and industries reducing their international competitiveness compared with those from countries which have lower environmental standards and regulations. The loss of competitiveness is said to be greater in the so called "pollution-intensive" industries. An entirely opposite view is that environmental regulations lead to productivity improvements because of a more cleaner environment and to innovations because of the stimulating effects of such regulations (see Porter, 1991; Deans, 1992; and Jaffe et al., 1995)[2].

Industrial flight hypothesis or pollution havens hypothesis

According to this hypothesis, "dirty" or environmentally sensitive industries are going to be located in developing countries with relatively low environmental standards. It is claimed that multinational firms shift their operations to these countries because of the high costs resulting from environmental regulations imposed upon them in their own countries. It is also believed that developing countries purposely undervalue environmental standards in order to attract more foreign direct investment (e.g. Deans, 1992).

Environmental regulations and innovations

One major view is that environmental regulation constrains strategic choices and limits innovations, thereby disadvantaging environmentally regulated firms (Sanchez, 1997). An opposing view is that environmental regulation enhances competitiveness by encouraging efficiency gains through innovation. Firms that develop technological expertise in response to environmental regulations hold an advantage over their competitors, who are obligated to purchase and learn to use the new technology (Porter, 1991; Porter and Linde, 1995).

Data and Methodology

Some of the issues mentioned above have been analysed using inter-industry data and the results are reported in this book (see chapters 3 and 5). However, the inter-industry approach is not satisfactory as it cannot identify industry specific factors affecting the linkages. For the purpose of investigating those linkages at industry level, data relating to trade and environmental variables, preferably at firm level is needed. Unfortunately, in New Zealand, these data are not available either at industry level or at firm level. The individual researchers including the author of the present study are not in a position to gather such data from large scale national survey due to financial constraints. Therefore, our investigation was based on a small scale survey of firms.

In order to investigate the issues described above in more detail at industry level, a sample survey of firms in three environmentally sensitive industries (plastics, iron and steel and paper) was conducted. The firms surveyed were selected randomly from the Manufacturers Association Yearbook and the sample was limited to the Auckland region due to financial constraints in administering the survey. The questionnaire used is given in the appendix to this chapter. The survey period was July 1996 to August 1996.

Generally, we found difficulties in obtaining data from small firms (turnover from $500,000 to $2 million). The impression given was that much of the information requested did not enter their "strategy" at all, if in fact they had a strategy. It was noticeable that the larger the company, especially the multinationals, the greater the level of knowledge regarding regulations, alternative approaches considered and the more professional, in terms of strategic planning, and helpful they became. It was as if they were willingly complying and had nothing to lose by doing so. The theory would say that these firms had attained size and competitive advantage by anticipating change, adapting to it and being efficient in their all round business approach.

The smaller company/operator was on the contrary wary of revealing information and clearly they were the ones whose profits and competitive position would likely suffer most, if regulations were tightened or additional charges levied. They were the "fidgety" survey participants, very unwilling, and uncooperative. One got the impression that they had something to fear and in general the loss would probably affect them personally. Contrariwise, the multinationals had power, global strategies, options, scope and access to finance. They would survive more easily if regulation became more stringent, or they would leave.

We were able to get responses from 55 firms after contacting 100 firms. Some of this was only partial in terms of the questionnaire requirements, nonetheless information was collected on other aspects of their dealings.

Industry Case Studies

We tabulated the data collected from the survey under each industry and analysed below.

The Plastics and Synthetics Industry

The coverage of this industry includes plastic materials suitable for further processing such as synthetic resins, plastic materials, solid and liquid resins, sheets etc. and man made fibres excluding glass. Information was obtained from 20 firms. Some of this was only partial in terms of the questionnaire requirements, as some companies refused to talk at all about their financial position.

Issue 1: *Environmental standards and international competitiveness*

Consensus was that the New Zealand regulatory regime, specifically environmental related, was currently not inhibiting either international or domestic competitiveness levels or influencing investment decisions. Companies that did not have a specific EMS (Environmental Management System) believed that they were complying with environmental standards by complying to general health and safety standards and through ISO 14,000. However, on a different tact, reservations were expressed about the proposed Carbon Tax. Fear over its repercussions, in an internationally competitive sense, was expressed. But in all cases this was more speculative than certain.

We tested the international competitiveness issue using the responses to question 14 of the survey, i.e. "How well adapted is the environmental regulatory system in New Zealand to maintaining your company's competitiveness in overseas markets?" The responses are tabulated in Table 8.1.

Table 8.1: Competitiveness Perceptions - Plastics and Synthetics

Response	Number of firms
Very Well Adapted	7
Well Adapted	3
Acceptable	7
Poorly Adapted	1
Very Poorly Adapted	2

Source: Prepared using survey data

As illustrated in Table 8.1, the majority of firms (70 per cent) think that either our environmental regulatory system is "Very well adapted" or "Acceptable".

Question 15 of the survey is related to the efficacy of the RMA (Resource Management Act). The main purpose of this act is to circumscribe environmental degradation. The responses to this question are summarised in Table 8.2. It can be seen that currently the RMA is having little direct effect on output levels of the companies participating in the survey. Either they complied without difficulty or had informal environmental strategies in place that did not hinder their production drive.

Table 8.2: RMA Impact Against Environmental Degradation - Plastics and Synthetics

Response	Number of firms
RMA has had *no effect* on behaviour	14
RMA has had *an effect* on behaviour	6

Source: Prepared using survey data

Issue 2: *Industrial flight hypothesis or pollution havens hypothesis*

Question 8 of the survey is used to test this hypothesis. The question is "...How significant a factor was the cost of compliance with New Zealand's environmental regulations in the decision to invest here?" The responses are presented in Table 8.3.

Table 8.3: Significance of Regulations in Investment Decisions - Plastics and Synthetics

Response	Number of firms
No significance	9
Moderate significance	1

Source: Survey data

New Zealand's environmental regulations were in 90 per cent of cases of "No significance" when it came to investment decisions in New Zealand.

Next, we tabulated the data in terms of the destination of New Zealand's exports (Table 8.4). In order to substantiate the theory of pollution haven hypothesis, one should be able to show that the major destinations of New Zealand's exports are developing countries where relatively lower environmental standards are claimed to be in place. The data given in Table 8.4 do not support this hypothesis.

Table 8.4: Destination of Exports - Plastics and Synthetics

Destination of Export	Number of Respondents
Advanced developed countries	19
Newly industrialised countries	1
Other developing countries	7

Source: Survey data

Those companies that are subsidiaries and parented overseas made decisions to invest in New Zealand that were not driven by the environmental standards in place at the time. Any investment, or takeover seems to have been driven by global strategic motives rather than regulation or environmental considerations. The actual motives for investment were not ascertained at the time of interview but certainly of those operating with overseas parentage, New Zealand's regulatory environment was not inhibitory or onerous to comply with. We may speculate that investment motives related to profit opportunities and cost structures. This is positively related to the light handed regime per se within New Zealand.

Issue 3: *Effects of environmental regulations on innovations*

We tested the effects of environmental regulations on innovations through Question 16, i.e. "How would [you] respond to more stringent environmental regulations?" The responses are given in Table 8.5. The firms surveyed stated that should additional regulations be imposed, then they would almost unanimously consider using different technology to combat this constraint, as a preferred strategy. The results were tempered by uncertainty as to exactly what form these additional regulations would take. This hypothetical strategic option proposed by firms indicates that the environment would benefit, and firms are prepared to invest to stay competitive, compliant and in business.

The implication of increased regulation was mixed though as to how purported technological change would affect product price. Mostly firms expected to pass envisaged increased production and compliance cost onto consumers, manifesting as a straightforward "cost pass through", process. The degree of pass through and capacity to absorb increased production (average costs) would probably see the more powerful and profitable firms survive.

Table 8.5:   Possible Responses to Regulations - Plastics and Synthetics

Response	Number of firms
Introduce new, cleaner technology	15
Reduce output or change output mix	1
Change input mix (if possible)	5
Other – relocate	1
Cost pass through (onto customers)	5

Source: Survey data

There was an indication that the Carbon tax was likely to have some impact in causing firms to reconsider their technology use. As nothing specific has been stated as to actual target areas and the way tax is imposed, answers given were hypothetical in nature. But indications were that changes to production methodology would be feasible options taken. Innovation may be viewed as a proxy for adaptation of production techniques, and this was the preferred indicative course of action most firms proposed.

Specific Comments made by Firms

- Adapt to the regulations (whatever they be) and comply, because the company believed in the need for a clean environment.
- Introducing new technology is the only option to stay competitive, anything else is an avoidance issue.

- Innovation is seen as the survival strategy response to the market but in the end costs would be passed on.
- Become more efficient users of inputs and resources.
- Adapt their processes and machinery to be compatible with environmental requirements.
- Introduction of new technology would be the most favoured option but expected it to be too expensive and that the cost would be assessed carefully to ascertain the viability of continuing business.

The Iron and Steel Industry

To begin with a historical note, the terms and conditions under which the iron and steel industry was to be established were formally set down in the Heads of Agreement between the government and New Zealand Steel (which was incorporated in July 1965). On these grounds is it fair to state the development of the steel industry through the 1960s and 70s was a joint venture between the government and New Zealand Steel.

The election of the Labour government in July 1984 signalled a major change in attitude of the government. A November Treasury report "Review of the Major Projects" stated that steel mill expansion (Glenbrook) had suffered from "construction delays, lower steel prices and increases in the economic cost of supplying coal". In line with divesting itself of non core business a Reconstruction Agreement was arranged such that the Crown transferred its shares to New Zealand Steel in what became a controversial transaction over price and timing, given the New Zealand sharemarket crash of October 1987.

New Zealand Steel is subsequently owned and operated by BHP Steel, an Australian parent. The industry has fallen on hard times with industry losses occurring as recent as 1988-89 and 1989-90. Like many industries post the 1995 market reforms, New Zealand's steel industry has been in a state of flux, with considerable controversy surrounding some market transactions regarding its stock and appropriate pricing level of assets. Steel is produced by the unique direct reduction process using indigenous ironsands at the BHP - New Zealand Steel works at Glenbrook, while Pacific Steel produces rod and bar using scrap.

The scope of this industry includes basic metal industries (manufacturing of primary iron and steel products and primary non-ferrous metal products), manufacturing of fabricated metal products (cutlery, hand tools, hardware, furniture etc.), and manufacturing of machinery.

Issue 1 : *Environmental standards and international competitiveness*

The question is whether "stringent environmental regulations impose significant costs on domestic firms and industries reducing their international competitiveness". We tested this hypothesis in the context of the steel industry using question 14 of the survey, i.e. "How well adapted is the environmental regulatory system in New Zealand to maintaining your company's competitiveness in overseas markets?" We tabulated the responses to this question in Table 8.6.

Table 8.6: Competitiveness Perceptions - Iron and Steel

Response	Number of firms
Very Well Adapted	2
Well Adapted	5
Acceptable	7
Poorly Adapted	1
Very Poorly Adapted	5

Source: Survey data

Opinions in this industry are divided, with the majority (35 per cent) saying regulations are "Acceptable" and 25 per cent saying they are either "Well adapted" or "Very poorly adapted".

Next, we look at the impact of RMA on firms (question 15). The responses for this industry are presented in Table 8.7. In this industry, RMA seems to have considerable impact on firms compared with plastics and synthetics industry.

Table 8.7: RMA Impact Against Environmental Degradation - Iron and Steel

Response	Number of firms
RMA has had *no effect* on behaviour	7
RMA has had *an effect* on behaviour	13

Source: Survey data

Specific Comments made by Firms

- It has been time consuming and has created more work for us.
- The RMA has diverted resources, i.e. capital away from new product development.
- As a result an environmental audit has been conducted.
- It is making the operating environment very difficult.

Issue 2: *Industrial flight hypothesis or pollution havens hypothesis*

According to this hypothesis, "dirty", or environmentally sensitive industries are going to be located in developing countries with relatively low environmental standards. We tabulated the responses to the question "How significant a factor was the cost of compliance with New Zealand's environmental regulations in the decisions to invest here?" in Table 8.8.

Table 8.8:   Significance of Regulations - Iron and Steel

Response	Number of firms
No Significance	0
Little significance	1
Moderate	1
Very significant	1

Source: Survey data

Of the three firms who responded there was a variation in response that makes any conclusions difficult. Specific circumstances would most likely be the most plausible explanation.

Table 8.9 presents the responses by the firms regarding destinations of New Zealand's exports. Data in this table again do not provide any support for the hypothesis.

Table 8.9:   Destination of Exports - Iron and Steel

Destination of Exports	Number of Respondents
Advanced developed countries	10
Newly industrialised countries	5
Other developing countries	2

Source: Survey data

Issue 3: *Effects of environmental regulations on innovations*

The responses by the firms to the question "How would your company respond to more stringent environmental regulations?" are presented in

Table 8.10. The majority of firms would like to introduce new cleaner technology.

Table 8.10: Possible Responses to Environmental Regulations – Steel

Response	Number of firms
Introduce new cleaner technology	14
Reduce output or change output mix	6
Change input mix (if possible)	9
Other – relocate	6
Cost pass through	0

Source: Survey data

Specific Comments made by Firms

- Try to innovate with new products for export.
- Recover costs through price increases in the hope it will be incurred entirely across all manufacturers and so not disadvantage their competitive position.
- They would take the necessary steps to see that they remained competitive.
- Most changes would probably be prohibitively expensive so if required they would have to relocate if a living was still possible out of the business.
- Price rises would probably occur and possibly they would lose customers, so any tougher regulations was a "horrible" thought and would severely test the viability of the firm.

The Paper Industry

The paper making industry began in New Zealand in 1876 with the New Zealand Paper Mills Limited Company emerging as the pioneer firm, starting mills at Mataura and Woodhaugh[3]. The years 1905 to 1946 saw consolidation of the industry but with the industry responding to international technological changes, subsequently more imported kraft pulp was used. Post Second World War saw the emergence in strength of New Zealand Forest Products with their production from the Kinleith mill and Tasman Pulp and Paper Company founded in 1952, using the Kawerau facility, spurring growth in the industry.

The Kinleith mill is now owned by Carter Holt Harvey Limited and overall the industry has struggled in the recent past with overcapacity in the global pulp markets significantly impacting on prices and industry profits[4]. Market sales are currently approximately 53 per cent domestic, 41 per cent Asia and 6 per cent to Australia.

This industry includes manufacture of pulp, paper and paperboard, manufacture of paperboard containers (corrugated board of primary paper) and manufacture of pulp, paper and paperboard articles.

Issue 1: *Environmental standards and international competitiveness*

We tabulated the responses to question 14 in relation to the paper industry in Table 8.11. As illustrated in the tables, the majority of firms (60 per cent) think the environmental regulatory environment is "Well adapted", or better.

Table 8.11: Competitiveness Perceptions - Paper

Response	Number of firms
Very Well Adapted	2
Well Adapted	3
Acceptable	2
Poorly Adapted	1
Very Poorly Adapted	0

Source: Survey data

Next, we look at the responses to question 15 of the survey, i.e. "How has your firm responded to recent changes in New Zealand's environmental regulatory regime?" (Table 8.12). The majority of firms stated that RMA has had no significant impact on their behaviour.

Table 8.12: RMA Impact Against Environmental Degradation - Paper

Response	Number of firms
RMA has had *no effect* on behaviour	5
RMA has had *an effect* on behaviour	3

Source: Survey data

Specific Comments made by Firms

- The RMA has inconsistent applications.
- The RMA is costly with obtaining consents and is time consuming.

Issue 2: *Industrial flight hypothesis or pollution havens hypothesis*

The responses to question 8 of the survey (how significant a factor was the cost of compliance with New Zealand's environmental regulations in the decision to invest here?) and Question 10 (the destination of exports) are presented in Table 8.13 and 8.14 respectively.

It can be seen in Table 8.13, New Zealand's environmental regulations are of "Moderate or No significance" when it comes to decisions to invest here. With regard to destination of exports, the data is inconclusive with both "advanced" and newly industrialised countries being the main recipients of exports of paper products. We assume advanced countries have stringent regulations and NICS more liberal regulations.

Table 8.13: Significance of Regulations - Paper

Response	Number of firms
No significance	2
Moderate significance	3

Source: Survey data

Table 8.14: Destination of Exports - Paper

Destination of Exports	Number of Respondents
Advanced developed countries	9
Newly industrialised countries	4
Other developing countries	1

Source: Survey data

Issue 3: *Effects of environmental regulations on innovations*

We use the responses of question 16 to test this hypothesis (Table 8.15). This table shows that 5 out of 14 respondents would consider introducing new technology as an innovative measure to meet tighter regulatory conditions.

Table 8.15: Possible Responses to Regulations - Paper

Response	Number of firms
Introduce new cleaner technology	5
Reduce output or change output mix	3
Change input mix (if possible)	6
Other - relocate	0
Cost pass through	0

Source: Survey data

Specific Comments made by Firms

- If the regulations were too tough they would just go out of business because they couldn't adapt to certain expensive technological requirements.
- It would most likely mean they would go out of business because of the intensity of competition from overseas interests (Asian mainly).
- Regulation would present opportunities to adapt their strategy but exactly how would be the "challenge".

Conclusion

In this chapter, we have tested three hypotheses relating to linkages of trade and environment in three industries using firm level data. Firstly, we tested whether stringent environmental regulations impose significant costs on international competitiveness of domestic firms and found no support for the hypothesis. The majority of firms were of the view that New Zealand's environmental regulatory system is very well adapted or acceptable. It was also found that the Resource Management Act has little direct effect on output levels of companies participating in the survey. Secondly, we tested whether "dirty" or environmentally sensitive industries are getting located in countries with relatively low environmental standards. The cost of compliance in all industries was found to be insignificant in investment decisions of New Zealand. The majority of firms in the survey exported their goods to advanced developed countries where relatively high environmental standards are in place. Thirdly, we have examined the impact of environmental regulations on innovations. The question asked was how would firms respond to more stringent environmental regulations. Again the majority of firms stated that they would introduce new technologies to combat this constraint.

Notes

1   Thanks to Jon Cotton for excellent research assistance.
2   See chapter 3 for details.
3   Labour Relations in the New Zealand Pulp and Paper Industry Since 1956, Roche, M. & Wooding, C., Working Paper 86/2.
4   Carter Holt Harvey Annual Report 1996.

References

Dean, J. (1992), "Trade and the Environment: A Survey of Literature", in P. Low (ed).

Jaffe, A.B., Peterson, S.R., Portney, P.R. and Stavins, R.B. (1995), "Environmental Regulation and the Competitiveness of U.S. Manufacturing: What does the Evidence Tell Us?", *Journal of Economic Literature*, XXXIII, 132-163.

Porter, M.E. (1991), "America's Green Strategy", *Scientific American*, April.

Porter, M. and Linde, C.V.D, (1995), "Towards a new conception of the environment-competitiveness relationship", *Journal of Economic Perspectives*, 9, 97-118.

Sanchez, C.M. (1997), "Environmental Regulation and Firm-level Innovation", *Business and Society*, 36 (2), 140-168.

SURVEY QUESTIONNAIRE

General Information

1) Company Name: ....

   Contact Name: ....

2) What area(s) of manufacturing is the company engaged in and what are your main products?

   ....

   ....

3) What are your company's total annual sales? $ ....

4) What are your company's total operating costs? $ ....

5) Please give the majority shareholder(s) share in the company and their nationality.

Name	Share	Nationality
....	%	....
....	%	....

Information on International Dealings

6) Does your company hold overseas assets?   YES / NO
   [if NO, please proceed to question 8]
   What is your company's total overseas investment? $ ....

7) How significant was the cost of compliance with the foreign country's environmental regulations in the decision to invest there?
   [please circle, if known]

   Very Significant   5   4   3   2   1   No Significance

What other factors were significant in the company's decision to invest overseas?

....

....

8) If you are the subsidiary or division of a foreign based firm, how significant a factor was the cost of compliance with New Zealand's environmental regulations in the decision to invest here?
[please circle if known]

Very Significant   5   4   3   2   1   No Significance

What other factors were significant in the company's decision to invest in New Zealand?

....

....

9) Are some inputs into your production sourced from outside New Zealand?   YES / NO

What is the total value of input(s) imported? $........................

10) Does your company export from New Zealand?   YES / NO

What is the total value of exports? $ ....

New Zealand Environmental Regulations

11) Does your company operate an Environmental Management System?   YES / NO

12) If possible, please supply the annual Environmental Compliance Costs faced by your company, either as approximate dollar values or as percentages of Total Costs: [see following page]

- Production Related Costs (eg. power, chemicals, transport and disposal, maintenance and depreciation on pollution control equipment) $ or ...... %
- Regulatory Costs (eg. permit processing charges) $ or ...... %
- Management Costs (eg. enviro-specialists salaries) $ or ...... %
- Total Environment Compliance Costs $ or ...... %

13) How significant is the cost of environmental regulatory compliance for your company when evaluated against total operating costs? [please circle, if known]

    Very Significant   5   4   3   2   1   No Significance

14) How well adapted is the environmental regulatory system in New Zealand to maintaining your company's competitiveness overseas? [please circle, if applicable]
    Very Significant   5   4   3   2   1   No Significance

15) How has your firm responded to recent changes in New Zealand's environmental regulatory regime? (such as the introduction of the Resource Management Act 1991).

....

....

....

16) How would your company respond to more stringent environmental regulations?
  1. Introduce new cleaner technology (innovation)   YES / NO
  2. Reduce output or change output mix   YES / NO
  3. Change mix of production inputs   YES / NO
  4. Other (eg. relocate overseas)

Why would you follow this course of action?
....
....

17) What are the main implications of the Resource Management Act for your firm in the future?

....

....

....

18) Would the introduction of a Carbon Tax affect your firm, and if so in what way?

....

....

....

Thank you for participating in this study - complete confidentiality of responses is assured.

9 Forestry Export Restrictions and Carbon Emissions in New Zealand

JOHN GILBERT

Introduction

Export restrictions on forestry (log) exports are in place in most of the major log producing regions of the world, with the most well known example being Indonesia. Export restrictions have also been proposed for New Zealand (usually with the objective of increasing the level of domestic processing). Most of the existing literature on the effect of export restrictions on the environment has focused on the tropical hardwood producing countries, and the impact export restrictions have on the rate of deforestation. In New Zealand the situation is somewhat different in that the vast majority of New Zealand exports of logs come from privately-owned plantations of exotic species. Moreover, the absorptive capacity of these plantations forms a cornerstone of the New Zealand government policy on reducing net carbon emissions under its FCCC (Framework Convention on Climate Change) obligations. In this chapter we therefore consider the issue of export restrictions from the perspective of their impact on net carbon emissions, and the policies required to meet the FCCC obligations. We develop a CGE model of the New Zealand economy, which explicitly incorporates emissions data from manufacturing and the absorptive capabilities of the forestry sector. We use the model to simulate the effect of log export restrictions on net carbon emissions, and development estimates of the carbon taxes required to fulfil FCCC obligations with and without log export restrictions. We demonstrate that inclusion of environmental costs in this manner strengthens the usual neo-classical case against export restrictions for the small economy.

In section 2 we provide a brief overview of the New Zealand forestry sector, and describe its role in the New Zealand economy. In section 3 we review the literature on trade and environmental policy which has focused on the forestry sector, as well as more general literature regarding CGE assessments of environmental policy and carbon emissions. In section 4 we present a computable general equilibrium model of the New Zealand economy, which we use to simulate the impact of export restrictions and carbon taxes, taking into account carbon emissions of industry (from both production and energy consumption activities) and the absorptive capacity of the forest resource. In section 5 we present the results of the simulations. A summary of the results and concluding comments follow in section 6.

An Overview of Forestry in New Zealand

Resource and ownership

New Zealand's forestry resources have been developed according to a principle of "dual" forest estates. There is separation of those resources coming from planted production forests, and those coming from natural production forests. These estates are distinct in terms of their legal, institutional and functional dimensions. The plantations consist mainly (approximately 89 per cent) state as a fast growing replacement for rapidly declining stocks of natural timber earlier this century. The plantation forests are largely commercial in nature (with some role in land stabilisation and recreation), with some overseeing but minimal intervention by the Ministry of Forestry.

Those resources which are classified in the natural forest category are in general managed by the New Zealand Department of Conservation with soil and water conservation and recreational values as the primary objectives. These forests can be broadly divided into two main types. These are the beech forests, dominated by one or more of the four indigenous species of Nothofagus, and the conifer-hardwood forests dominated mainly by Podocarps (Brown 1997, pp.10-11). Severe restrictions are placed on the utilisation of the natural forest resource, including those which have been set aside for production, by both the Resource Management Act 1991 (which covers all industries) and the Forest Amendments Act 1993.

Table 9.1 gives a relative description of the size of the New Zealand forestry resource. Forests occupy approximately 29 per cent of New

Zealand's total land area. Of this area, approximately 18 per cent, or about 1.388 million hectares (roughly five per cent of New Zealand's total land area), is in the plantations. While the majority of the natural forestry resource (79 per cent) is held by the State in the form of National parks, scenic reserves, the plantations are mostly privately owned, although this is a relatively new trend. Prior to the sales of state forestry assets which began in 1989, ownership of plantation forests was shared almost evenly between the public and private sectors, but at present, approximately 80 per cent of the plantation resource is in private ownership.

Table 9.1: Areas of New Zealand Forested and Non-Forested Land

Type of Land Cover	Estimated Area (000 hectares)		Percentage of Total NZ Land Area	
Natural Forest	6406		23.0	
Plantation Forest	1388		4.8	
Total Forested Land		**7794**		**28.8**
Grassland and Lucerne	9600		35.0	
Fruit, Vegetables and Nurseries	104		0.3	
Crops	309		1.2	
Tussock and Danthonia	3917		14.9	
Total Pasture and Arable Land		**13930**		**51.5**
Other Non-Forested Land	5246		19.4	
Minor Offshore Islands	83		0.3	
Total Non-Forested Land		**19259**		**71.2**
Total New Zealand Land Area		**27053**		**100.0**

Source: Ministry of Forestry, Forestry Statistics 1995

Industrial structure and production

The forestry sector can be broadly split into two component industries or sub-sectors, the timber industry and the forest products industry. The timber industry consists of the production of roundwood, the production of sawn timber, the production of wood chips, and timber preservation. The forest products industry is characterised by a higher level of value added production, and consists of the pulp and paper industry and the wood-based panels industry.

The roundwood sub-industry involves the removal for other purposes, either further processing or export, of the forestry resource. In 1995, an estimated 16 million cubic metres of roundwood were removed from New Zealand forests, an estimated 16 million, or 99 per cent, of which was from plantation forests. The output of this industry is used to support the sawn timber sub-industry, which produced 2.9 million cubic metres of sawn timber in 1995, approximately 97 per cent of which was produced from exotic plantation species. The wood chip sub-industry uses both native and exotic trees unsuitable for sawn timber production, in addition to forest and sawmill residues.

The pulp and paper sub-industry, concentrated in the North Island of New Zealand, takes approximately 28 per cent of total roundwood removals as fibre input, while the wood based panels sub-industry takes approximately 1.4 per cent in addition to waste residues. Total production of pulp reached just over 637 thousand air dry tonnes in 1995. Paper and paperboard production reached 876 thousand tonnes over the same period, while total production of veneer, plywood, particle board, and fibreboard reached 1.25 million cubic metres[1].

Contribution to the New Zealand economy

Together forestry and logging, manufacture of wood products, and manufacture of paper products contributed 4.63 billion dollars to GDP in 1994. This amounts to over 5.5 per cent of GDP. Comparing this to the proportion in 1990 of 4.5 per cent highlights not only the substantial contribution which the forestry sector makes to the New Zealand economy, but also the rapid growth the sector has experienced over the last few years, although it has frequently been argued that the recent improvements in the performance of the forestry sector have come about largely by increasing exports of unprocessed logs, rather than through attempting to add value within New Zealand.

Although the days of the forestry industry being used by the state as a form of social welfare by providing jobs for the unemployed are now over, the forestry sector also remains a not insignificant employer in New Zealand. In 1995, 25,415 people were engaged in forestry and first stage processing, up from 18,239 at the same time in 1990. The largest component of the industry in terms of employment is the forestry and logging industry itself (accounting for approximately one third of total employment in the sector). In terms of the New Zealand economy as a whole, approximately 1.5 per cent of the total labour force is employed in forestry and first stage processing.

Exports

Table 9.2 gives the Ministry of Forestry's regional base cut wood supply forecasts until the year 2025. The available wood supply from New Zealand plantation forests is expected to grow extremely rapidly over the next thirty years, with large supply volumes coming on line from the year 2000.

With respect to demand trends, Table 9.3 shows the estimated New Zealand consumption of forestry products in roundwood equivalents[2] for the years 1971 to 1995. Domestic consumption has been characterised by fluctuating cycles of between 4.5 and 6.8 million cubic metres per annum, the main cause being the boom/bust nature of the building industry. Observing the five-year moving averages confirms that for the past twenty years per capita consumption of roundwood has remained largely unchanged. Overall, consumption is not expected to increase greatly in the future. Given that supply is forecast to increase rapidly over the next twenty years, while demand is expected to remain largely constant, a large increase in the volume of roundwood available for export markets over the next few decades, directly or indirectly, can be expected.

The forestry sector has already in fact become New Zealand's third largest export sector. The increase in forestry exports has come about as New Zealand's traditional exports products, meat and wool, have declined in relative importance. In terms of volume, exports of forestry products have nearly tripled over the past two decades. The rate of increase in the value of exports also stands out spectacularly. The sector has maintained an average annual growth in value of exports of around 14 per cent, with extraordinary growth displayed in certain years[3]. In total, a twenty-five fold increase over the past two decades. The vast majority (67 per cent) of the increase in total export volume since 1987 has been in logs and poles.

Table 9.2: **New Zealand Regional Base Cut Wood Supply Forecasts (000m³ per year)**

Region:	2001-05	2006-10	2011-15	2016-20	2021-25
Northland	1756	3211	4303	4367	4692
Auckland	1530	1649	1654	1640	1985
Central North Island	11402	11737	12079	12272	12677
East Coast	1306	1885	2165	2547	3995
Hawkes Bay	1903	1943	2006	2018	3254
Southern North Island	1730	1837	1843	2282	4017
Nelson/Marlborough	2538	2792	2924	2932	3268
Canterbury	451	457	502	524	540
West Coast	935	1031	1005	1050	1363
Otago/Southland	2267	2331	2281	2809	4632
Total	**25818**	**28873**	**28873**	**32441**	**40403**

Source: Ministry of Forestry, Forestry Statistics 1995

Table 9.3: **Estimated New Zealand Consumption of Roundwood (000m³ RWE) 1971-1995**

Year	Mean NZ Population (000)	Total Removals	Imports	Exports	Total Apparent Consumption
1971	2831	8205	323	3251	5277
1972	2876	7970	286	3427	4829
1973	2931	8250	337	3640	4947
1974	2994	8585	486	3325	5746
1975	3058	8361	497	2733	6125
1976	3111	8272	207	3116	5363
1977	3136	9701	304	3907	6098
1978	3144	9243	219	4021	5441
1979	3143	8974	281	4537	4718
1980	3138	9911	301	5136	5076
1981	3147	10245	272	4904	5613
1982	3161	9753	348	4178	5923
1983	3190	9358	351	3880	5829
1984	3231	9266	422	4318	5370
1985	3259	9626	568	3911	6283
1986	3273	10195	656	3881	6970
1987	3282	9613	766	3670	6709
1988	3310	9688	566	4638	5616
1989	3318	10619	556	5630	5545
1990	3337	11744	626	6000	6369
1991	3373	13693	642	7876	6459
1992	3416	14136	700	9097	5739
1993	3452	14938	1070	9872	6136
1994	3491	15131	861	9119	6873
1995	3539	16437	996	10222	7211

Source: Ministry of Forestry, Forestry Statistics 1995

Table 9.4 summarises the major markets for New Zealand exports by value over the period 1985 to 1995, and has been organised according to the major economic entities within the Asia Pacific region. All countries not specifically mentioned have been included in the "Others" category. New Zealand has a relatively narrow export base. Export dependence on two major markets, Australia and Japan, is evident. Together these two countries account for approximately two thirds of the purchases of New Zealand's total forest products exports by value, with Japan recently becoming the largest single market (taking 29.9 per cent of New Zealand exports by value in 1995).

International perspective

In world terms New Zealand is a relatively small producer, accounting for only just over one per cent of total world production. However, while New Zealand is not currently significant as a producer of roundwood, it is a major exporter. New Zealand was the fifth largest exporter of industrial roundwood in the world in 1993, accounting for over six per cent of total world exports. The same dominance cannot be observed in the processed forest products markets. New Zealand is only the eleventh largest exporter of sawn timber, and is positively minute when compared with countries like Canada. It fails to register at all in the paper and paperboard markets. This confirms New Zealand's position in world markets as predominantly a raw materials supplier.

In terms of the global political perspective, New Zealand is characterised as a moderate country. According to Brown, its primary contribution in the international arena is often to act as an arbiter or conciliator, seeking ways to progress deadlocks between the more protagonistic countries. It also provides development assistance to the forestry sectors of the island states of the South Pacific, and plays an important role in international environmental initiatives, where its key aim is to ensure that plantation forestry as practised in New Zealand, continues to be internationally accepted as a means of achieving environmental objectives (Brown, 1997, p.42).

Table 9.4: Value of Exports of Forestry Products From New Zealand by Destination 1985-1995 ($000)

Destination	1985		1990		1995	
	Value	%	Value	%	Value	%
Australia	343014	45.02	550066	39.69	762431	29.16
Japan	173355	22.75	335201	24.19	781904	29.90
EANIEs[a]	61346	8.05	246120	17.76	615620	23.55
Korea	20815	2.73	125212	9.03	371466	14.21
Taiwan	6046	0.79	65696	4.74	145417	5.56
Singapore	6646	0.87	22780	1.64	29378	1.12
Hong Kong	27839	3.65	32432	2.34	69359	2.65
ASEAN-4[b]	68049	8.93	121101	8.74	204077	7.81
Indonesia	19665	2.58	57894	4.18	108581	4.15
Malaysia	17745	2.33	20663	1.49	34098	1.30
Philippines	14095	1.85	17090	1.23	25128	0.96
Thailand	16545	2.17	25454	1.84	36270	1.39
China	23185	3.04	21637	1.56	26870	1.03
NAFTA[c]	8401	1.10	24507	1.77	133468	5.10
USA	7855	1.03	22981	1.66	131583	5.03
Canada	543	0.07	1526	0.11	1885	0.07
Mexico	3	0.00	-	0.00	-	0.00
Others[d]	84603	11.10	87239	6.29	90259	3.45
Total	**761953**	**100.00**	**1385871**	**100.00**	**2614629**	**100.00**

[a] East Asian Newly Industrialising Economies
[b] Association of South-East Asian Nations
[c] North American Free Trade Area
[d] Others are all other countries to which New Zealand has exported forestry products during the year.

Source: New Zealand Forestry Statistics 1995, Ministry of Forestry and Department of Statistics INFOS EXI Series

Forestry Trade Restrictions and Environmental Issues

The tariffs applied to imports of forestry products in most countries are generally low and declining. The average trade weighted tariff rates for all wood and wood product imports into developed countries are around zero for wood in the rough, and have declined under the GATT from 2.4 per cent to 1.7 per cent for primary wood products, and from 7.8 per cent to 5.7 per cent for secondary wood products. Also, under the APEC Early Voluntary Sector Liberalisation (EVSL) programme, all tariffs in wood products are to be eliminated in the Asia-Pacific region, which include all of New Zealand's major export markets, by 2004. However, the sector is still characterised by tariff escalation as the level of processing increases. Moreover, it has been argued that additional non-tariff barriers, such as health, safety and technical standards, anti-dumping and countervailing duty investigations, and import licensing schemes, may have a role in reinforcing tariff barriers, and that these types of barriers are increasing under growing pressure from environmental advocacy groups (FAO 1994, p.319). While import bans have also started to appear in Europe and the United States, these apply to tropical timber, reflecting the common perception that tropical timber is produced in an environmentally unfriendly manner, and do not directly effect New Zealand, as a softwood producer[4].

It is difficult to determine the effects of import restrictions on the environment. The higher relative tariffs for processed products may restrict the ability of exporting countries to develop their own processing capabilities. It may therefore be argued that trade barriers are preventing the efficient utilisation of the forest resource. By keeping prices of logs artificially low import restrictions may also further exacerbate the disparity between stumpage prices and the real economic scarcity value of logs – resulting in excessive logging of old growth forests and insufficient investment in new plantations. Perhaps more importantly, import restrictions on processed wood products may prompt producer countries to argue for subsidies and log export restrictions to compensate their domestic producers. This has certainly been the case in New Zealand, where the role of escalating tariffs in lowering New Zealand's exports of processed forest products is frequently cited (e.g., Wije-wardana 1985), despite the fact that it is not clear that New Zealand has any comparative advantage in processed wood products.

Log export bans and other export restrictions are used in many producer countries to increase domestic processing by allowing industry access to lower cost logs. Gillis (1990) has reviewed the role of log export restrictions in encouraging industrialisation. The most well known example is Indonesia, which has become a major plywood supplier on the basis of the log export ban which it imposed in 1985. While several studies, including Fitzgerald (1986), Gillis (1988) and Lindsay (1989), have estimated the costs of the policy to be substantial, other countries, including Malaysia, the Philippines, and the United States, have also brought in log export restrictions. Indeed, New Zealand is one of the few major log producers which does not currently employ substantial export restrictions (with the exception of those applying to some West Coast native forests). However, New Zealand has used export restrictions in the past, and calls are still made for export restrictions to be reintroduced, the most recent being the efforts of the New Zealand Owned Sawmillers Group in 1993.

While in New Zealand the main incentive for the proponents of log export restrictions has clearly been the expansion of domestic processing, proponents here and overseas have also been able to argue that export restrictions are good for the environment. Perhaps the biggest environmental issue facing the global forestry industry is the unsustainable extraction of roundwood from forests to supply international trade in forest products, which can lead not only to a decline in the availability forest resources, but also wider environmental effects. These externalities include the loss of the resource for other consumptive uses (e.g., hunting or recreation), the loss of ecological functions (e.g., watershed protection, carbon storage and microclimatic roles) and the loss of other non-consumptive values (e.g., biodiversity and existence values) of the forest. It may be argued that export restrictions are helpful because falling external demand may reduce log harvests. Moreover, once the processing industries expand and become dependent on a regular wood supply, incentives to investment in reafforestation may expand.

Although this is clearly a complex issue, FAO (1994) argues that the current evidence does not support these arguments; log export bans have led to neither better forest conservation nor to the development of efficient processing industries, since the bans do not reduce the overall demand for logs, but rather shift the location of processing (p.318). While log export restrictions may stimulate short-term growth of domestic processing, over time they tend to result in undervaluing of logs, processing overcapacity and inefficient production processes. Barbier, et al. (1995) similarly, does not find support for the hypothesis that export restrictions lower the rate of deforestation (see also Barbier and Rauscher 1994). Moreover, some of the debate over the environmental impact of log export restrictions appears to be somewhat out of focus, taking as given the objective of reducing the rate of deforestation, since the environmental cost associated with forest products trade is not deforestation itself, but rather the impact which deforestation has on the environment. As discussed above, there may be a number of aspects to this, including decreased biodiversity, as well as the loss of recreational uses. Although they are difficult to measure and quantify, it is these costs which result from deforestation which are the objective of economic analysis, rather than the deforestation itself.

In New Zealand, these consequential costs of deforestation give the environmental argument for log export restrictions a further spin. As discussed above, the forest resource available for economic exploitation in New Zealand is not a natural forest, as is the case in most tropical hardwood suppliers, but rather commercial plantations of exotic softwood species. Log export restrictions are likely to result in lower levels of forestry output. However, as these forests are largely privately owned and planted, this reduction in output may not imply a reduction in deforestation, as may be the case with an existing natural resource (although this link may be somewhat tenuous, as discussed above), but rather a reduction in reafforestation. Furthermore, while the role of plantation forests in the ecosystem may be a subject of debate, there is no debate over the role of plantation forestry in the New Zealand strategy for achieving its carbon emission reduction targets under the FCCC. Article 4.2 of the FCCC contains specific commitments for Annex 1 parties (of which New Zealand is one), including a target to reduce the levels of CO_2 gas emissions to 1990 levels by the year 2000. At the core of the New Zealand strategy is increased plantations of forestry to act as "carbon sinks". Indeed, it was initially expected that some 80 per cent of the target reduction would be met by increasing absorption through forestry, with only 20 per cent through reduced gross emissions (voluntary reductions, increased energy efficiency, etc.) The New Zealand policy package announced in 1994 also includes the imposition of carbon charges in the event that the target will not be achieved by these other means.

The New Zealand response to the carbon emission debate is discussed in considerable detail in Ministry for the Environment (1996). There are a number of areas of interest, not the least being whether or not targeting net emissions is rational from a long term perspective (since growth rates in the forestry biomass cannot be expanded or even maintained indefinitely)[5], or scientifically valid (measurement of absorption is difficult, and there is some debate over whether a unit of carbon absorbed really is the same as a unit not emitted – since technically the forest is only a store of carbon). Since log export restrictions remain an area of debate in this country, also of considerable interest is the impact that log export restrictions might have on the level of gross carbon emissions as the industrial structure is changed, on the absorptive capacity of forestry in New Zealand, and on the steps necessary to ensure that the carbon emission targets are met and their associated costs.

The arguments put forward against export restrictions tend to suggest that the environmental impacts of log export restrictions spread far beyond the forest. Substantial increases in the level of processing may imply increases in the level of environmental degradation in general. Ideally, these costs should also be taken into account when analysing the impact of export restrictions. This points to a need for general equilibrium methods of analysis, rather than studies which focus only on the forestry sector. Computable general equilibrium (CGE) modelling therefore seems the most appropriate methodology. CGE models have already been used in numerous studies of trade and environment issues. In some cases existing models have been extended to include environmental analysis. One example of such an approach is Marks et al. (1991), who extend the ORANI model of Australia to examine the costs of carbon emission abatement. There are also numerous extensions of the GTAP model, such as Perroni and Wigle (1997), which uses side modules which calculate emission responses to various policies, using the GTAP results as inputs (in this sense the study is not truly general equilibrium), and a number of studies from ABARE (the Australian Bureau of Agricultural and Resource Economics). There is in fact a major effort to incorporate environmental costs directly into the next version (number 5) of the GTAP database. Other studies use models specifically built for environmental policy analysis, including various modified versions of the GREEN model, developed at the OECD (described in Burniaux et al. 1992), such as the Yang et al. (1996) ESSAM model. In the case of New Zealand the only published CGE estimates are derived from the multi-country WEDGE model, as described in Chisholm et al. (1994).

The models which have been used are both multi-region (for an early example see Whalley and Wigle 1991, Manne and Rutherford 1994 is a more recent piece), and single region, dynamic and static. Despite the differences in construction, all CGE models are essentially descriptive policy analysis tools, the results of which should be interpreted as indicative rather than predictive. In the remainder of this chapter we describe and use a computable general equilibrium model of the New Zealand economy.

The Model

The model we describe in this section is a static[6], neo-classical CGE model of the New Zealand economy which we modify to consider environmental issues. The fundamental model structure is quite standard, and so here we only describe the basic features of the model. The actual model equations and parameter values are presented in the appendices. We agree with the arguments of Clarete and Roumasset (1986), among others, that the neoclassical CGE, with its clear and well understood microeconomic foundations, is the policy tool best suited to facilitating intuitive understanding of economic adjustments and sectoral linkages which result from changes in trade and also environmental policy. Hence, on the production side, we make the standard assumptions that all markets are perfectly competitive, all firms operate under constant returns to scale, and that all factors of production are fully employed, available in fixed quantities, and internationally immobile[7]. We further assume that labour is mobile between sectors, while capital and natural resources are not (the implication being that current investment will add to capacity only in future periods)[8].

We have aggregated to nine sectors: agriculture, forestry, mining, light manufactures, wood processing, heavy manufactures, traded services, non-traded services and energy. The input-output data to which we calibrate our model is presented in Appendix 9.3 (the data is based on the 1993 input-output table of New Zealand). The production technology for all sectors except wood processing is modelled using generalised CES functions. In the wood processing sector we make use of a two-level CES function, with logs at one level, and all other inputs at the other. While many other CGE analyses of environmental issues have maintained the standard procedure of assuming all intermediate inputs are utilised in fixed proportions to output, in our model we allow energy to be utilised by industry in variable proportions along with capital and labour (all other intermediate goods are still assumed to be used in fixed proportions). The reason for taking this approach is that assuming fixed proportions in the use of energy (as in Strutt and Anderson 1998 or Perroni and Wigle 1997) limits the response of firms to carbon taxes (the implementation of which is discussed further below) where energy consumption is the main source of carbon emissions by industry. In a model where energy is used in fixed proportions to output the only response a firm can have to a carbon tax is to reduce its output (a point also noted by Beghin et al. 1995). With flexible proportions technology, the firm can respond not only by reducing the scale of its activities, but also by substituting less pollutive inputs (capital and labour) for more pollutive ones (energy). We believe that this flexibility is an important model feature.

On the demand side, we assume that households spend a constant proportion of their incomes on each commodity, and that their underlying preferences are identical (or alternatively, the specification can be interpreted as assuming one representative consumer). The underlying utility function is Cobb-Douglas in form. Our objective is primarily to analyse the effect of trade policy on sectoral production and overall economic welfare rather than the details of government spending and revenue collection, and hence there is no real role for the government in the model. The government collects tax revenue, but we assume that all of this revenue is transferred back to consumers in a non-distortionary manner (this could also be interpreted as assuming that the government spends the tariff revenue in a manner identical to the consumption pattern of households). Investment is treated in a similarly simple manner. We make the neoclassical assumption that investment is equal to savings (of the household and government), and hence final demand (the sum of household consumption, government purchases and investment demand) is a fixed proportion of national disposable income (which is equal to GDP minus an exogenous trade surplus or net capital outflow)[9]. The flexible exchange rate adjusts to maintain the exogenous trade surplus. Total demand is simply final demand plus intermediate demand. Unlike some other studies (Espinosa and Smith 1995, for example), we do not include demand side effects of pollution through indirect health links or direct traffic effects, etc. The only measure of the benefit of emission policies is the reductions in emissions themselves.

With respect to trade there are several features to note. First, we do not allow for monopoly power in trade. The small country assumption seems the most reasonable starting point for a country the size of New Zealand. Also, we incorporate what has become known as the Armington assumption into the model. This means that we treat imports and domestically produced goods in the same industrial category as imperfect substitutes. Fundamentally, the Armington assumption serves two purposes. The first is that it provides a simple way of allowing for intra-industry trade, a fact which we observe in the empirical data but which cannot be explained within the standard trade framework. The second is that it avoids the possibility of small changes in policy variables leading to unrealistically large production responses. Note that the aggregation is assumed to take place at the border, i.e., we do not trace imports to specific agents in the domestic economy. Note also that since we also maintain the small country assumption for both exports and imports, the inclusion of an Armington specification of the tradable sector raises some difficulties in interpretation, since equality of world and domestic prices adjusted for tariffs is no longer required. It is necessary to reinterpret the small country assumption to mean that the world prices of both exports and imports are exogenous.

We incorporate carbon emissions using 1993 New Zealand data, also presented in Appendix 9.3. In the model emissions can come from three distinct sources. The first is from the production process itself (e.g., fugitive fuel emissions). The second is from consumption of energy products for the purpose of production. Finally, we have emissions from final consumption of energy products. Note that different production processes lead to different levels of emissions by level of energy consumption, reflecting the fact that different industries use different sources of energy intensively. We also incorporate carbon absorption into the model, which is assumed to be related to the level of gross output of the forestry sector[10]. Carbon taxes are incorporated into the model by means of a specific tax on emissions, the rate of which is the same irrespective of the source of those emissions (hence the single carbon tax is in effect a combination of taxes on consumption, production, and inputs to the production process).

The model differs from that used by Chisholm et al. (1994) in several ways. The database is newer, and we use a slightly different production structure (in particular different sources of energy are assumed to be used in fixed proportions in each industry, and energy can be substituted at different rates for capital and labour in each industry – rather than at a constant rate across industries as in WEDGE). Emissions can come from productive processes directly, as well as energy consumption, and the model also incorporates, albeit somewhat crudely, carbon absorption (one of the main criticisms of Chisholm et al., 1994, found in Read 1994 is the lack of recognition of this mechanism). The model is single country and of a smaller scale. However, there is also a certain degree of complementarity – if we get similar results with models of different specifications we can feel more comfortable about the robustness of those results.

Model Results

The model described above is implemented in non-linear (levels) form, and utilised to consider three experiments. In the first we use the model to find the carbon tax which reduces net New Zealand carbon emissions to their 1990 level, as under the FCCC obligations. We next analyse the impact of a 25 per cent export tax on logs, which we assume is implemented for the purpose of increasing processing production. Finally, we consider the same export restriction in combination with a carbon tax to meet FCCC requirements.

The results of these experiments are contained in Tables 9.5 to 9.7. Table 9.5 gives the changes in production and exports, Table 9.6 gives the changes in consumption and energy usage by sector, and finally Table 9.7 contains carbon emissions and summary statistics. Consider first the impact of a carbon tax. The carbon tax required to reduce New Zealand's carbon emissions from 12449 kt in 1993 to the 1990 level of 7772 kt is NZ$67,410 per kt of carbon emitted. This figure is broadly consistent with existing estimates[11]. It is also a substantial tax, and not surprisingly the impact on production is substantial. All sectors except services respond to the tax by reducing output. As we might expect, it is the dirtiest industries (energy, mining and quarrying, and the manufacturing sectors) which exhibit the largest response. However, as the figures in Table 9.6 indicate, the production response is actually relatively small compared to the reduction in energy use by industries (see also the reduction in final energy consumption in the same table). As we might expect, all firms reduce their energy consumption substantially in response to the carbon tax. Moreover, in this model it appears that the effect of substituting energy for other factors of production dominates the production scale effect on emissions. In Table 9.7 we have the reduction in emissions by sector. Note that since the carbon tax marginally reduces the output of the forestry sector, absorption declines slightly. The equivalent variation or welfare cost of meeting the FCCC obligation is calculated at NZ$154.6 million, or approximately 0.2 per cent of GDP. Of course, the model places no values on the reduction in carbon emissions which the policy has induced, and hence the carbon tax may in fact be resulting in a welfare gain (if society does indeed value the improvement in the environment more highly than the loss of income).

Table 9.5: Production and Trade Effects

	Initial Equilib- rium	Carbon Tax	Export Tax	Carbon & Export Tax
		(Percentage Changes)		
Production				
(1) Forestry and Logging	2036	-0.20	-3.69	-3.92
(2) Light Manufacturing	19329	-6.30	-0.25	-7.37
(3) Non Traded Services	39391	0.58	-0.16	0.49
(4) Wood Product Manufacturing	2486	-3.83	16.02	11.28
(5) Heavy Manufacturing	19965	-4.39	0.30	-4.68
(6) Energy	8170	-11.82	-0.04	-13.47
(7) Agriculture, Fishing and Hunting	10679	-1.01	-0.04	-1.18
(8) Other Mining and Quarrying	480	-17.49	-0.38	-23.55
(9) Traded Services	49918	0.70	-0.15	0.69
Exports				
(1) Forestry and Logging	492	3.22	-51.98	-47.67
(2) Light Manufacturing	9654	-10.92	-0.42	-12.74
(3) Non Traded Services	0.0	-	-	-
(4) Wood Product Manufacturing	672	-11.73	51.40	36.88
(5) Heavy Manufacturing	4149	-15.37	0.98	-16.42
(6) Energy	226	203.06	-2.09	222.23
(7) Agriculture, Fishing and Hunting	1568	19.37	0.89	22.78
(8) Other Mining and Quarrying	175	-40.07	-1.45	-55.93
(9) Traded Services	6171	9.55	-1.27	9.98

Table 9.6: Final Demand and Energy Usage

	Initial Equilib- rium	Carbon Tax	Export Tax	Carbon & Export Tax
		(Percentage Changes)		
Final Demand				
(1) Forestry and Logging	442	0.29	24.68	25.04
(2) Light Manufacturing	6135	0.29	-0.18	0.11
(3) Non Traded Services	30793	0.84	-0.19	0.75
(4) Wood Product Manufacturing	582	0.29	-0.18	0.11
(5) Heavy Manufacturing	8283	0.29	-0.18	0.11
(6) Energy	2598	-17.94	-0.18	-20.31
(7) Agriculture, Fishing and Hunting	612	0.29	-0.18	0.11
(8) Other Mining and Quarrying	12	0.29	-0.18	0.11
(9) Traded Services	18700	0.29	-0.18	0.11
Energy Usage				
(1) Forestry and Logging	13	-22.78	-25.03	-44.00
(2) Light Manufacturing	343	-25.33	-0.24	-28.43
(3) Non Traded Services	715	-3.36	-0.14	-4.03
(4) Wood Product Manufacturing	56	-23.80	18.98	-12.33
(5) Heavy Manufacturing	617	-19.64	0.57	-21.48
(6) Energy	3352	-20.97	-0.04	-23.66
(7) Agriculture, Fishing and Hunting	312	-15.37	-0.02	-17.29
(8) Other Mining and Quarrying	32	-22.71	-0.38	-28.96
(9) Traded Services	800	-14.07	-0.14	-15.97

Table 9.7: Carbon Emissions and Summary Statistics

	Initial Equilib- rium	Carbon Tax	Export Tax	Carbon & Export Tax
		(Percentage Changes)		
Carbon Emissions by Sector				
(1) Forestry and Logging	73	-22.78	-25.03	-44.00
(2) Light Manufacturing	2604	-16.07	-0.25	-18.18
(3) Non Traded Services	506	-3.36	-0.14	-4.03
(4) Wood Product Manufacturing	418	-16.01	17.83	-3.12
(5) Heavy Manufacturing	4407	-15.11	0.49	-16.49
(6) Energy	7256	-20.18	-0.04	-22.78
(7) Agriculture, Fishing and Hunting	1035	-15.37	-0.02	-17.29
(8) Other Mining and Quarrying	286	-22.14	-0.38	-28.37
(9) Traded Services	2117	-14.07	-0.14	-15.97
(10) Final Energy Demand	8573	-17.94	-0.18	-20.31
Summary Statistics				
Total Gross Emissions (kt)	27275	22568.0	27323.4	22016.7
Absorption (kt)	-14826	-14796.0	-14279.0	-14244.6
Net Emissions (kt)	12449	7772.0	13044.4	7772.0
Equivalent Variation (NZ$millions)	0	-154.6	-27.0	-221.5
Carbon Tax Rate (NZ$/kt)	0	67410.0	0.0	78010.0
Log Export Tax Rate (%)	0	0.0	25.0	25.0

Consider next the effect of the imposition of an export tax on logs. The export tax lowers the domestic price of forestry, and hence production of forestry falls (Table 9.5). The policy has the desired effect on the processing industry. The lower price of forestry is effectively a subsidy to wood processing, which expands substantially. Production in other industries is less directly affected, we observe a small increase in the production of heavy manufactures and slight decreases in production in all remaining industries. A similar pattern follows through to exports. The misallocation of resources which the policy causes is estimated to have a welfare cost of NZ$27 million.

The export restriction also has implications for carbon emissions. The policy causes production in a relatively clean industry (forestry) to decline, while production in the relatively dirty wood processing and heavy manufacturing industries expand. Both of these industries also expand their use of energy in production, and hence carbon emissions in these two industries expand from both of these sources. The reduction in emissions from other sectors is not enough to offset this expansion, and hence gross emissions rise, albeit only slightly. Absorption by forestry also falls, resulting in an expansion of net emissions of 4.8 per cent.

Finally, consider the impact of a carbon tax to reduce net emissions to 1990 levels in the presence of the export tax. Since the export tax alters the production structure in such a way that net emissions rise, a larger carbon tax is now required to meet the FCCC obligations. The model calculates the required tax at NZ$78,010 per kt of carbon emitted, nearly 16 per cent higher than the tax required in the absence of export restrictions on forestry. The pattern we observe in production is much the same as before, although the declines in production are larger, as we expect with a larger carbon tax. The wood processing sector still expands as a result of the effective subsidy the export restrictions provide, but the expansion is offset considerably by the carbon tax. As in the case of the carbon tax alone, in addition to reducing output, all industries economise on the use of energy.

The estimated welfare cost of the carbon taxes and the export restrictions together is estimated at NZ$221 million, or 0.3 per cent of GDP. This implies that once the FCCC obligations are taken into account, the true welfare cost of export restrictions on forestry is in fact approximately NZ$66 million – more than double the welfare cost estimated without accounting for the obligations[12]. The entire difference between the welfare cost of the carbon tax with and without the export restrictions can be interpreted as the cost of the export restrictions, since the additional cost associated with the carbon tax comes about because of the distortions in the production structure which the export restrictions cause. Since these costs need not be incurred in order to reduce emissions to 1990 levels without the export tax, the issue of whether or not the reduction in emissions is beneficial to society overall is not relevant to this problem.

Concluding Comments

The forestry and wood processing sectors are very important to the New Zealand economy. The forestry sector is also a central component of New Zealand's strategy in meeting its FCCC obligations. Moreover, there continues to be debate in New Zealand as to the desirability of implementing export restrictions on logs for the purpose of increasing domestic processing, a policy which is common among the other major log producers. In this chapter we have used a computable general equilibrium model of the New Zealand economy to explore some of the issues involved. The model is a static, neo-classical trade model, with energy in all sectors and forestry in the wood processing sector used in variable proportions. The main findings can be summarised as follows. First, the carbon taxes required to meet FCCC obligations are substantial, and will result in considerable alterations to the New Zealand production structure and energy consumption patterns. Furthermore, since New Zealand's net emissions have in fact been growing steadily since 1993, the implication is that even higher taxes than estimated here will be required. If New Zealand is committed to meeting the FCCC obligations, it can therefore ill afford to implement any policy, such as export restrictions on logs, which would lower the incentive to expand the growth of plantation forestry and hence reduce carbon absorption potential. Second, implementing export restrictions on logs distorts resource allocation and results in welfare losses. While the policy may increase domestic processing, it does so at a net cost to society. Third, because export taxes on forestry distort production in such a way that production in dirty industries expands, and production in clean industries declines, they harm the environment in the New Zealand context (contrary to the arguments which have been used in most other markets where plantation forestry is not the norm). This distortion in the production structure greatly expands the cost of export restrictions where carbon taxes are required, since a much higher carbon tax then needs to be used to reduce carbon emissions to the desired level. Hence, this also provides an example of how the existence of environmental externalities in the presence of emission constraints may strengthen the neo-classical case against export restrictions.

Notes

1   It is also common to find the forest products industry separated according to definitions of the wood processing industry - which includes sawn timber and panel products, and the pulp and paper industry, which includes the production of wood pulp, paper and paperboard. This definition regards sawn timber (lumber) as a processed rather than an essentially unprocessed product.

2   Roundwood equivalent is a theoretical measurement unit giving the total amount of roundwood necessary for the production of one unit of a stated forestry product with existing technology as if only roundwood was used as a raw material; no allowance is made for the use of residues in the manufacture of the product. The roundwood equivalent conversion factors were derived by the New Zealand Forest Service in 1976 and may be subject to review to take into account technological change.

3   Value figures in this table and all others in this section are given in nominal New Zealand dollars, f.o.b.

4   New Zealand may however, face similar problems in the future, if it is argued that the New Zealand plantation forestry model is not environmentally sound due to a lack of biodiversity. The Aphid case may be an indication of things to come.

5   The New Zealand approach could be interpreted as being based on a sort of technological optimism, that improvements in technology will lower the cost of reducing gross emissions in the log run, and hence it is rational to lower net emissions in the short run by targeting absorption.

6   Most CGE analyses are static in nature, the results of policy simulations thus represent how the economy in question would have looked had the policy been in place in the base year. A number of studies use recursively dynamic CGE models (such as Brendemoen and Vennemo 1994), where the capital stocks are updated after each run, and the model projected forward. Such models can be poorly behaved, however. Another approach is to use a true

intertemporal model, but this expands the complexity of the model substantially (see Manne and Rutherford 1994).

7 The assumption of full employment of labour implies that the results should be interpreted as comparative static states for a given level of labour effort.

8 This obviously begs the question as to what exactly is meant by 'short run'? According to Dixon et al. (1982, p.65), the short run must be long enough for prices to fully adjust to policy increases, for users to decide on the optimal usage of domestic and imported goods, for domestic producers to hire labour and expand output with their existing plant and natural resources, and for price changes to be passed back into factor returns (and vice-versa). While the actual length of this time is difficult to know in practice, we take the same route as other CGE modellers in regarding the short run as being a period of 2-3 years.

9 An alternative would be to fix savings and investment levels and focus only on household and government consumption as an indicator of welfare (or indeed to fix government spending as well and consider only the household). However, we agree with Hertel et al. (1997) that forcing all of the adjustment in the economy's final demand into private consumption is rather extreme, and the assumption used here is preferable. That is, a rise in income implies an increase in savings and government expenditure, as well as private consumption. Moreover, the approach is backed up by the work of Howe (1975) who showed that the intertemporal extended linear expenditure system could be derived from an equivalent atemporal maximisation problem in which savings enters the utility function.

10 While incorporating emission coefficients related to production or consumption is quite reasonable, the use of a production absorption coefficient for forestry is somewhat less satisfactory. Indeed, in the context of an exhaustible forestry resource the absorptive capacity of the forest is likely to be negatively related to the level of output of the sector. The absorption of carbon dioxide in fact comes through growth of the forest biomass, hence we are assuming that the same factors which cause output to expand in this model will also cause an increase in the forest biomass (by encouraging new planting). Ideally we would need to model this issue in a dynamic framework – but the assumption we make here is probably a reasonable first approximation in the New Zealand plantation forestry context.

11 The Chisholm et al. figure is US$42, but this is a stabilisation from a projected equilibrium at 2000, rather than the cost at the base year as presented here. The Ministry for the Environment (1996) cites a contract report by Stroombergen and Terry (1994), which estimates the required carbon tax for New Zealand at approximately NZ$100 per tonne. Results for other developed countries are also available, and are in a similar range

US$20-150 for the United States and Canada and US$0-40 for the European Union (see Jacard and Montgomery 1996, and Krause 1996). Many of these results are from partial equilibrium studies with quite different approaches to that used here – so the level of consistency is revealing.

12   Note that we would reach the same conclusion even without relating absorption in forestry to output, since gross emissions rise. The effect would be less marked without this assumption, however.

References

Barbier, E.B. and Rauscher, M. (1994), "Trade, Tropical Deforestation and Policy Interventions", *Environmental and Resource Economics*, 4(1), 75-90.

Barbier, E.B. et al. (1995), "The Linkages Between the Timber Trade and Tropical Deforestation – Indonesia", *World Economy*, 18(3), 411-42.

Beghin, J., Roland-Holst, D. and van der Mensbrugghe, D. (1995), "Trade Liberalization and the Environment in the Pacific Basin: Coordinated Approaches to Mexican Trade and Environment Policy", *American Journal of Agricultural Economics*, 77.

Brendemoen, A. and Wennemo, H. (1994), "A Climate Treaty and the Norwegian Economy: A CGE Assessment", *The Energy Journal*, 15(1), 77-93.

Brown, C. (1997), "In Depth Country Study - New Zealand", *FAO Asia-Pacific Forestry Sector Outlook Study Working Paper No. APFSOS/WP/05*.

Buniaux, J., Nicoletti, G. and Olivira-Martins, J. (1992), "GREEN: A Global Model for Quantifying the Cost of Policies to Curb CO_2 Emissions", *OECD Economic Studies*, 19, Paris.

Chrisholm, A., Moran, A. and Zeitsch, J. (1994), "The Economic Costs of Stabilising Emissions of Carbon Dioxide in New Zealand", *New Zealand Economic Papers*, 28(1), 1-24.

Clarete, R.L. and Roumasset, J.A. (1986), "CGE Models and Development Policy Analysis: Problems, Pitfalls, and Challenges", *American Journal of Agricultural Economics*, 68(5), 1212-6.

Dixon, P.B., Parmenter, B.R., Sutton, J. and Vincent, D.P. (1982), *ORANI: A Multi-sectoral Model of the Australian Economy*, Amsterdam: North-Holland.

Espinosa, J.A. and Smith, V.K. (1995), "Measuring the Environmental Consequences of Trade Policy: A Non-Market CGE Analysis", *American Journal of Agricultural Economics*, 77, 772-77.

FAO (1995), "1945-1993...2010 Forestry Statistics Today for Tomorrow", FAO.

Gilbert, J. (1998), "Trade Policy, Processing and the New Zealand Forestry Industry", Unpublished PhD Dissertation, The University of Auckland.

Gillis, M. (1988), "Indonesia: Public Policies, Resource Management, and the Tropical Forest", in Repetto and Gillis (eds), *Public Policies and the Misuse of Forest Resources*, New York: Cambridge University Press.

Harrison, G. and Kimbell, L. (1985), "Economic Interdependence in the Pacific Basin: A General Equilibrium Approach", in Piggot and Whalley (eds), *New Developments in Applied General Equilibrium Analysis*, New York: Cambridge University Press.

Hertel, T.W. (ed) (1997), *Global Trade Analysis: Modeling and Applications*, Cambridge University Press.

Howe, H. (1975), "Development of the Extended Linear Expenditure System from Simple Saving Assumptions", *European Economic Review*, 6, 305-10.

Jacard, M. and Montgomery, W.D. (1996), "Costs of Reducing Greenhouse Gas Emissions in the USA and Canada", *Energy Policy*, 24(10), 889-916.

Krause, F. (1996), "The Cost of Mitigating Carbon Emissions: A Review of Methods and Findings from European Studies", *Energy Policy*, 24(10), 917-26.

Lindsay, H. (1989), "The Indonesian Log Export Ban: An Estimation of Foregone Export Earnings", *Bulletin of Indonesian Economic Studies*, 25(2), 111-23.

Manne, A.S. and Rutherford, T.F. (1994), "International Trade in Oil, Gas and Carbon Emission Rights: An Intertemporal General Equilibrium Model", *Energy Journal*, 15(1), 57-76.

Marks, R.E. et al. (1991), "The Cost of Australian Carbon Dioxide Abatement", *The Energy Journal*, 12(2), 135-52.

Ministry for the Environment (1996), "Climate Change and CO_2 Policy: A Durable Response – Discussion Document of the Working Group on CO_2 Policy".

Ministry of Forestry (1996), *New Zealand Forestry Statistics 1996*, Ministry of Forestry.

Perroni, C. and Wigle, R. (1997), "Environmental Policy Modeling", in Hertel (ed), *Global Trade Analysis: Modeling and Applications*, New York: Cambridge University Press.

Piggott, J. and Whalley, J. (1985), *New Developments in Applied General Equilibrium Analysis*, Cambridge University Press.

Read, P. (1994) "The Economic Costs of Stabilising Emissions of Carbon Dioxide in New Zealand: Comment", *New Zealand Economic Papers*, 28(2), 211-17.

Repetto, R. and Gillis, M. (eds) (1988), *Public Policies and the Misuse of Forest Resources*, Cambridge University Press.

Whalley, J. and Wigle, R. (1991), "Cutting CO_2 Emissions: Effects of Alternative Policy Approaches", *The Energy Journal*, 12(1), 109-24.

Whyte, A.G.D. (ed) (1989), *8th NZASIA Conference on Asia Studies Forestry Papers*, University of Canterbury: School of Forestry.

Wije-wardana, D. (1989), "Current Forest Products Trade Patterns in Asia and Pacific Rim Countries", in Whyte (ed), *8th NZASIA Conference on Asia Studies Forestry Papers*, University of Canterbury: School of Forestry.

Yang, A., et al. (1996), "The MIT Emissions Prediction and Policy Assessment (EPPA) Model", *MIT Joint Program on the Science and Policy of Global Change Report No.6*, Cambridge MA: MIT Press.

Appendix 9.1: Equations of the Model

Production Functions

1. $$X_1 = \frac{b_1}{(1 - \sum_{j=1}^{N} a_{1j})} \cdot [\delta_1 \cdot \{\delta_{1K} \cdot \overline{K}_1^{-\rho_1} + \delta_{1L} \cdot L_1^{-\rho_1} + (1 - \delta_{1K} - \delta_{1L}) \cdot EN_1^{-\rho_1}\}^{\rho_1/\rho_1} + (1 - \delta_1) \cdot XQ_1^{-\rho_1}]^{-\psi_1}$$

2. $$X_i = \frac{b_i}{(1 - \sum_{j=1}^{N} a_{ij})} \cdot [\delta_{iK} \cdot \overline{K}_i^{-\rho_i} + \delta_{iL} \cdot L_i^{-\rho_i} + (1 - \delta_{iK} - \delta_{iL}) \cdot EN_i^{-\rho_i}]^{-\psi_i} \qquad i = 2, \dots, N$$

Labour Market Equilibrium

3. $$\overline{L} = \sum_{i=1}^{N} L_i$$

4. $$W = PN_i \cdot \frac{\partial X_i}{\partial L_i} \qquad i = 1, \dots, N$$

Processing Demand for Logs

5. $$P_2 = PN_1 \cdot \frac{\partial X_1}{\partial XQ_2}$$

Demand for Energy by Industry

6. $$PEN_i = PN_i \cdot \frac{\partial X_i}{\partial EN_i} \qquad i = 1, \dots, N$$

Total Intermediate Use

7. $$V_2 = \sum_{j=2}^{N} a_{2j} X_j + XQ_2 \qquad j \neq 1$$

8. $$V_3 = \sum_{i=1}^{N} EN_i$$

9. $$V_i = \sum_{j=1}^{N} a_{ij} X_j \qquad i = 1, 4, \dots, N$$

Utility Function and Welfare Measure

10. $$U = \prod_{i=1}^{N} C_i^{\lambda_i}$$

11. $$EV = NDI^1 \cdot \left[\prod_{i=1}^{N} \left(\frac{PCT_i^0}{PCT_i^1} \right)^{\lambda_i} \right] - NDI^0$$

Appendix 9.1: Equations of the Model *continued*

Domestic Demand for Domestic Production

12. $C_i = \phi_i \cdot \dfrac{NDI}{PCT_i}$ $\qquad i = 1, \ldots, N$

13. $D_i = DR_i \cdot (C_i + V_i)$ $\qquad i = 1, \ldots, N$

Import Demand Equations

14. $Q_i = \overline{B}_i \cdot [\Delta_i \cdot M_i^{-\mu_i} + (1 - \Delta_i) \cdot D_i^{-\mu_i}]^{-1/\mu_i}$ $\qquad i = 1, \ldots, T$

15. $M_i = \left(\dfrac{\Delta_i}{1 - \Delta_i}\right)^{\eta_i} \cdot \left(\dfrac{PD_i}{PM_i}\right)^{\eta_i} \cdot D_i$ $\qquad i = 1, \ldots, T$

Price Equations

16. $PM_i = \overline{PW_i} \cdot (1 + tm_i) \cdot XR$ $\qquad i = 1, \ldots, T$

17. $PD_i = \overline{PWE_i} \cdot XR / (1 + te_i)$ $\qquad i = 1, \ldots, T$

18. $P_i = \overline{B}_i^{-1} \cdot [\Delta_i^{\eta_i} \cdot PM_i^{(1-\eta_i)} + (1 - \Delta_i)^{\eta_i} \cdot PD_i^{(1-\eta_i)}]^{1/(1-\eta_i)}$ $\qquad i = 1, \ldots, T$

Net Price Equations

19. $PN_1 = PDCT_1 - \sum_{j=1}^{N} a_{j1} \cdot P_j$ $\qquad j \neq 2,3$

20. $PN_i = PDCT_i - \sum_{j=1}^{N} a_{ji} \cdot P_j$ $\qquad \begin{aligned} &i = 2, \ldots, N \\ &j \neq 3 \end{aligned}$

Income Equations

21. $LI = \sum_{i=1}^{N} W \cdot L_i$

22. $KI = \sum_{i=1}^{N} PN_i \cdot X_i - LI - P_1 \cdot XQ_1 - \sum_{i=1}^{N} P_3 \cdot EN_i$

23. $TR = \sum_{i=1}^{T} tm_i \cdot \overline{PW_i} \cdot M_i \cdot XR + \sum_{i=1}^{T} te_i \cdot PD_i \cdot E_i - \sum_{i=1}^{N} CT \cdot PE_i - \sum_{i=1}^{N} CT \cdot CE_i$

24. $GDP = LI + KI + TR$

25. $NDI = GDP - \overline{F} \cdot XR$

Material Balance Equations

26. $X_i = D_i + E_i$ $\qquad i = 1, \ldots, T$

27. $X_i = D_i$ $\qquad i = T+1, \ldots, N$

Appendix 9.1: Equations of the Model *continued*

Balance of Payments

28. $\sum_{i=1}^{T} \overline{PW_i} \cdot M_i + \overline{F} = \sum_{i=1}^{T} \overline{PWE_i} \cdot E_i$

Price Normalisation

29. $\sum_{i=1}^{N} \Omega_i \cdot P_i = 1$

Carbon Emissions

30. $PE_i = PEC_i \cdot X_i$ $i = 1, \ldots, N$
31. $EE_i = EEC_i \cdot EN_i$ $i = 1, \ldots, N$
32. $CE_i = CEC_i \cdot C_i$ $i = 1, \ldots, N$
33. $PA_i = PAC_i \cdot X_i$ $i = 1, \ldots, N$

34. $GEM = \sum_{i=1}^{N} PE_i + \sum_{i=1}^{N} EE_i + \sum_{i}^{N} CE_i$

35. $NEM = GEM - \sum_{i=1}^{N} PA_i$

Carbon Taxes

36. $PDCT_i = PD_i + (ct \cdot PEC_i)$ $i = 1, \ldots, N$
37. $PCT_i = P_i - (ct \cdot CEC_i)$ $i = 1, \ldots, N$
38. $PEN_i = P_3 - (ct \cdot EEC_i)$ $i = 1, \ldots, N$

Appendix 9.2: Definitions of Variables and Parameters

Industrial Classification

1	Wood Processing Sector
2	Forestry Sector
3	Energy Sector
4,...,T	Other Traded Goods
T+1,...,N	Non-Traded Goods

Endogenous Variables

C_i Final demand

D_i Domestic demand for domestic production

DR_i Domestic use ratio

E_i Exports

EN_i Energy use

EV Equivalent variation

GDP Gross domestic product

GEM Gross carbon emissions

KI Total capital income

L_i Sectoral labour employment

LI Total labour income

M_i Imports

NDI Net disposable income

NEM Net carbon emissions

P_i Price of the domestic/import composite

PCT_i Consumer prices inclusive of carbon taxes

PD_i Price of domestically produced goods, expressed in domestic currency

$PDCT_i$ Producer prices inclusive of carbon taxes

PEN_i Energy prices inclusive of carbon taxes

PM_i Price of imported goods expressed in domestic currency

PN_i Net price expressed in domestic currency

Q_i Domestic/import composite

TR Tax component of GDP

Appendix 9.2: Definitions of Variables and Parameters *continued*

U	Social welfare
V_i	Intermediate demand
W	Wage rate per unit of labour
X_i	Gross output
XQ_2	Logs used in the processing industry
XR	Exchange rate
$\overline{F}$	Capital outflow
$\overline{K}_i$	Capital stocks (sector-specific)
$\overline{L}$	Total labour supply
$\overline{PW}_i$	World price of imports
$\overline{PWE}_i$	World price of exports

Policy Variables

ct	Carbon tax (specific duty – defined as negative)
te_i	Ad-valorem export taxes
tm_i	Ad-valorem import tariffs

Parameters

a_{ij}	Intermediate input-output coefficients
b_i	Scale parameter in production of good i
δ_i	Distribution parameters in CES production functions
ρ	Substitution parameters in CES production functions
Δ_i	Distribution parameters in CES Armington functions
μ_i	Substitution parameters in CES Armington functions
η_i	Elasticity of substitution between imports and domestic production
ϕ_i	Consumption expenditure shares
Ω_i	Weights for price index
CEC_i	Consumption emission coefficients
EEC_i	Energy use emission coefficients
PAC_i	Production carbon absorption coefficients
PEC_i	Production emission coefficients

Appendix 9.3: Input Output Database for New Zealand 1993

($million)	(1) Forestry and Logging	(2) Light Manufacturing	(3) Non Traded Services	(4) Wood Product Manufacturing	(5) Heavy Manufacturing	(6) Energy	(7) Agriculture, Fishing & Hunting	(8) Other Mining & Quarrying
(1) Forestry and Logging	608	4	9	314	152	0	5	0
(2) Light Manufacturing	10	3552	455	81	143	4	200	1
(3) Non Traded Services	18	287	5298	47	247	271	678	20
(4) Wood Product Manufacturing	2	22	718	368	169	6	24	1
(5) Heavy Manufacturing	92	1596	4576	296	7946	196	1165	31
(6) Energy	13	343	715	56	617	3352	312	32
(7) Agriculture, Fishing and Hunting	19	6528	83	5	29	0	1976	0
(8) Other Mining and Quarrying	9	15	39	1	1166	41	7	22
(9) Traded Services	220	2943	5662	459	3639	553	1730	74
(10) Sub Total (1)-(9)	991	15290	17555	1627	14108	4423	6097	181
(11) Labour	121	2700	13496	554	3376	818	1140	281
(12) Capital	924	1339	8340	305	2481	2929	3442	18
(13) Sub Total (11)-(12)	1045	4039	21836	859	5857	3747	4582	299
(14) Grand Total (13)+(10)	2036	19329	39391	2486	19965	8170	10679	480
(15) Emissions from Production	0	1267	0	163	1309	630	0	31
(16) Emissions from Energy Use	73	1337	506	255	3098	6626	1035	255
(17) Absorption	-14826	0	0	0	0	0	0	0
(18) Net Emissions	-14753	2604	506	418	4407	7256	1035	286

Appendix 9.3: Input Output Database for New Zealand 1993 *continued*

($million)	(9) Tradable Services	(10) Sub Total (1)-(9)	(11) Consump-tion	(12) Invest-ment	(13) Exports	(14) Imports	(15) Tariff Revenue	(16) Grand Total
(1) Forestry and Logging	16	1108	32	410	492	6	0	2036
(2) Light Manufacturing	1536	5982	5597	538	9654	2370	72	19329
(3) Non Traded Services	1732	8598	26248	4545	0	0	0	39391
(4) Wood Product Manufacturing	65	1375	395	187	672	134	9	2486
(5) Heavy Manufacturing	3817	19715	3071	5212	4149	12052	130	19965
(6) Energy	800	6240	2520	78	226	894	0	8170
(7) Agriculture, Fishing and Hunting	233	8873	544	62	1568	335	33	10679
(8) Other Mining and Quarrying	23	1323	8	4	175	1029	1	480
(9) Traded Services	14897	30177	16506	2194	6171	4879	251	49918
(10) Sub Total (1)-(9)	*23119*	*83391*	*54921*	*13230*	*23107*	*21699*	*496*	*152454*
(11) Labour	13756	35766						
(12) Capital	13043	33298						
(13) Sub Total (11)-(12)	*26799*	*69063*						
(14) Grand Total (13)+(10)	**49918**	**152454**						
(15) Emissions from Production	0		0					
(16) Emissions from Energy Use	2117		8573					
(17) Absorption	0		0					
(18) Net Emissions	2117		8573					

Appendix 9.4: Parameter Values

Industry	Value	Source
Production Substitution Elasticities		
(1) Forestry and Logging	0.80	Harrison and Kimbell (1985)[a]
(2) Light Manufacturing	0.90	Harrison and Kimbell (1985)
(3) Non Traded Services	0.73	Harrison and Kimbell (1985)
(4) Wood Product Manufacturing[b]	0.48 and 0.84	Gilbert (1998)
(5) Heavy Manufacturing	0.57	Harrison and Kimbell (1985)
(6) Energy	0.84	Harrison and Kimbell (1985)
(7) Agriculture, Fishing and Hunting	0.78	Harrison and Kimbell (1985)
(8) Other Mining and Quarrying	0.15	Harrison and Kimbell (1985)
(9) Traded Services	0.97	Harrison and Kimbell (1985)
Armington Elasticities		
(1) Forestry and Logging	2.0	Dixon, et al. (1982)[c]
(2) Light Manufacturing	1.7	Dixon, et al. (1982)
(4) Wood Product Manufacturing	1.7	Dixon, et al. (1982)
(5) Heavy Manufacturing	1.4	Dixon, et al. (1982)
(6) Energy	1.7	Dixon, et al. (1982)
(7) Agriculture, Fishing and Hunting	1.7	Dixon, et al. (1982)
(8) Other Mining and Quarrying	2.0	Dixon, et al. (1982)
(9) Traded Services	2.0	Dixon, et al. (1982)

a Figures are weighted averages of the estimates used by Harrison and Kimbell (1985).
b Internal and external elasticities of the two-level CES function.
c Figures are weighted averages of the estimates used by Dixon et al. (1982).

10 Reconciling Trade and Environment Concerns: Summary of Policy Conclusions

RAVI RATNAYAKE

Until recently, the promotion of multilateral trading system and the protection of environment have been seen as two different objectives. One objective has always been seen counter productive to the other. The environmental community believes that international trade is always environmentally damaging while the trade community argues that international trade is beneficial to the environment. This conflict of interest has led to an intense debate on the linkages between trade and environment. However, recently, one can witness some signs of compatibility of trade and environmental objectives at international policy making forums such as WTO. Now it is accepted in principle that international trade can be promoted while protecting the environment. The recent discussions at the WTO Committee on trade and environment have centred on the ways in which this single objective can be achieved. What is needed now is greater integration of trade and environmental policies so that they will be mutually supportive in the pursuit of sustainable development. For this purpose, the examination of the linkages between trade and environment empirically is of paramount importance in order to formulate national perspectives leading to an international perspective on trade and environment. The chapters in this book were intended to fill the knowledge gap in this area by undertaking detailed empirical investigations into the important issues involved in the debate in the context of New Zealand. We below summarise some of the important policy conclusions arising from the preceding studies.

Firstly, in general, trade liberalisation can have either negative or positive effects on environment dependent largely on whether there are appropriate environmental policies. The negative effects in general arise from the expansion of trade, production and consumption. Trade liberalisation can stimulate polluting industries and reduce national welfare. On the positive side, trade liberalisation would lead to higher incomes which ensure more resources for environmental protection and greater demand for environmentally friendly goods. In particular, in developing countries higher incomes mean lower population growth and more employment which can affect environmental degradation effectively. It has been shown that the negative effects associated with liberalisation can be substantially reduced if proper environmental protection measures are in place in order to internalise some of the externalities associated with the expansion of production. Therefore, the key to environmentally friendly trade liberalisation is the introduction of optimal environmental policies along with trade reforms.

For instance, the case study on agriculture has shown that trade liberalisation in general as well as in agricultural goods results in improved economic efficiency and economic growth. These effects may be fed into improved environmental quality, but that outcome is not automatic and an increased efficiency is a necessary but not sufficient condition. What is required for the improvement in environmental quality is that environmental policies are put in place as first-best instruments to deal with environmental degradation. In short, trade liberalisation cannot be used as a substitute for environmental policies although it could be used as a remedial policy or as a second-best instrument in a limited number of cases.

Policy responses for environmental effects of trade liberalisation can vary depending on:

- whether the product concerned is importable (import competing local production), exportable (produced for both local and export market), only for exports (no production for local market) or non-tradeable (no exports and imports), and
- whether the environmental damage arises from production or consumption.

In terms of these two factors, the environmental effects of trade liberalisation together with some policy responses are listed in Table 10.1. These policy responses can be used as general policy guidelines for integrating trade and environmental policies.

In terms of policy responses given in Table 10.1, trade policy instruments are treated as most less effective measures of environmental protection. A number of arguments have been presented against the use of trade policy measures for environmental purposes.

- It has been shown that trade policy measures do not attack "the root causes of environmental problems and provide no positive incentives for sustained improvement" (Drake-Brockman and Anderson, 1994).

- These measures can violate the important principles of GATT/WTO as they are discriminatory in most cases where there are differences in environmental standards between the WTO member countries.

- There are instances where trade restrictions have been applied on imports on the basis of production process and methods. A well-cited example is the US ban on Mexican tuna fish because they do not use dolphin-safe nets. Sometimes these restrictions can be extended to goods which are entirely unrelated to the goods being restricted; i.e., cross retaliation. For example, advanced developed countries can restrict imports of textiles and clothing from certain developing countries where logging of tropical timber is carried out in an unsustainable manner.

Table 10.1: The Environmental Effects of Trade Liberalisation and Policy Responses

Environmental damage is from	Type of product	Environmental effects of trade liberalisation	Policy response
Production	Importable	Positive if trade liberalisation replaces environmentally-damaging local production with imports	(a) Reduce quantitative restrictions and tariffs on environmentally damaging products to encourage more imports (b) Impose a production tax to discourage local production
	Exportable	Negative if trade liberalisation leads to more production for exports. However, it is possible that efficiency effects of trade liberalisation will be greater than the negative environmental externality	Tax on production for both local and export market. Export bans and export taxes can worsen the environmental damage. For example, export restrictions on timber in Indonesia have led to more intensive use of logs in production resulting from lower domestic prices of timber. A tax on all timber at the logging stage would have reduced the environmental damage.
	Only for exports	Negative because production generates the damage. However, trade liberalisation of this particular product will not have a direct effect on environment	Production tax to reduce production

Table 10.1: The Environmental Effects of Trade Liberalisation and Policy Responses *continued*

Environmental damage is from	Type of product	Environmental effects of trade liberalisation	Policy response
	Non-tradeable	Negative because the damage is due to production. A general trade liberalisation can encourage the non-tradeable production	Tax to reduce production
Consumption	Importable	Negative if trade liberalisation increases imports and consumption	Consumption tax on both imports and locally produced goods
	Exportable	Positive if trade liberalisation encourages more exports and less local consumption	Consumption tax to reduce local consumption
	Only for exports	No effects. However, exports of these goods will face severe restrictions overseas. Therefore, in the long run, it may be beneficial for the country to move away from such production	No action required. However, since there will be negative effects on global environment, an international action may be needed to stop or reduce such production

Secondly, the use of trade restrictions on the grounds that stringent environmental regulations impose significant costs on domestic firms and industries reducing their international competitiveness in terms of declining exports, increasing imports compared with those from the countries which have lower environmental standards and regulations can not be justified. Our research found no evidence to suggest that New Zealand has lost its comparative advantage of environmentally sensitive (ES) goods during the period under consideration. It was also shown that it was not an important determinant of New Zealand's international competitiveness.

Thirdly, it has been suggested that stringent environmental regulations and standards may induce multinational corporations (MNCs) to relocate their investment and production in the countries with laxer environmental regulations. As the environmental control costs are part of total production costs, the relocation of production to lower cost countries can give distinct comparative advantage to those relocating firms over the firms located in environmentally rich countries. This argument has been closely associated with the capital/industrial flight hypothesis that increasing the stringency of domestic environmental regulations, which adversely affects the competitive position of domestic firms, will push investment out of the national boundaries. These policies are known as "push factors" to FDI. An alternative view is that some governments allow foreign MNCs a moratorium from domestic environmental regulations which act as "pull factors" for FDI. This view is known as the pollution haven hypothesis which suggests that when the relative stringency of environmental regulations is different between countries, capital will relocate to those countries where regulations are relatively less stringent. The empirical investigation on issue has shown that environmental regulation is not a significant determinant of foreign direct investment. The other factors such as cheap labour and availability of markets appear to be much more important than environmental factors in decisions of locations.

Fourthly, there are two major views regarding the relationship between environmental regulations and innovations. First, there is a positive relationship between environmental compliance costs and environmental abatement technology. The second view is that environmental regulations undermine innovations and restricts firms in pursuing cutting-edge technology. Neither of these views is supported by the empirical research. However, the introduction of "good type" environmental regulations is needed in order to make sure that such regulations stimulate R&D on environmental technology. The regulations that are in place usually are of "command and control type" which highly depend on tough administrative and legal legislation to control polluting behaviour of firms. These poor regulations constrain the choice of technologies and depend on end-of-pipe and clean up measures rather than market incentives.

Fifthly, the use of trade restrictions in achieving environmental objectives have serious problems. Most of the time they can be environmentally counter productive. For example, first the study on trade restrictions in the forestry industry has found that export restrictions on logs, would lower the incentive to expand the growth of plantation forestry and hence reduce carbon absorption potential. Second, implementing export restrictions on logs distorts resource allocation and results in welfare losses. While the policy may increase domestic processing, it does so at a net cost to society. Third, because export taxes on forestry distort production in such a way that production in dirty industries expands, and production in clean industries declines, they harm the environment in the New Zealand context (contrary to the arguments which have been used in most other markets where plantation forestry is not the norm).

Domestic environmental protection measures which address the root causes of environmental problems are much more effective than trade measures. Given the well-known problems associated with the use of trade measures, it is important to make sure that these trade measures are necessary and effective in achieving environmental goals. If there is no other alternative, it is important to use the least restrictive trade measures which do not violate GATT/WTO principles.

Sixthly, trade policies are likely to affect environment favourably if property rights are in place. The case study on fisheries shows that in New Zealand the management regime of regulated access coupled with subsidies contributed to serious depletion of high value fish stocks and minimal economic surplus in the fishing industry. Subsidies and non-transferable property rights had combined to produce unsustainable outcomes. Since 1986, an unsustainable and unprofitable fishing industry has been converted to a dynamic profitable industry within the framework of rights-based fishing. In terms of biological sustainability and economic wealth in the fishery, the new fisheries management system easily out-performs regulated access.

Finally, harmonisation of environmental policies will be crucial in preventing unjustified interruptions to free movement of international flows of trade. In the cases where there are no valid reasons such as different stages of industrial development and different assimilative capacities for diversity of national environmental standards, the governments should get together and establish common standards for such environmentally damaging products. International cooperation in the context World Trade Organisation (WTO) appears to be extremely important in reconciling trade and environmental concerns.